Villy Tsakona
Recontextualizing Humor

Language Play and Creativity

Editor
Nancy Bell

Volume 4

Villy Tsakona

Recontextualizing Humor

Rethinking the Analysis and Teaching of Humor

ISBN 978-1-5015-2693-0
e-ISBN (PDF) 978-1-5015-1192-9
e-ISBN (EPUB) 978-1-5015-1152-3
ISSN 2363-7749

Library of Congress Control Number: 2019954491

Bibliographic information published by the Deutsche Nationalbibliothek
The Deutsche Nationalbibliothek lists this publication in the Deutsche Nationalbibliografie;
detailed bibliographic data are available on the Internet at http://dnb.dnb.de.

© 2021 Walter de Gruyter Inc., Boston/Berlin
This volume is text- and page-identical with the hardback published in 2020.
Typesetting: Integra Software Services Pvt. Ltd.
Printing and binding: CPI books GmbH, Leck

www.degruyter.com

Acknowledgments

I would be stating the obvious by saying that many people have contributed to this book, even if it appears to be a monograph by a single author. I therefore feel lucky and privileged not to be alone in this endeavor. First, I would like to thank the publishers I have collaborated with in the past for granting me permission to reproduce extracts from previous papers of mine, modified here to suit the purposes of this book. This is the list of these papers:

- Tsakona, Villy. 2013. Okras and the metapragmatic stereotypes of humor: Towards an expansion of the GTVH. In Marta Dynel (ed.), *Developments in linguistic humor theory* (Topics in Humor Research 1), 25–48. Amsterdam: John Benjamins. https://benjamins.com/catalog/thr.1
- Tsakona, Villy. 2015. "The doctor said I suffer from vitamin € deficiency": Investigating the multiple social functions of Greek crisis jokes. *Pragmatics* 25(2). 287–313. https://benjamins.com/catalog/prag.25.2.07tsa
- Tsakona, Villy. 2017. Genres of humor. In Salvatore Attardo (ed.), *The Routledge handbook of language and humor* (Routledge Handbooks in Linguistics), 489–503. New York: Routledge. https://www.routledge.com/The-Routledge-Handbook-of-Language-and-Humor/Attardo/p/book/9781138843066
- Tsakona, Villy. 2018. Online joint fictionalization. In Villy Tsakona & Jan Chovanec (eds.), *The dynamics of interactional humor: Creating and negotiating humor in everyday encounters* (Topics in Humor Research 7). Amsterdam: John Benjamins, 229–255. https://benjamins.com/catalog/thr.7

Examples (3.3, 3.32, and 5.1) come from the corpus compiled during the research project "Investigating the sociolinguistic status of young people in Patras with data coming from their narrative discourse", funded by the University of Patras, Greece (*K. Karatheodoris* 2425, project coordinator: Argiris Archakis).

I have also benefited from the constructive and encouraging feedback from the audience of the 31st Conference of the International Society for Humor Studies, at the University of Texas at Austin, USA, in June 2019, where a part of Chapter (4) was first presented.

I am grateful to Salvatore Attardo, Nancy Bell, Jan Chovanec, Marianthi Georgalidou, Dionysis Goutsos, and the anonymous reviewer for offering their generous and precious support at various stages of the writing process. Special thanks go to Argiris Archakis for his friendship and collaboration through the good times and the bad times. My family and my friends are always around with their loving care and support, without which I would not survive.

This book is dedicated to Marios and Andreas, the two more recently arrived humorous "informants" in the gang of charming princes. The first one was born on a cold Wednesday night while I was teaching a sociolinguistics course at Alexandroupoli, and the second on a sunny Friday morning during my presentation at the IPrA conference in Antwerp.

Contents

Acknowledgments —— V

List of Tables —— XI

List of Figures —— XIII

Transcription conventions for the Greek oral data and its translation —— XV

Introduction —— 1

1 Context in humor research —— 7
1.1 Introductory remarks —— 7
1.2 Conceptualizing context within humor research —— 8
1.3 The focus of the present study —— 13
1.4 Summary —— 17

2 Humor and metapragmatics —— 19
2.1 Introductory remarks —— 19
2.2 On metapragmatics —— 19
2.3 Some methodological notes on metapragmatic research —— 26
2.4 Metapragmatic research on humor —— 28
2.5 The sociopragmatic functions of metapragmatic comments —— 33
2.5.1 Creating solidarity through metapragmatic comments on crisis jokes —— 33
2.5.1.1 Some examples of the crisis jokes —— 35
2.5.1.2 Speakers' metapragmatic comments on crisis jokes —— 41
2.5.1.3 Comparing speakers' metapragmatic stereotypes with scholarly analyses of political jokes —— 45
2.5.2 Metapragmatic debates on humor —— 48
2.5.2.1 A controversial humorous (?) advertisement —— 48
2.5.2.2 Two conflicting metapragmatic stereotypes on humor —— 52
2.5.2.3 Comparing speakers' metapragmatic stereotypes with scholarly analyses of humor —— 58
2.5.3 Summarizing the sociopragmatic functions of metapragmatic comments and stereotypes —— 62
2.6 Summary —— 63

3	**Genres with/and humor — 65**
3.1	Introductory remarks — 65
3.2	On the interplay between genres and humor — 66
3.3	Classifying the genres of humor — 69
3.4	Humor and the recontextualization of generic conventions — 79
3.4.1	The emergence of new humorous (sub)genres — 79
3.4.2	The transformation of humorous genres — 85
3.4.2.1	The generic structure and sociopragmatic goals of oral joint fictionalization — 85
3.4.2.2	The data of the online fictionalization case study — 88
3.4.2.3	Jointly constructing the online fictionalization — 90
3.4.3	Recontextualizing generic conventions to create humor — 100
3.5	Summary — 102

4	**Towards a "contextualized" theory of humor — 103**
4.1	Introductory remarks — 103
4.2	The Semantic Script Theory of Humor and the General Theory of Verbal Humor: The competence theories of humor — 104
4.3	Expanding the General Theory of Verbal Humor — 109
4.4	Building a performance theory of humor — 114
4.4.1	Humorous discourse as dynamically constructed and negotiated — 115
4.4.2	Contextual parameters within the General Theory of Verbal Humor — 117
4.4.3	The Analytical Foci of the Discourse Theory of Humor — 123
4.5	Accounting for humor failure and humor quality — 126
4.6	An example of analysis using the Discourse Theory of Humor — 130
4.7	Summary — 138

5	**Teaching about humor within a critical literacy framework — 139**
5.1	Introductory remarks — 139
5.2	Humor in education — 140
5.3	Humor in language teaching — 143
5.4	What is critical literacy? — 148
5.5	Why teach about humor within a critical literacy framework? — 155
5.6	Addressing some reservations concerning critical literacy and humor — 158

5.7	Using humorous texts in critical literacy courses —— 163	
5.8	Designing critical literacy courses on humor —— 168	
5.9	Tentative proposals for teaching about humor within critical literacy —— 171	
5.9.1	Critically reflecting on political jokes and political reality —— 171	
5.9.2	Scrutinizing humorous representations of gender roles and identities —— 175	
5.9.3	Unveiling racism in contemporary migrant jokes —— 181	
5.10	Summary —— 188	

6   Conclusions —— 189

References —— 195

Subject Index —— 221

Author Index —— 225

List of Tables

Table 1.1 Accounts of context within humor research —— **14–15**
Table 2.1 The two opposing metapragmatic stereotypes on humor, as expressed during the public debate concerning the Greek advertisement —— **58**
Table 2.2 Humor researchers' positionings and findings concerning the (non) humorous quality of a text, the sociopragmatic functions of humor, and its limits —— **61**
Table 4.1 Accounts of context within humor research (also including Attardo 2017b) —— **119–121**
Table 4.2 Aspects of context associated with the knowledge resources of the General Theory of Verbal Humor —— **122**
Table 4.3 Accounting for humor failure or low quality within the Discourse Theory of Humor —— **129**

List of Figures

Figure 1.1	The interconnection between metapragmatic stereotypes and genres —— 16	
Figure 2.1	The relationship between metapragmatic awareness, stereotypes, indicators, and their sociopragmatic functions —— 25	
Figure 3.1	Cover photo and profile photo of the Facebook page *The Crocodile of Amari Should Remain in the Potami Dam* —— 91	
Figure 3.2a	Sifis' post on the arrival of the herpetologist —— 92	
Figure 3.2b	Comments (3.18–3.26) —— 93	
Figure 3.2c	Comments (3.27–3.29) —— 94	
Figure 3.2d	Comments (3.30–3.31) —— 94	
Figure 3.3	'16,400 points, wonderful Rethymno, here I come!' —— 97	
Figure 3.4	Map of Greece with crocodile instead of Crete —— 98	
Figure 3.5	'Sifis the crocodile wanted' —— 98	
Figure 4.1	The interplay of factors in a theory of humor performance (Attardo 2017b: 96) —— 113	
Figure 4.2	The Analytical Foci of the Discourse Theory of Humor —— 125	
Figure 5.1	'The Pakistani lucky winner of Joker [i.e. a popular lottery game] is thinking of buying Amygdaleza [i.e. a refugee camp near Athens]' —— 183	
Figure 5.2	'The parade on March 25th, 2020' —— 183	
Figure 5.3	'You get on the metro. It is packed with people. You get on your knees. You start praying in Arabic. Allahu Akbar. The metro wagon is evacuated. You rule' —— 184	

Transcription conventions for the Greek oral data and its translation

/	self–correction
//	interruption
( )	incomprehensible parts of utterances
[ ]	overlapping talk
xxx	stressed parts of utterances
xx:: x:	prolongation of a sound
{xxxx}	comments and contextual information added by the author
.	falling intonation
,	ongoing intonation
;	rising intonation in the Greek text
?	rising intonation in the English translation

Introduction

Humor is everywhere (or almost everywhere) in public and private discourse, online communication, etc. Raskin (1985: 17) is correct in pointing out that "[a]s virtually everything else in human society, humor turns out to be a convention created and legitimized by society and imposed by it on its members (so early in their lives (...) that no human who is totally unfamiliar with the phenomenon can actually be found)". Humor surfaces in numerous and diverse contexts, while at the same time context determines to a significant extent how humor will work, its form, and its functions and consequences for interlocutors.

The main theories of humor more or less explicitly consider context to be a significant parameter for defining humor. *Incongruity theories* suggest that humor originates in the perception of something that seems to be incompatible or unexpected *in a given context*. It is *in specific circumstances* that something violates our expectations, is judged as irrelevant or abnormal, and hence triggers a humorous effect or response. Then, *aggression/superiority theories* perceive humor as an expression of (usually mitigated or covert) hostility against something or someone deviating from what is socially expected. The target of humor is denigrated or attacked for not complying with the conventions or rules that are dominant *in a specific context*. Finally, *relief theories* of humor maintain that humor enables individuals to circumvent or defy the social rules imposed *within a specific sociocultural context*. In this sense, it allows individuals to speak "freely" and express themselves in ways that are stigmatized or forbidden within that context. Thus, even momentarily, humor releases the tension caused by social (i.e. *contextual*) conventions and restrictions.[1]

Yet, for several decades, linguistic humor research has often neglected context as a parameter accounting for the construction and meaning(s) of humor. Such a tendency appears to be related to the fact that for humor scholars the most common and popular humorous texts for analysis have been canned jokes which are supposed to be "verbatim" reproduced in various communicative settings and whose meaning has been perceived as stable across contexts (see also Bell 2018: 291–292). Hence, context appears to be left out of the theoretical and analytical parameters taken into consideration by the most influential linguistic theories of the past few decades, namely the *Semantic Script Theory of Humor* (Raskin 1985) and the *General Theory of Verbal Humor*

---

[1] For more detailed descriptions of the main theories of humor, see Bergson ([1901] 1911), Freud ([1905] 1991), Raskin (1985), Attardo (1994), Palmer (1994), Billig (2005b), Morreall (2009), Larkin-Galiñanes (2017), and references therein.

(Attardo and Raskin 1991; Attardo 1994, 2001). All this is in line with more general trends in theoretical linguistics, most notably Chomsky's (1965) generative theory, which programmatically refrained from a contextualized view of linguistic phenomena. Drawing on Chomsky (1965), both the Semantic Script Theory of Humor and the General Theory of Verbal Humor described an ideal speaker's competence in identifying and understanding humor in idealized circumstances where, for example, everybody shared the same sense of humor and reached identical interpretations of humorous texts.

Within linguistics, it was mostly in sociolinguistic and discourse analytic approaches to humor (see among others Norrick 1993; Norrick and Chiaro 2009) that the analysis of humor concentrated on real speakers' actual performances in social settings, thus highlighting the significance of context in the production and interpretation of humor. Furthermore, discourse analytic and sociolinguistic approaches to humor reminded and still remind us that nothing can be "universally accepted" as humorous: speakers co-construct and negotiate humor in interaction and may more or less differ in their perceptions of what can be considered and framed as humorous. This is why some attempts at humor prove to be successful, namely accepted by all interlocutors, while others may fall flat or even cause intense disaligning reactions by at least some of them. Such diverse reactions underline the fact that not all of us perceive the same behaviors or aspects of social reality as incongruous; we do not therefore agree on the selected targets to be attacked through humor and/or on the reasons for such "humorous" aggression. Furthermore, we do not think that the same topics, behaviors, actions, etc. are "appropriate" for humorous framing; in fact, the violation of some social conventions, norms, or restrictions is not unanimously welcome by the members of a sociocultural community, even if it makes some of them feel temporarily "released" or "free" from social impositions. In short, *in situ* humorous performances could involve diverse, even opposing senses and interpretations of humor.

Given the above, and adhering to the sociolinguistic and discourse analytic perspective, the present study will try to explore the variety of forms humor may take in different communicative settings, the wide range of sociopragmatic functions it may serve, as well as the more or less dissimilar perceptions speakers may have concerning what humor is, what it means, and how it works. To this end, the Chapters of this book will try to contribute to building a new theoretical approach to the analysis of humor placing emphasis on context. Such an approach presupposes that language is not perceived as a limited set of rules and units with predetermined meaning (cf. Chomsky 1965). Instead, it is based on the premises that meaning is perceived as co-constructed and negotiated in context by participants and that linguistic creativity and the possibility for multiple interpretations are considered to be key aspects of human communication (see among others Linell 1998; Bell and Pomerantz 2015; Chovanec and Tsakona 2018). Therefore, the proposed approach will try to take into consideration not only the sociocultural environments where humorous texts are created and interpreted, but also the meanings derived from them and the reactions to humor by real interlocutors in real settings.

The importance of context for the production and interpretation of humor has repeatedly been underlined in humor scholarship during the past few years: from decontextualized canned jokes or other printed material, many humor scholars have re-oriented themselves towards more contextualized approaches to humorous texts and genres, so as to examine them in their own terms. This means that it becomes increasingly significant and unquestionable that there is no way we can account for the situated, local meanings of humorous texts/genres unless we take into consideration a number of factors that constitute their context. So, the first Chapter of this book is dedicated to the theoretical description of what context is, by placing particular emphasis on how humor scholars account for those contextual aspects that they consider significant for analyzing humor (see among others Raskin 1985; Norrick 1993; Oring 2008).

Among other things, context includes speakers' reactions to humor, which may confirm or cancel the humorously intended meaning proposed by the humorist. Such reactions seem to depend on speakers' own perceptions and assessments of humor and eventually on differences and preferences concerning what can qualify as humor, when, why, etc. Such perceptions and preferences are shaped by the sociocultural background speakers interact in: social habits and customs, widespread stereotypes, shared knowledge concerning humorous phenomena are all responsible for our reactions to humor and for the interpretations we derive from it. In Chapter (2), all these will be discussed in terms of the metapragmatic study of language, which involves the analysis of speakers' knowledge and discourse about pragmatic phenomena (see among others Jaworski, Coupland, and Galasiński 2004; Agha 2007; Bublitz and Hübler 2007; Culpeper and Haugh 2014). After an overview of some main concepts, topics, questions, methodologies, and goals of metapragmatic research, the analysis will concentrate on the metapragmatic comments on humor, particularly on how such comments work in terms of creating or reinforcing solidarity and intimacy among speakers who share similar interpretations of humorous texts; or, on the contrary, in terms of dividing them into opposing groups defending different views and evaluations of humorous texts and humor in general. The data examined here comes from humorous texts circulated online (an advertisement and canned jokes) and, most importantly for the metapragmatic analysis, also includes authentic, spontaneous reactions to them, which reveal how these texts are understood and evaluated.

Chapter (3) is dedicated to issues related to the genres of humor, thus highlighting not only the presence of humor in numerous and diverse communicative settings, but also the different forms it may take therein. After a brief theoretical overview on genres and humor, I offer a taxonomy of humorous genres and then discuss how humorous genres may be transformed in time, mostly due to the new needs arising in online communication and the new media. New genres may emerge, while old ones may transform to adjust to the new environments of (humorous) communication. As the data analysis is intended to demonstrate, such transformations may be attested in prototypical humorous texts such as canned jokes, as well as in oral humorous genres, such as joint fictionalizations (Kotthoff 1999), which are adapted to online environments. It will therefore be confirmed that genre is indeed one of the key contextual features affecting humor production and interpretation.

In view of the above, the discussion in Chapter (4) turns to the two linguistic theories of humor, namely the Semantic Script Theory of Humor and the General Theory of Verbal Humor (see above), and to some recent efforts to expand the latter, so as to include aspects of context which were left out of its initial version. This discussion will lead to the development of a performance theory of humor, which will attempt to encompass most (if not all) aspects of context that are significant for the creation and interpretation of humor (as presented in Chapters 1–3). Moreover, a performance theory of humor cannot but account for humor failure and humor quality issues as well, hence I will try to address these topics (drawing, among others, on Bell 2015). A tentative application of the proposed analytical model is also included in this Chapter exploiting the humorous advertisement discussed earlier (in Chapter 2) and viewers' reactions to it.

So far, we have placed particular emphasis on speakers' multiple ways of conceptualizing and interpreting humor (Chapter 2) as well as on the variety of settings and genres it may occur (Chapter 3). Such aspects of humor use are not only relevant to humor theory (as has been suggested in Chapters 1 and 4), but also to language teaching, especially to teaching about humor. So, in Chapter (5), I explore how we can teach about humor in language courses while taking into serious consideration that humor may indeed yield multiple and often opposing interpretations, and that it surfaces in most communicative settings and texts/genres. This means that we need to adopt an educational/teaching framework opening the door to multiple perceptions of humorous discourse and simultaneously creating space for everyday texts with humor and not limiting students' linguistic/textual experiences in class to the texts/genres proposed by the official curriculum. One such educational/teaching framework is, I suggest, that of *critical literacy* (see among others Fairclough 1992a; Comber and Simpson 2001; Wallace 2003).

So, in Chapter (5), after an overview of recent research on teaching with/about humor, I elaborate on what critical literacy is and how it is usually practiced within educational settings. I also argue for the exploitation of humorous texts in critical language courses, trying to diffuse common or potential reservations or objections. Particular emphasis is placed on teaching about humor through the exploitation and analysis of humorous texts in class rather than on teaching with humor, which is often proposed to improve learning outcomes. To this end, I finally present some tentative proposals for a critical approach to humorous texts in language classes. The main aim of these critical proposals is to enhance students' critical awareness of what humor is, how it works in various contexts and genres, and what are its (positive or negative) social implications for interlocutors and/or the targeted individuals or groups. The teaching proposals are based on the analysis of everyday humorous texts referring to current sociopolitical affairs, gender issues, and migration. In addition, I intend to demonstrate that the analytical model described in Chapter (4) is not only meant for theoretically-oriented approaches to humor, but it is also helpful for designing and implementing critical analyses and discussions about humor in educational settings.

The conclusions at the end of the book (Chapter 6) summarize its content and explores further areas of inquiry.

1 Context in humor research

1.1 Introductory remarks

The importance of context for the interpretation of humor has repeatedly been summarized by most of us when we say "You just had to be there" to apologize for an utterance or a story whose humor has not been understood by our recipients, despite our best efforts. It is also clearly reflected in (linguistic or other) humor scholarship during the past few years: from decontextualized canned jokes or other printed material, which are supposed to be repeated "verbatim" in different contexts, many humor scholars have re-oriented themselves towards more contextualized approaches to humorous texts and genres, so as to examine them "in their own terms". This implies that we can account for the situated, local meanings of humorous texts/genres only if we take into consideration a number of factors that constitute its context.

So, why this study begins (and emphasizes in its title) the concept of *context*? If context has become the *sine qua non* for a significant number of humor analyses, why do we need to read more about it? Various studies on humorous phenomena seem to presuppose and exploit different aspects of context and, in my view, it would be interesting to discuss and bring together different approaches. In addition, as our above-mentioned excuse "You just had to be there" indicates, lack or overlooking contextual information may lead to the failure of humor. Successful or unsuccessful humor and, in general, multiple perceptions of humor due to diverse and sometimes incompatible contextual presuppositions are another area of study that has recently attracted the attention of humor scholars.

Admittedly, context is notoriously hard to define. It is not accidental that, under the influence of anthropological conceptualizations and approaches to it (see among others Malinowski [1923] 1989; Duranti and Goodwin 1992), innumerable pages have been written and innumerable debates have taken place on its definition and significance for the analysis of discourse within pragmatics, discourse analysis, and sociolinguistics (to name but a few). It is not among the aims of this book to contribute to such debates and discussions (see Brown and Yule 1983; Fetzer 2004; Georgakopoulou and Goutsos 2004; Widdowson 2004; Predelli 2005; van Dijk 2008a; Fetzer and Oishi 2011; Finkbeiner, Meibauer, and Schumacher 2012, and references therein). Instead, here I would like to begin with bringing together those aspects of context that have been considered as significant specifically for the analysis of humorous discourse. These aspects are not, of course, specific to humorous discourse, but they can help us frame and develop our research questions and their discussion in the present book.

So, in what follows, I will briefly refer to some main approaches to context put forward by humor scholars.

1.2 Conceptualizing context within humor research

In his seminal work on the linguistic mechanisms of humor, Raskin (1985) offers a linguistic theory which deliberately and programmatically disregards context; it is instead designed to account for *speakers' competence* to identify a text as humorous based on its semantic structure. Drawing on Chomsky (1965), Raskin discusses the ideal speaker's competence in identifying and understanding humor in idealized circumstances where everybody shares the same sense of humor and reaches identical interpretations of humorous texts (for a more detailed description of Raskin's theory, see Chapter 4). This, however, does not mean that Raskin underestimates or totally overlooks the importance of context for processing humor. Quite on the contrary, he presents a quite detailed account of the factors constituting context (Raskin 1985: 3–5, 11–19, 63–64). These are the following:

1. the *human participants* in the humor act, namely the speaker, the perceiver/hearer, and the addressee. In an effort to underscore the significant role of the perceiver for constructing and identifying humor, Raskin (1985: 3) states: "It is the perceiver's presence, of course, which makes a humor act a humor act, simply because it is the perceiver who laughs";
2. the *humorous stimulus*: "something must happen in a humor act. An utterance has to be made, a situation has to develop or to be perceived – in short, a new stimulus should be presented and responded to humorously" (Raskin 1985: 4). The stimulus must involve a failure, a violation of a rule/the social order, or a deviation from what is expected; in other words, an incongruity or script opposition;
3. the *participants' life experiences* including their preferences or tastes for humor, their feelings or beliefs about what can be humorously framed or not, and their previous experiences with humor. Such experiences are related to differences in humor from one generation or era to another;
4. the *participants' dispositions to humor*, namely the psychological mood allowing them to participate (or not) in a given humor act;
5. the *physical environment or situation* where a humorous stimulus occurs;
6. the *social and cultural background* of a humor act including shared social values, norms, etc. Such a common background renders humor effective. To elaborate on the significance of this factor, Raskin (1985: 17) quotes Viktoroff (1953: 146), among others: "society determines the circumstances

under which laughter is recommended, tolerated or forbidden, as well as its duration, intensity, etc.".

Raskin's account of context appears to resonate Freud ([1905] 1991: 282–285) who offered a list of "accompanying factors" for humor including, among other things, a cheerful mood, the absence of a "serious" mental activity, the absence of feeling, and the presence of a pleasurable circumstance where humor is expected (see Raskin 1985: 11–13). All these are reminiscent of what Raskin refers to as participants' dispositions and the physical environment or situation of a humor act (see above).

In addition, Raskin (1985: 59) underlines the fact that the script-based semantic theory on which he builds the Semantic Script Theory of Humor has "a strong *contextual* emphasis" and belongs to "*contextual* semantics" (see also Raskin 1985: xiv, emphasis mine). He further supports the contextual nature of the Semantic Script Theory of Humor in his account of semantic scripts: "[t]he script is a cognitive structure internalized by the native speaker and it represents the native speaker's knowledge of a small part of the world. Every speaker has internalized rather a large repertoire of scripts of 'common sense' which represent his/her knowledge of certain routines, standard procedures, basic situations, etc." (Raskin 1985: 81). It should also be underlined here that, even though he concentrates on speakers' competence (i.e. their potential to recognize and interpret humor), Raskin (1985: 63) admits that "every sentence is perceived by the hearer already in some context. If the context is not given explicitly by the adjacent discourse or extralinguistic situation, the hearer supplies it from his previous experience. If the hearer is unable to do that he is very unlikely to comprehend the sentence". In other words, Raskin (1985: 59–98) recognizes and actually capitalizes on the significance of context for processing humor, since context forms the basis for evoking or building the scripts that need to be opposed for creating and comprehending humor.

In one of the earliest discourse analytic approaches to humor, Norrick (1993: 3–6) discusses the significance of context for knowing when to produce humor and for grasping its meaning(s). In his account, context involves:
1. the *cultural lore* (Norrick 1993: 4) about places, customs, and interactions as well as the stereotypes that may be evoked in humorous discourse;
2. *interactants' assumptions about when, where, about what, and with whom to use humor*; such assumptions include information about a community's habits concerning the use of humor or its avoidance or prohibition;
3. the *physical setting*, the *participants* (including their social roles, relationships, and interactional history), and the *co-text* (i.e. the surrounding linguistic/discourse context) of humor; in other words, the local circumstances of humor production and reception; and

4. the *contextualization cues* provided by the participants (e.g. intonation, prosody, code-switching, smiles, laughter, facial and body movements; see Gumperz 1982).

In a similar vein, but from an anthropological and folklorist perspective, Oring (2008: 196–202) suggests that there are four different categories of context which are perceived as relevant to the analysis of humor:
1. the *cultural context* including cultural knowledge, concepts, values, and attitudes contributing to processing humor;
2. the *social context* referring to the social circumstances where humor emerges: time, setting, participants and their relationships, as well as the nature of their interaction, all relating to how humor functions and what message(s) it conveys;
3. the *individual context* highlighting aspects of humor that may more or less deviate from one person to another. Under the influence of previous experiences and inclinations, participants may exhibit specific preferences as to what kind(s) or topics of humor they prefer and disseminate, as well as whether and how they recontextualize humorous texts. This results in the development of different habits or even tastes in humor use (cf. Kuipers 2006); and
4. the *comparative context* mostly referring to humor research methodology and tradition rather than to participants' real-life circumstances, practices, and concerns. Humor scholars have often adopted comparative approaches to humorous discourse by examining similar practices or texts across sociocultural communities (see among others Davies 1998).

Oring's (2008) classification is quite compatible with Raskin's (1985) and Norrick's (1993) accounts in terms of the cultural and the social context.[2] Their main difference involves the emphasis both Raskin and Norrick place on linguistic aspects of context (i.e. the humorous stimuli or the co-text and the contextualization cues respectively). On the other hand, Raskin and Oring underline the individual differences in humor creation, dissemination, and perception, while Oring is the only one who discusses an analyst-oriented aspect of context, that is, the comparative context.

Without offering such comprehensive accounts of context, Canestrari (2010) and Tsakona (2013a) highlight the same contextual aspects as significant for the

---

[2] El Refaie (2011: 90) also distinguishes between "the immediate interpersonal setting in which a particular joke is created, communicated and received, and the broader social, political and historical context, which determines what is considered to be funny in the first place".

analysis of humor. Canestrari argues for the importance of contextualization cues for processing humor, while Tsakona (2013a: 42) argues for the centrality of its "sociocultural presuppositions", namely the culturally-specific background knowledge necessary for its processing. In addition, both concur that verbal reactions to, or comments on, humor are to be closely examined as part of the context, since they reveal participants' perceptions of discourse intended as humorous and (more or less directly) reflect their views on when or whether something is humorous, why it is (not), how humor is (not) to be used, etc. (cf. Oring's *individual context* above; see also Shilikhina 2017, 2018).

An interesting, and more elaborate in a sense, proposal is put forward by Filani (2017), who distinguishes between the *context-of-the-joke* and the *context-in-the-joke*. More specifically, the *context-of-the-joke* refers to the circumstances within which humor emerges and is interpreted, and includes three components:
1. the *shared situational knowledge*, that is, participants' mutual perception of their own ongoing activities (which give rise to humor);
2. the *shared cultural knowledge* pertaining to the beliefs, history, events, actions, presuppositions, attitudes, values, and behaviors that may influence the use of humor in a specific sociocultural community. Such factors may be more or less different across communities and may result in multiple forms, topics, and targets of humor; and
3. the *shared knowledge of code* including the linguistic choices made for a humorous utterance/text, which must be accessible to its recipient(s).

The *context-in-the-joke* refers to what happens *inside* the humorous text and forces recipients to evoke background assumptions and knowledge to process it. This kind of context comprises the following:
1. the *joke utterance*;
2. the *participants-in-the-joke*, namely the characters and the targets, as well as the stereotypes surrounding them;
3. the *activity-in-the-joke*;
4. *conversational joke cues*, that is, devices used to engage recipients in the humorous exchange, contextualization cues;
5. *nonverbal cues* (see 4 above); and
6. *voicing* referring to characters' speech representation.

As Filani (2017: 458) himself suggests, "[t]he context–in–the–joke (...) is embedded in the context–of–the–joke", thus underlining their close interconnection. His proposal is partially compatible with Norrick's (1993) and Oring's (2008), especially when it comes to his account of the context–of–the–joke and its components, as well as the conversational and nonverbal cues of the context-in-the-joke. The other components of the context-in-the-joke have not been adequately discussed before, so this model directs our attention also to how the content of humorous texts represents social reality or builds fictional realities through entextualizing aspects of the context-of-the-joke.

Recently, Chovanec and Tsakona (2018: 3–8) attempt to capture in (often overlapping) categories some aspects of context that matter for humor scholars. So, they discuss the following categories:

1. *framing devices of humor*, which include laughter and smile, prosodic and intonational features and patterns (pauses, pitch, speed, etc.), movements, gestures, and facial expressions, as well as code-switches and metalinguistic devices indicating the transference from the serious to the humorous mode and back (Shilikhina 2018), and in general explicit statements or descriptions concerning the humorous intention or quality of an utterance;

2. *reactions* to humorous discourse revealing whether or not the audience understood the intended humorous message, what was their exact interpretation of it (which may deviate from what the speaker initially intended), and whether they evaluate it positively (e.g. they like/agree with it) or negatively (e.g. they do not like/agree with it). Such reactions may be non-verbal (e.g. laughter, smile, facial expressions of approval or disapproval; see framing devices above) or verbal. In the latter case, the reactions may even take institutionalized forms such as the publication of journalistic and scholarly articles discussing and negotiating the meaning(s) and repercussions of a text intended as humorous;

3. *sociocultural parameters of humor* relating, on the one hand, to participants' social characteristics and identities (age, gender/sexual orientation, ethnicity, religion, social class, political affiliation, profession, etc.); and, on the other, to the sociocultural particularities of the community where a humorous text is circulated and interpreted. Different sociocultural communities have different preferences and norms concerning in which contexts humor is expected (or not expected) to be used, which humorous topics and targets are considered appropriate or inappropriate for each audience and in each setting, whether there are institutional restrictions on the use of humor, and how they are imposed on the members of the community (cf. the *normative communities of humor* in Kuipers 2008a);

4. the *reasons* why humor is employed and the *goals/functions* it is meant or perceived to achieve. Among other things, humor brings to the surface shared values and views, thus highlighting the boundaries between the ingroup and the outgroup; creates solidarity and reinforces intimacy; contributes to a pleasant atmosphere; expresses criticism; mitigates aggressive or face-threatening

moves/acts; disparages the "Other"; breaks social relationships; attracts the attention of the audience; enhances the popularity of the humorist; contributes to building specific social identities (e.g. gender, ethnic, political ones), etc. (see among others Norrick 1993; Attardo 1994: 322–330; Bell 2018). This means that humor is never "innocent" and devoid of emotional impact and social consequences, whether positive or negative ones; and

5. the *genres* where humor is included. Taking generic particularities into account could assist participants in making sense of a humorous text's content and purposes. By becoming familiar with the genres circulating in a sociocultural community, participants learn to use humor in specific ways so as to be able to participate in specific activities. They also learn to opt for humorous devices and strategies that are considered "conventional", "appropriate", and eventually effective in achieving certain goals or completing certain tasks. Still, the normativity and conventionality of genres does not necessarily constrain speakers' freedom in humor use; it can actually provide a meaningful background for creative uses and recontextualizations.

All these parameters, Chovanec and Tsakona (2018) suggest, underlie speakers' dynamic negotiations and perceptions of humor in real settings. Although this proposal exhibits similarities with all the previous ones, it seems to place particular emphasis not only on the *reactions* to humor (see also Canestrari 2010 and Tsakona 2013a above), but also on the *functions* and *genres* of humor, which are tacitly subsumed under Oring's (2008) *cultural context*, Norrick's (1993) "assumptions about where, when, about what and with whom to use humor", and Filani's (2017) *shared situational knowledge*. On the other hand, in Chovanec and Tsakona's (2018) classification, Oring's *cultural* and *individual contexts* are merged into the category of *sociocultural parameters*.

All these approaches could be presented in a concise way in Table (1.1), so as to demonstrate more clearly their similarities and differences:

1.3 The focus of the present study

Needless to say, not all aspects of context can be examined in detail in a single monograph. Moreover, even if we cho(o)se one or two of them, we would not be able to cover all related topics. The focus of the present study will be, first, on participants' verbal reactions to humorous discourse and their sociocultural assumptions (see Table 1.1, columns G and A respectively) and, second, on the genres of humor (see Table 1.1, column B).

Table 1.1: Accounts of context within humor research.

	A	B	C	D	E	F	G	H
	Sociocultural assumptions on humor use	Genres of humor	The specific communicative setting where a certain humorous utterance/text occurs	Text and co-text	Contextualization cues	The characters of the humorous text, their actions and speech	Reactions to and comments on humor	Preferences and differences in humor use among different speakers/hearers
Raskin (1985)	(6) social and cultural background		(1) human participants of the humor act (5) physical environment or situation	(2) humorous stimulus				(3) participants' life experiences (4) participants' dispositions to humor
Norrick (1993)	(1) cultural lore about places, customs, interactions, and stereotypes	(2) interactants' assumptions about when, where, about what, and with whom to use humor	(3) the physical setting and the participants	(3) co-text	(4) contextualization cues			

Oring (2008)[3]	(1) cultural context	(2) social context: nature of their interaction and functions of humor	(2) social context: time, setting, participants and their relationships			(3) individual context
Canestrari (2010)				(1) contextualization cues		(2) reactions to humor
Tsakona (2013a)	(1) sociocultural presuppositions of humor					(2) reactions to humor
Filani (2017)	(1.2) shared cultural knowledge	(1.2) shared cultural knowledge	(1.1) shared situational knowledge	(1.3) shared knowledge of code, (2.1) joke utterance	(2.4) conversational joke cues (2.5) nonverbal cues	(2.2) participants-in-the-joke (2.3) activity-in-the-joke (2.6) voicing
Chovanec and Tsakona (2018)	(3) sociocultural parameters of humor: community characteristics	(4) reasons and goals/functions of humor (5) genres of humor		(1) framing devices of humor		(2) reactions to humor (3) sociocultural parameters of humor: participants' social characteristics

3 Oring's (2008) *comparative context* is omitted here as it mostly refers to humor research methodology and tradition rather than to participants' real-life circumstances, practices, and concerns.

Participants' reactions to, and comments on, humor are one of the most important sources of information we have at our disposal to explore what they think of humor, how they perceive specific humorous utterances, texts, or genres, how they assess humor functions in specific real–life situations. In this sense, participants' comments on humor stem from, and reflect, their more or less diverse views and attitudes towards its use, all of which are directly related to their sociocultural assumptions concerning the use of humor: when and why it may be used, what its topics may be, what background knowledge is presupposed or taken for granted for its processing. All these can be considered as part of what Agha (1998, 2007) calls a *metapragmatic stereotype*. The metapragmatic stereotypes of a specific pragmatic phenomenon (e.g. humor) are participants' internalized models on what this phenomenon consists of, how it should be used, when, why, and for what purposes. Participants' metapragmatic stereotypes of humor constitute their positionings towards widely held beliefs on what humor is and how it is expected to be used and function in communication (for a more detailed discussion, see Chapter 2).

A significant part of the metapragmatic stereotypes of humor involves the communicative settings where humor is (or is not) expected to appear, that is, the *genres* of humor. In other words, metapragmatic stereotypes pertain to when and where the use of humor is deemed (in)appropriate, (in)dispensable, and hence (in)effective or not (their strong interconnection is depicted in Figure 1.1). Even though humor has by now become an integral part of the public sphere, popular culture, and certainly of private interactions, its presence turns out not to be welcome in certain cases (see among others Lockyer and

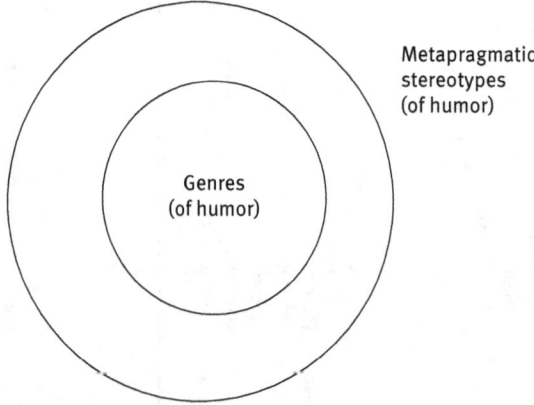

Figure 1.1: The interconnection between metapragmatic stereotypes and genres.

Pickering 2005). As a result, there may be controversies arising from divergent perceptions about where and when humor can or cannot be used. Even though humor seems to surface in increasingly more genres than in earlier times (e.g. even in courtroom decisions in the USA; see Hobbs 2007) and to become a main ingredient in new (often mediated) genres (e.g. memes, online posts in the social media), research on the genres of humor is still scarce: "[t]he consequences of genres and form for the interpretation and appreciation of humor is [an] understudied field in humor scholarship" (Kuipers 2008b: 388; see also Attardo 2001: 23; Tsakona 2017d).

So, in what follows, I first discuss the main tenets and goals of metapragmatic research, as well as recent research on the metapragmatics of humor, and how the latter can be explored through participants' verbal reactions and comments on humor use in context (Chapter 2). Then, we move on to discussing and classifying the genres where humor is more or less expected to occur as another significant parameter for the contextualized analysis of humor (Chapter 3).

1.4 Summary

This Chapter provided an overview of some main accounts of context offered by humor scholars. The comparison between the different approaches to context brings to the surface not only significant similarities from one approach to another, but also the wide variety of factors that are deemed important for the contextualized analysis of humor. The present study chooses to focus on two of them: first, speaker's reactions revealing their interpretations of humor and their sociocultural assumptions on humor use; and, second, the genres where humor is more or less expected to occur. The following Chapter is dedicated to the study of the metapragmatics of humor, which will allow us to account for the more or less diverse interpretations and sociocultural assumptions of it.

2 Humor and metapragmatics

2.1 Introductory remarks

Humor scholars often underline the importance of speakers' reactions to humor, since such reactions may confirm or cancel the humorously intended meaning proposed by the humorist (see among others Raskin 1985: 3). Such reactions seem to depend on speakers' own perceptions and assessments of humor and eventually on differences and preferences concerning what can qualify as humor, when, why, etc. Such perceptions and preferences are shaped by the sociocultural background speakers interact in: social habits and customs, widespread stereotypes, and shared knowledge concerning humorous phenomena are all responsible for our reactions to humor and for the interpretations we derive from it. All these parameters belong to what is called *context*, as explained in Chapter (1) (see also columns A and G in Table 1.1).

In this Chapter, these aspects of context will be discussed in terms of the metapragmatic study of language, which involves the analysis of speakers' knowledge and discourse about pragmatic phenomena (such as humor). To this end, we begin with a brief overview of some main concepts, topics, questions, methodologies, and goals of metapragmatic research (Sections 2.2–2.3), so as to demonstrate that these could help us explain the multiple ways the above–mentioned parameters influence the production and reception of humor in real settings. A second overview will follow including some recent studies on the metapragmatics of humor, covering a relatively wide range of phenomena and methodologies (Section 2.4). Then, by focusing on sets of data including metapragmatic comments on humor, I will try to investigate how such comments could broaden the scope of the analysis (and eventually the theory) of humor, and why it is not only interesting but also useful for humor scholars to examine various (even opposing) interpretations of humor. Furthermore, the two case studies discussed here will allow us to see how metapragmatic comments work in terms of creating or reinforcing solidarity and intimacy among speakers who share the same humorous texts, or, on the contrary, in terms of dividing them into opposing groups defending different views and evaluations of humorous texts and humor (Sections 2.5–2.5.3).

2.2 On metapragmatics

Metapragmatic research has concentrated mostly on phenomena such as politeness, register, deixis, and honorofics. Drawing on such previous research

(Agha 1998, 2004, 2007; Bublitz and Hübler 2007; Culpeper 2011: 71–112; Kádár and Haugh 2013: 181–206; Culpeper and Haugh 2014: 235–263) will enable us to clearly delineate the scope of the present Chapter and the respective research questions concerning the metapragmatics of humor.

So, *what is metapragmatics?* Metapragmatic research is premised on the inherent *reflexive* capacity of language, namely its capacity to refer to itself, to describe and evaluate its features, structures, uses, functions, etc. (Jakobson [1957] 1971; Lucy 1993; Mauranen 2010).[4] As Caffi (1994) suggests, a metapragmatic perspective on language involves "the investigation of that area of speakers' competence which reflects the judgments of appropriateness on one's own and other people's communicative behavior", namely the investigation of "the 'know how' regarding the control and planning of, as well feedback on, the ongoing interaction" (Caffi 1994: 2464, 2461, as cited in Hübler and Bublitz 2007: 7; see also Kádár and Haugh 2013: 181). Another term used to refer to such competence is *metapragmatic awareness*, which has been defined as "a discursive 'monitoring' based on the speakers' ability to explicitly reflect on their message and to organize it seeking to prompt certain perlocutionary effect on the part of the addressee" (Timofeeva–Timofeev 2016: 274). Metapragmatic awareness is therefore directly related to speakers' efforts to effectively shape their utterances/texts depending on their communicative goals in specific contexts. Based on their linguocultural experiences, speakers have acquired and/or recontextualize specific context–dependent ways of using language, namely specific norms guiding their own discourse production and interpreting or assessing that of others.

However, it is often pointed out that metapragmatic awareness remains quite abstract as a notion: "[a]wareness is not measurable, and the notion lends itself to easy speculation" (Verschueren 2000: 445; see also Culpeper and Haugh 2014: 237–239; Timofeeva–Timofeev 2016: 274–275). In an effort to better account for such awareness, Culpeper and Haugh (2014: 239–240, 252–253) distinguish between *metapragmatic awareness* and *metapragmatic comments*: metapragmatic comments or other such resources reflect speakers' metapragmatic awareness. A similar distinction is proposed by Preston (2004): his *Metalanguage 1* (i.e. metapragmatic comments/resources) refers to "folk linguistic comments

---

4 There definitely is a close interconnection among linguistic reflexivity, metapragmatic awareness, folk linguistics, and knowledge about language in general. In this sense, metapragmatic research is very closely related to metalinguistic research. A detailed discussion of such interconnections lies far beyond the scope of this book (see among others Lucy 1993; Verschueren 1999, 2000; Coupland and Jaworski 2004; Jaworski, Coupland, and Galasiński 2004a; Preston 2004; Hübler 2011: 120–125; Kádár and Haugh 2013).

(...) based on the respondent's awareness of a difference between his or her language use and that of some others" or, more generally, to "attitudinal responses to language" (2004: 79, 94); and his *Metalanguage 3* (i.e. metapragmatic awareness) refers to "the presuppositions which lie behind much *Metalanguage 1* use", namely "underlying folk beliefs speakers of a language have about the nature of the object itself" (2004: 87, 94; emphasis in the original).

Within metapragmatic research, scholars have identified several metapragmatic resources or, to use Culpeper and Haugh's (2014: 240) terminology, *metapragmatic indicators*, such as the following:
1. language description (whether scholarly or not),
2. speech representation (including stylization),
3. deixis,
4. hedges,
5. contextualization cues (e.g. intonation, prosody; see also Section 1.2),
6. references to, and the labeling of, previous or prospective (speech) acts,
7. cohesive devices (e.g. discourse/pragmatic markers), and
8. explicit comments on language use (e.g. evaluative or prescriptive acts).[5]

All such features provide recipients with more or less subtle guidelines concerning how they (are expected to) interpret an utterance/text in given circumstances and, in general, how language is (expected to be) used therein.

Why is it important to study metapragmatics? Metapragmatic research seems to grant researchers access not only to speakers' implicit views and norms concerning language use (i.e. their metapragmatic awareness), but also underlines the inseparability between speakers' conceptualization of pragmatic/sociolinguistic phenomena and their own practices in various contexts. Jaworski, Coupland, and Galasiński (2004b: 3) provide a comprehensive account of what metapragmatics can tell researchers interested in pragmatics, discourse analysis, and sociolinguistics:

> How people represent language and communication processes is, at one level, important data for understanding how social groups value and orient to language and communication (varieties, processes, effects). This approach includes the study of folk beliefs about language, language attitudes and language awareness, and these overlapping perspectives have established histories within sociolinguistics. Metalinguistic representations may enter public consciousness and come to constitute structured understandings, perhaps even

---

[5] On metapragmatic indicators, besides the seminal works of Jakobson ([1957] 1971), Bateson ([1955] 1972), Lucy (1993), Silverstein (1993), see also Caffi (1994), Verschueren (1999, 2000), Coupland and Jaworski (2004), Preston (2004), Hübler and Bublitz (2007), Culpeper (2011), Hübler (2011), Culpeper and Haugh (2014), Ruiz-Gurillo (2016c: 84), Chun (2017).

"common sense" understandings – of how language works, what it is usually like, what certain ways of speaking connote and imply, what they *ought* to be like. That is, metalanguage can work at an ideological level, and influence people's actions and priorities in a wide range of ways, some clearly visible and others much less so (emphasis in the original).[6]

It therefore seems that metapragmatic research does not only bring to the surface more or less latent norms of language use, but also reveals how such norms are circulated, debated, and eventually become entrenched and often naturalized among speakers. Metapragmatic research may help us trace the *interplay* between pragmatic norms (implicit or explicit ones) and actual use: pragmatic norms and conventions shape actual use which in turn reinforces or weakens the dissemination and validity of the norms, depending on whether speakers decide to comply with them or challenge them. In other words, speakers' perceptions and attitudes towards aspects of language use are directly related to how they themselves tend to speak or write – and vice versa. As a result, theorizing about pragmatic phenomena cannot but take into consideration speakers' metapragmatic awareness as encoded through metapragmatic indicators. In Verschueren's (1999: 196) words, "in social life, *conceptualizations and practices* are inseparable. Consequently, there is no way of understanding forms of social behavior without gaining insight into the way in which the social actors themselves habitually conceptualize what it is they are doing. Preconceived theoretical frameworks just do not suffice" (emphasis in the original).[7]

Relevant to the present discussion is the concept of *metapragmatic stereotypes* (Agha 1998, 2004, 2007). Agha claims that speakers internalize models of language use which guide their own linguistic behavior and enable them to make judgments about their own language use or that of others. Such models aim at fixing and stabilizing the variation attested in language use so that specific pragmatic phenomena are easily recognizable to speakers.[8] Metapragmatic stereotypes influence speakers' linguistic performance and interpretation of discourse in real settings, and are culturally–specific and context–dependent. They are shaped by the sociocultural context speakers interact in and, more specifically, by the ways discourse is used and evaluated therein. It could therefore

---

6 See also Culpeper (2011: 73–74) and Kádár and Haugh (2013: 181, 183–186).
7 See also Verschueren (2000: 451), Agha (2000: 216), Kádár and Haugh (2013: 183).
8 It should be noted here that the word *stereotype* does not imply that the respective categorizations are necessarily false or inaccurate. Nor do they try to distort the representation of sociolinguistic reality. The specific term indicates the ideological nature of language use and of the norms and rules speakers form and tend to follow in discourse (Agha 2007: 157; see also Moschonas 2005: 112–117, 122–123; Tsakona 2013b: 13–16).

be suggested that metapragmatic stereotypes on specific pragmatic phenomena are part of speakers' metapragmatic awareness.

Metapragmatic stereotypes can be observed and recorded via speakers' metapragmatic activities and statements, namely through metapragmatic indicators (see above). However, speakers seem to have different *ideologies* on how language is or should be used: the metapragmatic stereotype of one speaker may, to greater or lesser degree, deviate from, or even compete with, that of the other, thus leading to conflicts and negotiations on the "(un)common", "(un)desirable", "(in)appropriate", and "(in)correct" language use as well as to defending specific interpretations as "the only valid/correct ones". A single speaker's metapragmatic stereotype may even exhibit differences from one communicative setting to another. As a result, metapragmatic stereotypes may mark group boundaries (e.g. between those who agree and those who disagree on the definition and/or functions of a pragmatic phenomenon) and may acquire an exclusive/inclusive potential and function in context.[9]

For example, a metapragmatic stereotype on humor precedes any scholarly definition of humor, as every speaker has certain opinions and attitudes concerning what qualifies as humor and what does not, how, when, and where humor is used or should be used, what are its desired or attested effects, etc. Such a relatively stable mental model accounts for what speakers do (or think they do) and is evoked to assess humorous phenomena. In other words, each speaker has shaped their own metapragmatic stereotypes on humor which allows them to reach conclusions concerning its "success" or "failure", the "(in)appropriateness" of its use, its "positive" or "negative" effects, etc.

---

9 It should be noted here that two other concepts perhaps more commonly employed to refer to such internalized models of language use are *language ideologies* and *(social or meta-)discourses on language*. These consist of "habitual ways of thinking and speaking about language and language use" (Verschueren 1999: 198); or of "persistent frames of interpretation related to the nature and social functioning of language" (Verschueren 2000: 450; see also Cameron 2004: 316; Coupland and Jaworski 2004: 36–37; Preston 2004: 86–95; Moschonas 2005; Kádár and Haugh 2013: 200–204). Like metapragmatic stereotypes, language ideologies and social discourses influence language use and practices, are politically charged, and can be publicly contested. Thus, they are employed to categorize speakers (e.g. denigrate those who use language in a "non-standard" or "deviant" manner) and exhibit an inclusive/exclusive function through connecting language use with moral orders. The discussion of the similarities and subtle differences (if any) between *language ideologies*, *social discourses*, and *metapragmatic stereotypes* lies beyond the scope of the present study, while the latter term will be used throughout the book for ease of reference.

Given the above, metapragmatic indicators encoding metapragmatic stereotypes may fulfill sociopragmatic functions. As Hübler and Bublitz (2007: 3–4, 17–18) suggest, metapragmatic indicators may be:
1. evaluative,
2. conflictual (e.g. face-threatening),
3. organizing (e.g. turn-taking, topic management, coherence),
4. defending communicative norms,
5. creating and modifying identity.[10]

The use of such indicators becomes particularly relevant and salient when something "goes wrong" in interaction and participants feel the need to do some repair or management moves. For instance, metapragmatic indicators often occur when audience expectations are breached, when disagreement occurs, or when it becomes helpful or necessary to monitor interaction or to point to certain meanings (Preston 2004: 78–79; Hübler and Bublitz 2007: 8, 12, 16; Mauranen 2010: 18–20; Kádár and Haugh 2013: 199).

To sum up, speakers' knowledge, views, and stances concerning language use constitute their metapragmatic awareness which can also be conceptualized as the sum of metapragmatic stereotypes, each of which refers to a different pragmatic phenomenon. Such stereotypes become accessible through specific metapragmatic indicators, which are employed by speakers as more or less explicit guidelines addressed to recipients concerning how their utterances/texts are to be interpreted. Since, as metapragmatic research has shown, speakers may not share the same metapragmatic stereotypes on a specific pragmatic phenomenon, but instead they may possess different or even competing ones, the respective metapragmatic comments may be used to enact and underline such similarities or differences. As a result, metapragmatic indicators acquire multiple sociopragmatic functions themselves. The following Figure (2.1) represents the relationship between metapragmatic awareness, stereotypes, indicators, and their functions:

To recontextualize all these in humor theory terms, metapragmatic awareness involves, among other things, speakers' metapragmatic stereotypes on what humor is (or is not), how, why, when it should (or should not) be used, etc. Such views become explicit not only through speaker's own production of humor in specific communicative settings (and their avoidance of humor in certain others), but also through their contextualization cues and reactions to

---

10 See also Cameron (2004: 313), Jaworski, Coupland, and Galasiński (2004b: 3–4), Culpeper and Haugh (2014: 258–260).

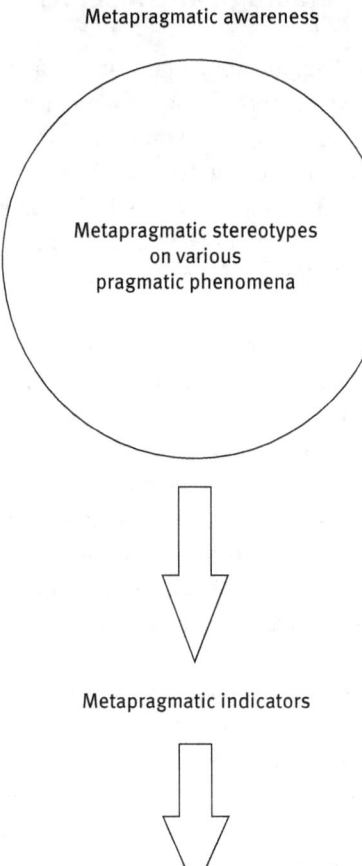

Figure 2.1: The relationship between metapragmatic awareness, stereotypes, indicators, and their sociopragmatic functions.

humor, that is, through metapragmatic indicators. Given that there can be differences in what speakers assess and/or frame as humorous as well as in how they choose to react to humor, they may converge or diverge as to their use of humor. Thus, the metapragmatic indicators of humor may eventually bring speakers closer together if they are used in a more or less similar manner and/ or convey compatible meanings; or, on the contrary, they may drive speakers apart if they are used differently or in opposing ways. This is how metapragmatic indicators acquire sociopragmatic functions.

2.3 Some methodological notes on metapragmatic research

There appear to be several ways to trace and collect metapragmatic data. Kádár and Haugh (2013: 192–204) discuss a wide variety of methodological approaches including corpus analysis, lexical/conceptual mapping, metapragmatic interviews and questionnaires, naturally occurring discourse (e.g. face-to-face interactions, media commentary, historical documents/texts), or elicited discourse (e.g. interviews, diaries, reports; see also Verschueren 1999: 196; Kristiansen 2004: 167; Preston 2004: 85; Sinkeviciute 2017, 2019; as well as the Chapters in Bublitz and Hübler 2007).

The investigation of metapragmatic indicators is not, however, without limitations and challenges. First of all, even though participants have implicit models on language use, they do not always encode them in their discourse. Moreover, the context-dependent and culturally-specific nature of such models does not allow for generalizations across texts, genres, communicative settings, or communities. Metapragmatic indicators may provide information on participants' perceptions within a specific communicative setting or linguocultural community at most (see Coupland and Jaworski 2004: 25–26; Kristiansen 2004; Kádár and Haugh 2013: 185–186, 192–204; Culpeper and Haugh 2014: 263; Tsakona 2017e).

Another restriction relates to the methodology of their collection: in case metapragmatic indicators are elicited (via questionnaires, interviews, etc.), they may be influenced by what Labov (1972) calls *observer's paradox*, namely the effect the presence of a researcher has on the collected data. Speakers are more or less likely to conform to (what they think are) the expectations of the researcher, whether consciously or subconsciously (see also Kristiansen 2004: 187). On the other hand, authentic, spontaneous data which would be preferable is not particularly easy to spot. It is often difficult to know in advance when and where participants will spontaneously discuss pragmatic or sociolinguistic phenomena, and to manage to record such discussions.

In addition, the distinction between pragmatic and metapragmatic analyses may still be a controversial issue in some cases. It often seems to be necessary to make a clearer distinction between analytical levels and foci when researchers aim at exploring metapragmatic phenomena (Hübler 2011: 4; Tsakona 2016a, 2017a). This could be attributed to the fuzziness of the concept of *metapragmatic awareness* (see Section 2.2).

Finally, given that scholarly linguistic descriptions and linguistics/pragmatics in general constitute metapragmatic activities themselves (see Caffi 1994: 2461), researchers tend to implicitly or explicitly suggest that their own methodogically-sanctioned and theoretically-informed analyses are the only "correct" and "valid" ones. Hence, there is often bias against speakers' metapragmatic activities and analyses, which are, subsequently, framed by scholars as "ideological" and not actually significant for linguistic analysis (see among others Cameron 2004: 317; Kristiansen 2004: 187; Preston 2004: 81–82).

The present investigation of the metapragmatics of humor is based on the premise that speakers' perceptions on humor are as ideological as researchers' ones. After all, researchers are predominantly language users. Whether we realize it or not, our research hypotheses and questions more often than not stem from our own experiences with language use and from potential discrepancies between real-life linguistic data and the theoretical frameworks and concepts employed for their analysis (Verschueren 2000: 452; Coupland and Jaworski 2004: 24; Tsakona 2013b, 2017e). This further suggests that theoretical frameworks and their analytical concepts and tools could actually be enriched and become more effective if we take into serious consideration speakers' perceptions and assessments of linguistic/pragmatic phenomena. And this is why I insist on a metapragmatic perspective on humor here.

More specifically, in the present study, emphasis will be placed on authentic, spontaneous *metapragmatic comments*, namely "expressions conventionally understood within a speech community to refer to an evaluation of certain behavior-in-context" (Culpeper 2011: 74; see also Section 2.2).[11] The analysis of such comments will allow us to trace speakers' metapragmatic stereotypes on humor, that is, their views and stances concerning what humor is, how humor is expected to be used in specific contexts, how it functions, what are the differences between a humorous utterance/text and a non-humorous (e.g. serious or offensive) one, etc. It will also be shown how similarities or differences in such metapragmatic stereotypes may respectively bring speakers closer together or may drive them apart via dividing them into opposing groups fighting over the "correct" interpretation of humor. Eventually, the analysis of metapragmatic comments could lead us to confirm, refute, or revise prefabricated theoretical schemas concerning the nature and use of humor and reinforce or undermine their validity. Understanding what humor is and how it works will always be partial without considering its users' views and attitudes concerning their own practices and habits.

Before we proceed with the analysis of metapragmatic comments on humorous texts, first, let's take a look at recent metapragmatic research focusing on humor and related phenomena.[12]

---

11 See also *descriptive metapragmatic comments* in Sinkeviciute (2019).
12 Following Ruch (1998) and Attardo (2011: 135), the word *humor* is used as an umbrella term covering all related phenomena.

2.4 Metapragmatic research on humor

Recently humor scholars have started to investigate various aspects of the metapragmatics of humor, not only bringing to the surface diverse perceptions of humor *per se*, but also testing different methodological approaches that could foster further research in the area.

Ruiz-Gurillo and the contributors to her edited volume (2016b) explore humor as metapragmatic awareness or, as the editor herself puts it, as "metapragmatic ability" (Ruiz-Gurillo 2016a: 1), namely as a means to gain insight on how speakers monitor and plan their own language use. Explicitly or implicitly drawing on Verschueren's (1999, 2000) conceptualization of *metapragmatic awareness* (see Section 2.2), the authors of the volume scrutinize specific strategies or devices speakers resort to, when producing and negotiating humorous utterances and texts, depending on their potential recipients and communicative settings. Such strategies or devices are expected to be recognized and appropriately interpreted by the recipients. The studies explore various metapragmatic indicators such as prosody, (dis)fluency markers, and facial expressions, while they also discuss humorists' metalinguistic/metapragmatic ability to manipulate linguistic/pragmatic conventions.

Metapragmatic comments as metapragmatic indicators are explored by researchers such as Kramer (2011), Laineste (2011), Stewart (2013), Constantinou (2019), and Dynel and Poppi (2019), who analyze online public debates on specific humorous texts. In their studies, these authors collect spontaneous, authentic reactions to humorous discourse by participants in online environments, who offer multiple perspectives on the meanings and the potential functions of specific texts. Such perspectives could lead to more or less intense conflicts which often turn out to be futile, as Kramer (2011) suggests, because participants do not appear to be willing to concede, converge, or even consider the arguments of the opposite side. Among the topics discussed in these debates are the following:
1. What is humor?
2. When does humor succeed or fail – and why?
3. How does humor function?
4. Should there be limits to humor (e.g. in the form of self- or other-censorship) or not? Does freedom of speech mean no limits to humor?
5. Do humorous texts reflect social reality?
6. Do humorous texts influence social stances and views (e.g. via promoting racism, aggression, or bigotry), or are they perceived as "simply amusing" and "inconsequential" discourse?
7. What is the relationship between humor and offense?

8. Is laughter a controllable/voluntary reaction to humor or an uncontrollable/involuntary one?
9. What does it mean to laugh or not to laugh with a text intended as humorous which may, however, be interpreted as aggressive or offensive?

The different stances participants adopt in such debates on the metapragmatics of humor divide them in opposing groups through the construction of opposing identities for themselves and the "Others". Specific texts and the multiple and ambiguous meanings derived from them thus bring to the surface different *humor ideologies* (Kramer 2011: 138) or different *tastes* of humor (Laineste 2011; cf. Kuipers 2006). The public defense of such ideologies on humor seems to acquire a *ritual* character as "identities and beliefs are performed and naturalized under the guise of a debate" (Kramer 2011: 163). In other words, such studies demonstrate that divergent metapragmatic stereotypes encoded through metapragmatic comments on specific humorous texts have significant sociopragmatic functions (see Figure 2.1).[13]

Humor ideologies or metapragmatic stereotypes conceptualized as humor ethics are also the focus of Lockyer and Pickering (2001) who investigate reactions to humor that has been interpreted as offensive. The reactions examined come from letters of complaint sent to, and published in, the satirical magazine *Private Eye*. Researchers suggest that speakers disapprove of humor, which they find exaggerated and beyond the limits of "propriety", while at the same time defend themselves against potential accusations of lacking a sense of humor. Through their comments on humor, speakers attempt to draw the boundary between humor and ethics, humor and offense, as well as between serious and humorous discourse (see also Lockyer 2006).

Kerkkänen (2006) has attempted to describe the humor–related topics focused upon in Finnish newspaper articles. The corpus analyzed includes articles reporting on Kerkkänen's own research on humor and elaborating on related phenomena. His conclusions indicate that journalists are not so much interested in research findings concerning humor; instead, they tend to concentrate mostly on whether such findings confirm or refute widely circulating views on humor, such as its subversive character or function and its positive

---

[13] A slightly different perspective is adopted by a number of studies investigating how humor is used to mitigate or disguise racist meanings or intent (see Billig 2001, 2005a; Park, Gabbadon, and Chernin 2006; Chun and Walters 2011; Malmquist 2015; McKinney and Chun 2017, and references therein). Such studies examine recipients' metapragmatic comments on humorous discourse, but their main focus is on the discursive construction and dissemination of discriminatory views and practices, not on the conceptualization of humor.

influence on health. Newspaper articles also tend to promote evaluative accounts of humor (e.g. which is the "best" kind of humor or whether humor is related to optimism). It therefore seems that press texts may often refer to widespread metapragmatic stereotypes on humor, thus further disseminating them and perhaps increasing their perceived validity (see also Kersten 2019).

Based on the same premise that the media significantly contributes to disseminating metapragmatic stereotypes on humor, Tsakona (2013b) aims at tracing the similarities and differences between scholarly accounts and findings on humor (i.e. etic perceptions of humor), on the one hand, and views or stances expressed by journalists and other professionals such as comedians, cartoonists, writers, scholars from outside humor research, literary or theater critics, on the other (i.e. emic perceptions of humor).[14] Her corpus includes interviews and articles from Greek newspapers and magazines (whether print or online) published and collected from 2000 until 2013 and referring to humor and related phenomena. The analysis of the metapragmatic comments on humor concentrates on six thematic areas:

1. the definition of humor and its relationship with related phenomena such as laughter, satire, and the comic;
2. the negative and positive attitudes towards humor and its research;
3. the sociopragmatic functions of humor in various genres;
4. the relationship between humor and politics;
5. the limits of humorous expression;
6. the role of humor in education.

The comparison between journalistic articles and research findings on humor reveals both similarities and differences between emic/lay and etic/scholarly perceptions of humor, thus confirming the inseparability between humor conceptualizations and humor practices (see Verschueren 1999: 196 in Section 2.2). It seems that not only may journalists and professionals be familiar with scholarly approaches to humor (e.g. in the framework of the research necessary to fulfill their professional roles or out of personal interest), but also that humor scholars may, on the other hand, rely on their lay perceptions of humor more than they would be willing to admit.

Besides spontaneous metapragmatic data, elicited ones could turn out to be revealing for humor research. Sinkeviciute (2017) investigates how funniness is conceptualized in interaction and what are, in her informants' views, the preferred reactions to funniness. Interviews are therefore used to detect emic

---

14 For the distinction between *etic* and *emic* analyses, see Pike ([1954] 1967).

understandings of funniness. The findings of this study suggest that participants may offer positive or negative evaluations of funniness depending on the point of view adopted each time, namely the humorist's, the target's, or the non-participant's in interaction. Yet, only positive (i.e. light-hearted or humorous) reactions to funniness are considered to be preferred and expected in all such cases. Sinkeviciute (2019) also explores metapragmatic comments coming from the same set of data and functioning as identity claims. She demonstrates how her informants construct collective, individual, or situated identities while interpreting and commenting on humorous instances. More specifically, informants may build collective identities when they align themselves with a linguocultural group in their assessment of what is (not) funny and, on the contrary, they may build individual identities when they differentiate themselves from what others belonging to a specific group perceive as humorous. Situated identities are constructed when speakers underline the importance of a certain local context and of participants' relationships therein for evaluating whether something can be considered to be funny or not (see also Sierra 2019).

Sørensen (2016: 85–96) also uses interviews to investigate the sociopragmatic functions of humorous political stunts, namely humorous activist performances taking place in public spaces to attract general attention and undermine dominant discourses on various sociopolitical issues. Specifically asked to comment on the role of humor in such contexts and in the communication within such groups, the interviewed activists come up with a variety of sociopragmatic functions of humor. Among other things, they employ humor in their stunts to reach out to, and mobilize, the wider audience, to reduce their fear and apathy, to attract and recruit new members, to render their messages more appealing and memorable, to convey undesirable or unpleasant truths, and to break well-entrenched patterns of thinking. Within the activist groups examined, humor helps members to sustain their culture of resistance, to enhance their self-respect, group cohesion, and motivation, to cope with feelings of fear, anxiety, depression, and burn-out, to lower the levels of aggression they experience, and to create and maintain a pleasant atmosphere in their meetings and joint activities. Humor thus appears to be an important multifunctional resource for activists, at least according to their own metapragmatic comments on it.

Metapragmatic research of humor may also be based on scripted discourse reflecting language use and potentially putting into wider circulation specific views on humor (on the interplay between metapragmatic stereotypes and discursive practices, see Section 2.2). Dynel (2017) examines the differences between emic/lay and etic/scholarly perceptions of two closely related phenomena: irony and sarcasm. In particular, she uses the terms *irony* and *sarcasm* as metapragmatic labels revealing speakers' perceptions of these phenomena in

American English, and she compares speakers' labels to theoretical definitions and approaches to irony and sarcasm. Such a comparison indicates that "the label 'irony' is typically used with reference to situational irony, whereas 'sarcasm' denotes the presence of the rhetorical figure [of irony]" (Dynel 2017: 84). Moreover, "contrary to the prevalent view in the scholarly literature that sarcasm (...) promotes disharmony and conflict or is simply offensive", in the data examined it appears to be "perfectly innocuous" and "carries no (intended or perceived) aggression" (Dynel 2017: 84). Needless to say, this line of research could bring to the surface more such intriguing mismatches between emic and etic understandings of humorous phenomena, that is, between speakers' metapragmatic stereotypes on humorous phenomena and the respective theoretical approaches and scholarly definitions of them.

Studies in the lexical field of the word *humor* could also be considered part of its metapragmatic research. Hempelmann (2017) offers a detailed discussion of the meanings of terms such as *humor*, *wit*, *laughter*, *comic*, *smile*, *amusement*, and *exhilaration* mostly in English but also in other European languages such as German, French, and Spanish (see also the references therein). His suggestions align with previous research on the terminology of other pragmatic phenomena (e.g. politeness; see Culpeper 2011: 74; Kádár and Haugh 2013: 189–194; Culpeper and Haugh 2014: 263) to the effect that there usually are significant differences in the meanings and uses of such terms not only across languages and cultures, but also within the same language due to polysemy and/or language change in time. As already mentioned (see Section 2.3), the use of such terms is always culture–specific and context–dependent, hence generalizations across contexts, languages and/or cultures could prove confusing and misleading. Even though previous such research may sometimes have been based (besides scholarly sources) on dictionaries or researchers' own intuition, use, and agenda, nowadays the use of large electronic corpora could facilitate and eventually encourage more research on the terminology and lexical fields of humor.

Whether based on spontaneous or elicited metapragmatic data, such studies offer solid evidence on the multiple interpretations of humor in context and could perhaps lead us to reconsider the strong emphasis placed on humorous intention by earlier studies. A humorous text is not humorous *per se* only because its producer intended it as such; its humorous dimension has to, and is indeed, negotiated by all participants (see also Pickering and Lockyer 2005: 9; Chovanec and Tsakona 2018). Furthermore, both types of methodology seem to have their strong and weak points: on the one hand, interviews providing us with elicited metapragmatic data are easier to design and conduct, but usually focus on specific, well–defined questions and hypotheses; on the other, authentic, spontaneous metapragmatic comments on humor are harder to find and collect, but they may offer insights on a wide variety of topics deemed significant by the participants themselves in relation to humor and its conceptualizations. Moreover, spontaneous metapragmatic data is not influenced by the presence of the researcher (see Section 2.2). Finally, scripted data or prescriptive texts (such as dictionaries) may promote specific meanings and uses of humor-related terms, thus entrenching or, on the contrary, contradicting common use and/or scholarly definitions. All methodologies on the metapragmatic research on humor seem to come with their pros and cons, hence researchers are expected to be aware of the limitations of their analyses and findings. Still, the variety of approaches to the metapragmatic of humor appears to be promising and paving the way for more interesting studies to come.

2.5 The sociopragmatic functions of metapragmatic comments

As already mentioned (in Sections 2.2 and 2.4), divergent metapragmatic indicators/comments reflecting different metapragmatic stereotypes may drive speakers apart, that is, divide them into ingroup and outgroup. On the contrary, converging metapragmatic indicators/comments stemming from compatible metapragmatic stereotypes may contribute to creating consensus and bonding among speakers. Such sociopragmatic functions will be discussed in the following Sections. In the first case presented here (Sections 2.5.1–2.5.1.3), it will be shown that speakers' metapragmatic comments on humor contribute to creating ingroupness and consensus, as they emphasize their common experiences and perceptions as represented in the humorous texts commented upon. In the second case (Sections 2.5.2–2.5.2.3), however, the metapragmatic comments on humor appear to have the opposite effect: they bring to the surface opposing perceptions and functions of humor, and hence speakers are divided into groups offering contrasting interpretations of a humorous text.

2.5.1 Creating solidarity through metapragmatic comments on crisis jokes

The first set of data comes from the online exchange of contemporary political jokes on the Greek debt crisis.[15] After a brief presentation of the political

---

15 Sections (2.5.1–2.5.1.3) draw from Tsakona (2015, 2017c, 2017f) with appropriate modifications to adjust to the purposes of the present book.

jokes exchanged among speakers, so as to demonstrate their main topics and targets, I will concentrate on the metapragmatic comments speakers offer on such jokes, and discuss how these comments put forward common views on the sociopragmatic functions of such humor, thus creating consensus among speakers.

The jokes discussed here come from a large corpus of humorous texts (1,662 texts) referring to the Greek financial crisis and collected from January 15, 2010 until December 12, 2013. The corpus includes both multimodal texts (i.e. internet memes, political cartoons; 1,066 texts, 64.13%) and exclusively verbal ones (i.e. jokes; 596 jokes, 35.86%). All of them were sent to the author's personal email account by friends and relatives.[16] The verbal jokes presented here could be divided into two broad categories: a) jokes directly targeting and discrediting Greek or, less often, foreign politicians and their political decisions and actions concerning the Greek debt crisis (322 jokes, 54.02%; see examples 2.10–2.15 in Section 2.5.1.1); and b) jokes referring to Greek people's everyday lives and problems due to that crisis, thus only indirectly and by implication targeting politicians and their policies (274 jokes, 45.97%; see examples 2.1–2.9 in Section 2.5.1.1).[17]

The main, however, focus here is not the crisis jokes *per se*, but the comments speakers offer after reading and before forwarding them. Such comments are inserted in the emails forwarding the jokes and constitute authentic, spontaneous reactions to them and could offer us some information on how speakers perceive such jokes and why they choose to forward them. In other words, they could reveal what are the sociopragmatic functions and purposes served by disseminating such material, and eventually grant access to speakers' metapragmatic stereotypes on this kind of humor. Out of the 167 emails including the jokes examined here, only in 72 cases (43.11%) did speakers offer their evaluations and views on such humor, either on the title of the email or exactly before the joke(s)

---

16 None of the emails sent was excluded from the collection and, at the same time, no other material was added by the author (e.g. downloaded from websites or coming from printed collections). Although the corpus does not claim representativeness, it could be suggested that this selection was not biased by the author's personal preferences.
17 These two categories are reminiscent of the ones identified by Raskin (1985: 222–237) in his discussion of political jokes:
1. *denigration jokes* targeting "a person, a group, an idea, or the whole society"; and
2. *exposure jokes* targeting "a political regime as a whole and contain[ing] a reference to an event or series of events, which are not widely publicized, and quite often actively suppressed by the regime" (Raskin 1985: 222).

began. In the rest of the emails (i.e. 95 emails, 56.88%), no comment was found: the email title included either an abstract of the joke or one of its utterances (e.g. the punch line or the opening phrase) or the word ανέκδοτο/α 'joke(s)' or an utterance not directly related to the content of the email (e.g. a greeting).

2.5.1.1 Some examples of the crisis jokes

In general, crisis jokes revolve around what are deemed as "incongruous" aspects of living in Greece during the past few years as well as politicians' "incongruous" behaviors.[18] Their brief presentation here will allow us to take a glimpse at the sociopolitical conditions Greek people experience and, most importantly, at how they perceive and evaluate these conditions and represent them in their discourse. Such representations (i.e. the crisis jokes) are in turn commented upon and critically discussed through speakers' metapragmatic comments on this kind of humor. Such comments, as we will see in the following Sections (2.5.1.2.1–2.5.1.2.3), indicate speakers' efforts to share their views and feelings through humor, thus supporting each other.

Many crisis jokes in my corpus refer to the lack of money (due to unemployment or cuts in salaries and pensions), which has had several repercussions on people's lives; the cost of living has increased and people cannot afford to pay for their everyday expenses:[19]

(2.1) Σε λίγο θα πηγαίνουμε σούπερ μάρκετ, δεν θα αγοράζουμε τίποτα και θα κάνουμε μόνο like.
Soon we will go to the super market, we will not buy anything and we will only "like" the products [i.e. as we do on Facebook].

(2.2) Έλεγα να πάρω σκύλο στο σπίτι αλλά τι φταίει το δόλιο να κρυώνει; Θα πάρω πιγκουίνο.
I thought of getting a dog at home but why should the poor animal be cold? I'll get a penguin instead.

---

18 On crisis jokes in a different sociocultural context, see Akinola (2018).
19 All the Greek data presented in this book was translated by the author. In humorous texts in particular, some humor may have been lost on the way. Unconventional spelling was maintained in the Greek original texts, but was not reproduced in the English translations. Square brackets include additional explanatory material. It should also be noted that short jokes were usually preferred to longer ones (which were more than one page long in several cases), as they proved relatively easier to translate.

In example (2.1), the joker complains about the high prices at the super market, where soon we will only "like" the products (as we do on Facebook), but will not be able to buy anything. The lack of money also results in the lack of heating at home, where only a penguin (and not a dog) could survive during the winter (example 2.2).

Crisis jokes often involve job scarcity and unemployment, bad working conditions and relations, and (forced) migration as a solution to the above:

(2.3) Αν ακούσετε τίποτα για καμιά θέση εργασίας ενημερώστε με σας παρακαλώ... ψάχνω δεύτερη δουλειά γιατί πρώτη δεν βρίσκω με τίποτα!!
If you hear anything about a job post, please let me know... I am looking for a second job, because I can't find a first one no matter what!!

(2.4) Στην τρίτη λυκείου θα πρέπει να προσθέσουν μάθημα «Πως να ζήσετε στο εξωτερικό»...
In the third class of Lyceum [i.e. the final year of Greek secondary education] they should add a course on "How to live abroad [as a migrant]"...

Such jokes focus, among other things, on the difficulty to find a job (example 2.3) and on the fact that young people may be forced to leave Greece to support themselves (so Greek education needs to prepare them for this; example 2.4).

Greek people also criticize themselves for their current situation:

(2.5) Οι νεοέλληνες ξοδεύουν χρήματα που δεν έχουν για να αγοράσουν αντικείμενα που δε χρειάζονται ώστε να εντυπωσιάσουν ανθρώπους που δεν εκτιμούν.
Greeks spend money they do not have to buy things they do not need so as to impress people they do not appreciate.

(2.6) Δεν είναι ότι δεν είμαστε επαναστάτες. Απλά είμαστε άτυχοι που δεν είναι όπλο ο καναπές.
It is not that we are not rebels. We are just unlucky that the couch is not a weapon.

Greek people are self-portrayed as wasting their money to satisfy their vanity (example 2.5) and as lazy and self-indulgent (i.e. lying on the couch all day; example 2.6), hence they do not care for, and do not fight against, the austerity measures imposed on them.

Moreover, crisis jokes identify incongruities in the general conditions of living and in the Greek public health and education systems (due to recent reforms), while they also critically comment on the Greek media, corruption in both the public and the private sector, monetary insecurity, elections, banks, demonstrations, etc. The following examples are indicative:

(2.7) Η διαφορά μεταξύ ελληνικής οικονομίας και Τιτανικού:
Στον Τιτανικό είχε και ορχήστρα.
[What is] the difference between the Greek economy and the Titanic?
On the Titanic there was also an orchestra.

(2.8) Ο χρόνος είναι ο καλύτερος γιατρός. Γιαυτό στο ΙΚΑ σου κλείνουν ραντεβού για μετά από 4 μήνες.
Time is the best doctor. This is why at IKA [i.e. the then largest social security organization in Greece] they give you an appointment for 4 months later.

(2.9) Συνομιλία μητέρας–γιού στην Ουγκάντα το 2011:
–Αμπντούλ διάβασε τα μαθήματά σου παιδί μου. Τα παιδάκια στην Ελλάδα δεν έχουν ούτε βιβλία..
A mother–son conversation in Uganda in 2011:
–Abdul dear, do your homework. Children in Greece do not even have textbooks...[20]

Greek economy seems to be sinking like the Titanic but without an orchestra playing music (example 2.7). Due to recent cuts, the public health system does not work properly (example 2.8) and, in Greek schools, students do not have textbooks (example 2.9).

In the jokes presented so far, Greek people complain about their deteriorated living conditions and unemployment, and seem to feel deprived of goods and services available to them before the crisis (e.g. house heating, health services, school textbooks). At the same time, they criticize themselves, among other things, for a luxurious lifestyle beyond their means and for not reacting dynamically against all the measures imposed by the Greek government and the members of the Troika (i.e. the International Monetary Fund, the European Central Bank, and the European Commission). It could therefore be suggested that via crisis jokes Greek people express their criticism and indignation for

---

[20] School textbooks are given to all students of Greek public schools for free at the beginning of each academic year. However, in September 2011, when the academic year began, the books were unavailable, hence teachers and students had to work with photocopied material for a few months.

their current situation, implying that things should not be like they actually are. What is more, they critically recognize (and laugh at/with) their own irresponsibility and inadequate behavior in preventing and/or solving such problems.

On the other hand, politicians' actions, statements, practices, policies, omissions, etc. are more often than not judged by joke-tellers as unexpected and incompatible with their institutional role. More specifically, a significant amount of the jokes discussed here considers incongruous, and hence disapproves of, the ways Greek politicians handle various aspects of the crisis. So, politicians are often represented as unsuitable for the job:

(2.10) Πώς καταφέρνει ο Γιωργάκης να κάνει τόσο πολλές βλακείες σε μία μόνο μέρα;
– Σηκώνεται νωρίς το πρωί!
How does little George [i.e. George Papandreou, the then Prime Minister] manage to do so many stupid things in only one day?
– He wakes up early in the morning!

The then Prime Minister George Papandreou from the socialist party PASOK is represented as stupid and thus incapable of, and even dangerous for, ruling the country. The nickname *Γιωργάκης* 'little George' further reinforces a widely circulating stereotype referring to Papandreou's allegedly limited political skills.

Opposition parties and their members are also attacked via humor:

(2.11) Πάει ο Τσίπρας και ο Στρατούλης στην Αγγλία για μία συνάντηση με τον Κάμερον. Πηγαίνουν στο ξενοδοχείο και ανοίγουν την ντουλάπα να βάλουν μέσα τα ρούχα τους και βλέπουν ένα ποντικό. «Ρε συ», λέει ο Τσίπρας, «ξέρεις πως είναι ο ποντικός στα αγγλικά για να πάρουμε τηλέφωνο στην Reception να τους πούμε ότι βρήκαμε ένα;» «Όχι» λέει ο Στρατούλης, «εσύ»? «Ούτε εγώ» λέει ο Τσίπρας, «αλλά άσε, θα πάρω εγώ να εξηγηθώ!».
– Yes, Reception?
– Yes, how can I help you?
– Do you know Tom and Jerry?
– Yes, of course.
– Jerry is here.
Tsipras and Stratoulis [i.e. the Leader and a prominent member of the then major Opposition party, SYRIZA] go to England to meet [David] Cameron [i.e. the then British Prime Minister]. They check in the hotel and they open the closet [in their room] to put in their clothes and they see a mouse. "Dude", says Tsipras, "do you know how they say 'mouse'

2.5 The sociopragmatic functions of metapragmatic comments — 39

in English so that we call the reception and tell them that we found one?" "No", says Stratoulis, "do you?" "Me neither", says Tsipras, "but let me call [them] to explain myself!".
<u>– Yes, Reception [there]?</u>
<u>– Yes, how can I help you?</u>
<u>– Do you know Tom and Jerry?</u>
<u>– Yes, of course.</u>
<u>– Jerry is here.</u>[21]

In joke (2.11), the Leader and a prominent member of the left party of SYRIZA are targeted for their inability to recall a rather common English word, and/or possibly for the limited skills in English stereotypically attributed to them.[22] It is thus implied that they may not be suitable for the job as they may not be able to discuss and negotiate with our EU partners and other international institutions.

In addition, politicians are targeted for corruption, power hunger, and criminal behavior:

(2.12) Ψήφισε Αλί Μπαμπά. Έχει μόνο 40 κλέφτες.
Vote for Ali Baba. He has only 40 thieves.

Joke (2.12) humorously represents Greek parliamentarians as thieves stealing Greek people's money and property. Thus Greeks are advised to vote for Ali Baba instead, who only has 40 thieves, while the Greek parliament has 300 members/thieves.

A few jokes from this corpus attack foreign politicians and institutions for interfering with Greek politics:

(2.13) Η Μέρκελ θα μιλήσει προεκλογικά στο Καστελόριζο στις 5 Ιουνίου, στο Δίστομο στις 10 Ιουνίου και στο Πεδίο του Άρεως 15 Ιουνίου.
Merkel is going to give pre-election speeches in Kastellorizo on June 5th, in Distomo on June 10th, and in Pedion tou Areos on June 15th.

During pre-election campaigns, Greek political leaders speak in open rallies in Athens and other big cities around Greece. So, in joke (2.13), the German Chancellor Angela Merkel is humorously portrayed as a "Greek" political leader touring Greece to deliver speeches, thus implying that she makes decisions and

---
21 The underlined extract appears in English in the original Greek joke.
22 See also Spilioti (2016: 71–72), Vladimirou & House (2018).

rules the Greek state. The humorous potential and connotations of this joke are enhanced by the selection of the places where she is supposed to deliver her pre-election speeches: Kastellorizo is a small island in the Dodecanese from where the then Prime Minister George Papandreou officially announced that the country would have to ask for help from the EU institutions to avoid bankruptcy; Distomo is a village in mainland Greece, whose inhabitants were slaughtered by the Nazis in 1944; and Pedion tou Areos is a big park in the centre of Athens where open rallies but also protests often take place. All three places are heavy with symbolism not only in relation to the Greek crisis and politics (Kastellorizo, Pedion tou Areos), but also in terms of the relationship between the Germans and the Greeks (Distomo).

Greek people's disappointment and mistrust are sometimes encoded as violent behavior against politicians:

(2.14) 1 φλιτζάνι καφέ, αξία: 5EURO
  1 ποτό στο μπαρ, αξία: 10EURO
  1 λίτρο βενζίνη, αξία: 1,70EURO
  1 γιαούρτι στα μούτρα ενός κουστουμάτου, ψεύτη πολιτικού, αξία: ΑΝΕΚΤΙΜΗΤΗ!
  1 cup of coffee, price: 5 euro
  1 drink at the bar, price: 10 euro
  1 liter of gas, price: 1.7 euro
  1 yogurt at the face of a well-dressed, lying politician: priceless!

Joke (2.14) constitutes a parody of the Mastercard "Priceless" advertisements and explicitly suggests that it is priceless, namely particularly satisfying, to throw yogurt at the face of "lying" politicians. Such a gesture constitutes an act of protest and denigration against people who are perceived as deceitful and worthless. Instead of a product or something that could be paid by a Mastercard and please us, the punch line involves a more violent type of "pleasure". In the same joke, the product prices may also allude to the incongruous increase of prices during the crisis due to heavy taxation.

Greek people occasionally blame themselves for voting for their politicians, thus in a sense sharing responsibility again (cf. jokes 2.5–2.6) for what is happening in the country:

(2.15) Βλέποντας αυτούς που εξέλεξαν οι Έλληνες στη Βουλή, σκέφτομαι πως δεν πρέπει να μας διώξουν από την ευρωζώνη αλλά από τον πλανήτη.
  Watching those elected in the parliament by the Greek people, I am thinking that we should not be expelled from the Eurozone but from the planet.

Joke (2.15) blames Greek people for voting the wrong people for the parliament, thus proposing that they should be even forced to leave the planet for such wrong choices.

So, crisis jokes targeting politicians depict the negative opinions Greek people seem to have for them, and convey their mistrust and disapproval towards them. Politicians are blamed for not being able to handle the problems of the country effectively and for defending their own interests instead of the country's ones. Concurrently, Greek people seem to feel responsible for electing such politicians, but they also tend to become aggressive towards them, even in a humorous frame.

2.5.1.2 Speakers' metapragmatic comments on crisis jokes
Together with crisis jokes, speakers seem to disseminate online their own opinions on such texts, namely their metapragmatic stereotypes on how and why humor works in such cases. In the set of data examined here, speakers tend to focus on the sociopragmatic functions of crisis jokes. So, in what follows, I will discuss the metapragmatic comments offered by those who read and circulate the jokes presented above. Speakers' own perceptions and evaluations of crisis jokes are equally (if not more) important with researchers' analyses, as they could confirm, enrich, or even refute etic conclusions.

2.5.1.2.1 Crisis jokes as sources of amusement
First of all, it should be noted that forwarding an email including jokes could be considered an indication of their positive evaluation in and of itself. We would not easily spend time recycling texts that we do not approve of; on the contrary, we share information and material that we find interesting and potentially enjoyable as a means of bonding with our peers (see among others Laineste 2008: 35). This seems to be confirmed by *all* the comments collected and examined here: no negative evaluation of such jokes is attested in the 72 comments offered on them.

More specifically, crisis jokes are evaluated via adjectives such as *(αρκετά/ πολύ) καλό/ά* '(quite/very) good', *φανταστικό* 'fantastic', *κορυφαίο* 'top (joke)', *καταπληκτικά* 'great', *φοβερά* 'amazing', *σοφό* 'wise', *φιλοσοφημένο* 'sagacious', *τέλειο* 'perfect', *νόστιμα* 'cute', *χαριτωμένα* 'delightful', *έξυπνα* 'clever', etc. A crisis joke also seems to be appreciated because it is *(πολύ) επίκαιρο* '(very) timely'. Furthermore, a positive evaluation of such jokes is implied when the emails including them are titled with phrases such as *γελάμε* 'we laugh', *ΧΑΧΑΧΑΧΑΧΑ* 'HAHAHAHAHA', *(και) (λίγο) γέλιο* '(and) (some) laughter', *πλάκα έχουν* 'they are fun', *τρελό γέλιο* 'crazy laughter', etc. Such metapragmatic comments also reveal that crisis jokes are circulated to provoke laughter and to share the amusement speakers feel when reading them. Thus, they become a means of entertainment and bonding among speakers (see also Piata 2018).

Moreover, metapragmatic comments such as "wise", "sagacious", and "clever" underline that such jokes are appreciated for their to-the-point and perceptive commentary on the sociopolitical reality in crisis-ridden Greece. This brings us to the second sociopragmatic function of crisis jokes pointed out by my informants.

2.5.1.2.2 Crisis jokes as "accurate" representations of a "tragic" reality

Speakers often comment on the "realism" of crisis jokes: the jokes are thought to be reflecting reality and proposing ways of interpreting and dealing with it. The following metapragmatic comments are illustrative:

(2.16) ΑΝΤΙΜΕΤΩΠΙΣΗ ΤΗΣ ΚΡΙΣΗΣ !
DEALING WITH THE CRISIS!

(2.17) δεν θα ηθελα να ηταν ετσι αλλα δυστυχως ΕΙΝΑΙ!!!!!!!!!!!!!!!!!!!!!!!!
I wouldn't like things to be like this but unfortunately THEY ARE!!!!!!!!! !!!!!!!!!!!!!!

(2.18) ΚΑΛΗΜΕΡΑ ΣΑΣ. . . . . . .ΕΤΣΙ ΕΙΝ'Η ΖΩΗ. . . ..
GOOD MORNING TO YOU. . . THAT'S LIFE. . .

(2.19) Gia na gelasoume ligaki me ta xalia mas!!
Let's laugh a bit with our mess!!

(2.20) ΜΗΝ ΓΕΛΑΣ . Η ΚΑΤΑΣΤΑΣΗ ΕΙΝΑΙ ΤΡΑΓΙΚΗ !!!
DON'T LAUGH. THIS IS A TRAGIC SITUATION!!!

(2.21) Ανέκδοτο για γέλια και για . . .κλάματα!
A joke to laugh and to. . . cry!

Not only are the situations described in these jokes perceived as "realistic" (at least by some speakers; see examples 2.16–2.19), but also as "tragic" (examples 2.19–2.21). Speakers imply that crisis jokes are in a sense "accurate" representations of what happens in Greece ever since the crisis began – and this seems to be one of the reasons why they choose to forward such jokes. Even if we do not adopt a literal interpretation of examples (2.16–2.19) but a figurative one (i.e. if we interpret them as exaggerations), the message conveyed remains that one of the reasons for recycling such jokes is that their incongruities seem at least "plausible" to Greek speakers.

Only in one metapragmatic comment are crisis jokes framed as a means for awakening the Greek people:

(2.22) Προωθήστε το μπας και ξυπνήσουν κάποιοι
Forward this just in case some people wake up.

This implies that crisis jokes as "accurate" representations of reality could contribute to cultivating Greek people's awareness of the circumstances and events that led to the current "tragic" situation, and could perhaps incite them to react against it.

All the metapragmatic comments presented so far show that, for Greek speakers, there is a strong interconnection between the hard reality of the financial crisis and the comicotragic reality of the jokes. Even though Greek speakers are aware of the fact that these texts are humorous and meant for entertainment (see Section 2.5.1.2.1), their evaluations underline the similarities between real life and its humorous representation.

2.5.1.2.3 Crisis jokes as a coping mechanism

It seems that crisis jokes and the ensuing laughter also function as a coping mechanism, namely as a way to survive the crisis (at least from a psychological point of view), as the following examples indicate:

(2.23) ΤΕΤΑΡΤΗ ΒΡΑΔΥ ΤΟΥ ΑΗ ΔΗΜΗΤΡΗ!!!
ΠΕΡΙΜΕΝΟΝΤΑΣ ΤΗΝ ΨΥΧΡΟΛΟΥΣΙΑ ΑΠΟ ΤΗΝ ΕΕ.............ΑΣ ΤΟ ΔΙΑΣΚΕΔΑΣΟΥΜΕ
με πολυ αγαπη (διοτι μονον αυτη θα μας μεινει στο τελος)
IT'S WEDNESDAY NIGHT, [the feast day] OF ST. DEMETRIUS!!! [i.e. October 26th]
WAITING FOR THE BAD NEWS FROM THE EU... LET'S HAVE SOME FUN
With lots of love (because this is the only thing we'll be left with at the end)

(2.24) Καλή σας μέρα και περαστικά μας!
Good morning and let's get well soon!

(2.25) και λιγο γελιο!!!!!!!!!!!!!!!!! χρειαζεται σε ολους μας.............
And some laughter!!!!!!!!!!!!!!!! We all need it............

(2.26) το χιούμορ και το γέλιο δεν θα το πάρουν απο τα χείλη μας !!!!!!
They won't take humor and laughter from our lips!!!!!!

(2.27) Γελάστε γιατί χανόμαστε!!!!!
Laugh or perish!!!!!

(2.28) Μπορεί να μην έχουμε λεφτά, μπορεί να είμαστε στα πρόθυρα της χρεοκοπίας, αλλά έχουμε. χιούμορ και αυτοσαρκασμό! Διαβάστε κορυφαίες ατάκες που κυκλοφορούν τα κρίσιμα αυτά χρόνια.
We may not have money, we may be on the verge of bankruptcy, but we have [a sense of] humor and self–sarcasm! Read top punch lines circulating during these critical years.

Such metapragmatic comments reveal that speakers reproduce crisis jokes in their effort to help themselves make it through the hardships. They admit that they may have been deprived of their money (example 2.28) or their hope for the future (examples 2.23, 2.26, 2.27), but they have managed to maintain their sense of humor and their ability to laugh as a means for keeping things in perspective. They seem to suggest that exchanging emails with crisis humor and the ensuing laughter will help them to endure the bad living conditions they find themselves in (examples 2.23, 2.25, 2.27) and to recover from the crisis (example 2.24).

To sum up, the analysis of speakers' metapragmatic comments on crisis jokes reveals their metapragmatic stereotypes on political humor, in particular on political jokes produced in times of crisis and circulated via email among Greeks. First, it seems that such humor is positively evaluated by Greek people as entertaining, clever, wise, and timely, and aimed at producing laughter. Moreover, it is considered to involve more or less "plausible" or even "accurate" representations of a "tragic reality". Speakers also perceive crisis jokes as a way to psychologically cope with the consequences of the austerity measures and to bolster their morale. Hence such jokes are shared as a means of self– and other–encouragement and of making people aware of the critical circumstances surrounding them and, less often, of their own responsibility therein. In my informants' views, these appear to be the main sociopragmatic functions of crisis jokes.

It should also be noted that *consensus* is built among participants, as they seem to offer similar or compatible accounts of the sociopragmatic functions of these jokes. In the present set of data, no negative evaluation of the jokes and their content was attested and, in general, speakers did not challenge or dispute the metapragmatic comments or stereotypes of their interactants. Such metapragmatic convergence may be related to the specific circumstances where these jokes were circulated and processed: each participant read the jokes in their own private space and could choose between further forwarding them and merely deleting them without accounting for such a choice. Hence, due to its design, this case study could not take into consideration speakers who may actually not enjoy such jokes, as they would most probably not forward (or perhaps not even read) emails including it – and this is one of the limitations of this set of data. Diverse and opposing metapragmatic stereotypes appear to be more often attested in public debates on humorous texts that are assigned different interpretations, and are thus considered controversial. To such a debate is our attention turned in Sections (2.5.2–2.5.2.3).

In the next Section, I will briefly refer to the sociopragmatic functions usually attributed to political jokes by the scholars who investigate them. Thus, I will try to bring to the surface similarities and differences between emic/lay perceptions and etic/scholarly approaches to political jokes.

2.5.1.3 Comparing speakers' metapragmatic stereotypes with scholarly analyses of political jokes

Besides provoking laughter, jokes in general grant access to cultural preferences and norms and to how people interpret "an array of the economic, social and ideological contexts that make up a society" (Laineste 2008: 27). Political jokes in particular offer useful insights on how people's minds interact with sociopolitical reality and reconstruct it (Laineste 2008: 28–29). Political jokes seem to be generated in oppressive political regimes, where people are more or less deprived of their right to express themselves openly, and in times of political transition, where abrupt and radical political changes take place. In both cases, political jokes allow people to express their anxieties and protests against their oppressors and/or their living conditions. They also seem to help people cope with everyday hardships by allowing them to laugh their troubles away: they bolster people's morale and strengthen their hope for the future. Sharing such texts contributes to creating a sense of community and to reinforcing the solidarity among those who share them.[23]

---

[23] On political jokes, see among others Obrdlik (1942), Brandes (1977), VanLoan Aguilar (1997), Shehata (1992), Kanaana (1995), Davies (1998: 77–83, 176–181), Van Boeschoten (2006), Laineste (2009), Stanoev (2009), Hong (2010), Badarneh (2011), Klumbytė (2011), Sheftel (2011), Tsakona

Besides these sociopragmatic functions, some scholars have claimed that political jokes also function as a means of resistance and rebellion against oppressive regimes, leaders, and respective sociopolitical changes (Obrdlik 1942; Shehata 1992; Van Boeschoten 2006; Klumbytė 2011).[24] This interpretation of political jokes as rebellion has, however, been strongly criticized, as humor has hardly ever resulted in subverting any political changes or regimes (see among others Brandes 1977: 345; Davies 2007: 300; Tsakona and Popa 2011b; Takovski 2016; Kersten 2019). Stein (1989: 88–90) maintains that claims to the effect that political jokes constitute a form of resistance are not supported by contextual information or solid empirical evidence, but rather reflect researchers' own ideological positionings (see also Stanoev 2009: 186–187; Hong 2010: 28, 31, 61). In a similar vein, Billig (2005b: 213) frames political jokes as "alibis for those who do not dare to rebel" enabling them to live with their conscience. In his view, by laughing at incongruous aspects of reality and momentarily disrupting the social order, humorists enhance their awareness of the restrictions imposed on them, and hence affirm and further reinforce the authority's power over themselves. In short, what is considered as rebellious humor may in fact be disciplinary humor ensuring compliance with the prevailing social order (Billig 2005b: 200–235; see also Badarneh 2011). This brief disruption of the social order and the subsequent affirmation of authority's power are reminiscent of Bakhtin's (1984a, 1984b) *carnival*, that is, the brief, regular, and state-sanctioned escape from the repression and restrictions imposed by the political status quo, during which people could defy social hierarchies and norms of etiquette, build a "second world" outside the regime, and mock the political order. In Bakhtin's (1984b: 10) own words, "carnival celebrated temporary liberation from the prevailing truth and from the established order; it marked a suspension of all hierarchical rank, privileges, norms, and prohibitions".

The crisis jokes examined here indeed seem to grant access to how Greek speakers perceive and evaluate their own lives and politicians' performances in crisis-ridden Greece. The analysis of speakers' metapragmatic comments on these jokes (see Sections 2.5.1.2.1–2.5.1.2.3) confirms that these texts are produced and disseminated as sources of amusement attenuating people's negative feelings and as a means of coming to terms with the "tragic" reality they live in. In this sense, perhaps the most prominent sociopragmatic function of

---

and Popa (2011a, 2013), Boxman-Shabtai and Shifman (2015), Moalla (2013), Takovski (2016), Kersten (2019).

[24] See also the relevant discussion in Sørensen (2016).

such jokes is their use as a coping mechanism by speakers who are disappointed and face serious problems on a daily basis.

Furthermore, both practices of exchanging emails containing such texts and commenting on them appear to contribute to the carving of a restricted, symbolic space, namely a *carnival*, in Bakhtin's (1984a, 1984b) terms, where joking about the crisis is allowed, positively evaluated, and eventually encouraged. In this restricted and relatively private space and time, Greek speakers are permitted to create more or less amusing, comicotragic conceptualizations of the financial crisis and to laugh at its dark(est) sides and its failed politicians. But when people close or delete their emails, or when they log out of their email accounts, they are back to the hard reality of financial and other problems. This is further confirmed by the fact that no metapragmatic comment offered by Greek speakers refers to such jokes as acts or discourses of rebellion or as practices liberating from political and economic oppression.

In sum, the similarities between speakers' own perceptions and metapragmatic accounts of political jokes, on the one hand, and researchers' analyses and findings, on the other, appear to be significant. The only point of divergence seem to involve the resistance/rebellion function of humor, which has been problematized among researchers anyway (see above). It therefore seems that speakers' spontaneous metapragmatic comments in the present case provide solid empirical evidence *confirming* previous scholarly interpretations on how political jokes work. This, however, does not mean that political jokes coming from different linguocultural environments or historical eras will follow the same pattern and exhibit the same sociopragmatic functions. It should not be forgotten that not only the socipragmatic functions of humor but also speakers' metapragmatic stereotypes on what humor is and how it works are context–dependent and culture–specific (see Section 2.2).

It could also be suggested that such similarities between emic/lay perceptions and etic/scholarly interpretations of political jokes could be due to the fact that humor scholars are often influenced by their own emic/lay perceptions of such texts as they usually belong to the communities where the humorous texts they analyze are circulated. Such influences are inevitable but at the same time enlightening when investigating social practices such as language use (on the inseparability of metapragmatic conceptualizations and linguistic/pragmatic practices, see Section 2.2).

In general, the present case study highlights the importance of the specific communicative setting where a certain humorous text occurs (see column C in Table 1.1), for determining their sociopragmatic functions and eventually their meanings. The fact that the jokes under scrutiny were circulated in times of crisis via emails among intimates makes their entertainment, bonding and morale boosting functions most relevant. If, for instance, some of them were delivered orally in the Greek parliament by members of the Opposition addressing members of the government, the above-mentioned functions would be most irrelevant. In that case, their critical, confrontational, and aggressive functions would be considered most salient. The opposition would most probably use such jokes to attack, denigrate, and eventually ridicule governmental policies as well as to side with "the common people" (cf. Archakis and Tsakona 2011).

2.5.2 Metapragmatic debates on humor

Even though humor researchers often tend to presuppose that humorous texts will normally be perceived as such by recipients, this is not always the case. Different people may have different interpretations of humorous texts, which means that the same humorous text may be perceived as hilarious, successful, disgusting, offensive, discriminating, etc. Such different interpretations are often expressed through metapragmatic comments on specific humorous utterances/texts. Previous research has shown that online public spaces may turn into humor battlefields, where participants defend their own interpretations of, and metapragmatic stereotypes on, humor and simultaneously question or even reject those of others (see Section 2.4). In what follows, I will discuss the diverse metapragmatic stereotypes evoked by speakers commenting on a controversial Greek advertisement.[25]

2.5.2.1 A controversial humorous (?) advertisement

The opposing metapragmatic comments examined here come from a public debate over a Greek television advertisement which was considered humorous and/or sexist. Here is a brief account of the advertisement and its side effects.

At the beginning of 2011, the Greek mobile phone seller company Germanos launched a television advertisement to promote the following service: customers who would buy a mobile phone and, after a certain period of usage time, would not be satisfied with it and wished to return it to the store, were given the opportunity to do so and take their money back in cash (instead of replacing the product with another one or taking a voucher to spend in the same store). The advertisement was based on a metaphor involving a young, recently married couple: the man was not satisfied with the food his wife cooked for them and

---

[25] The following Sections draw from Tsakona (2013a, 2013b, 2017e) with appropriate modifications to adjust to the purposes of the present book.

dreamt of returning her to her mother, while also asking back the money he had spent for/with her. The advertisement goes as follows (see the transcription conventions at the beginning of the book):

(2.29) Ά(ντρας): Τι::::ναυτό; {ειρωνικά προς τη γυναίκα του που φέρνει τις μπάμιες στο τραπέζι}
Γ(υναίκα): Μπάμιες! {με ενθουσιασμό}
Α: Μπάμιες! {με ψεύτικο ενθουσιασμό} Μπάμιες πάλι. {Ήχος που δηλώνει ότι ξεκινά η φαντασίωση του άντρα} Σήκω πάνω! Σήκω πάνω ρε! {με θυμό}
{Βλέπουμε το ζευγάρι να πηγαίνει στο σπίτι της μητέρας της και να χτυπούν την πόρτα. Η πεθερά ανοίγει χαρούμενη που τους βλέπει.}
Π(εθερά): Καλώς [τα]
Α: [Α::::]χαχα:. Λοιπόν πεθερούλα τη βλέπεις; Ε, στην επιστρέφω όπως την πήρα. Απείραχτη, αφόρετη και στη συσκευασία της.
{Η πεθερά δείχνει έκπληκτη.}
Α: Μου έχει κοστίσει 650 καφέδες, 152 γεύματα, 1 δώρο γενεθλίων και 2 γιορτής, Μαράκι {απευθύνεται στη γυναίκα του}, δε μου λες, εκείνη τη σπουδαία ταινία «Ο έρωτας στη Ζουαζιλάνδη» μαζί δεν τη είδαμε; {η γυναίκα γνέφει καταφατικά} Ε, και 39 σινεμά.
{Ήχος που δηλώνει ότι τελειώνει η φαντασίωση του άντρα.}
Γ: Μπάμιες! {με ενθουσιασμό}
Α: Ε; {συνερχόμενος από τη φαντασίωση}
Γ: Όπως τις κάν' η μανούλα μου.
Α: Α:::::
(*Germanos advertisement–mpamies [money back]* 2011)
M(an): Wha::::t's that? {ironically to his wife who brings okras to the table}
W(oman): Okras! {with enthusiasm}
M: Okras! {with fake enthusiasm} Okras again. {Sound signaling that the man starts fantasizing} Get up! Get up you! {in an angry tone}
{We watch the couple go to her mother's house and knock at the door. The husband's mother-in-law opens the door happy to see them.}
Mother-in-law: Wel[come]
M: [A::::]haha:. So dear mother-in-law do you see her? Well, I am bringing her back [exactly] as I took her [from you]. Untouched, unworn, and in her packaging.
{The mother-in-law looks surprised.}
M: She has cost me 650 coffees, 152 meals, 1 birthday present and 2 name day ones, Maria dear {he addresses his wife}, can you tell me, did

we watch it together that great movie "Love in Swaziland"? {his wife nods positively} <u>Well, plus 39 movie tickets.</u>
{Sound signaling that the man's fantasy is over.}
W: Okras! {with enthusiasm}
M: Uh? {waking up from the fantasy}
W: Like my mum cooks them.
M: U:::::hhhh

The analogy between returning the mobile phone to the store and returning the wife to her mother in the Greek sociocultural context evokes well known phrases such as *Θα σε γυρίσω στη μάνα σου* 'I will return you to your mother' or *Αν δε σ' αρέσει, να γυρίσεις στη μάνα σου* 'If you don't like [it], go back to your mother'. Such male chauvinist phrases are reminiscent of the patriarchal structure of the Greek society and were used (or may sometimes still be used) as threats by husbands who were/are not satisfied with their wives' behavior or who want/ed to respond to their wives' complaints. A few decades ago (and sometimes even today), women (together with their dowries) were/may still be part of a financial transaction between the woman's parents and the future son–in–law; women could not/cannot have a say in such transactions, and thus they were/are incapable of defending themselves. Such values and practices form the presupposition of the metaphorical mapping: just as a mobile phone cannot react to its owner's decision to take it back to the store and get his money back, Greek wives can be taken back to their parents and the sons–in–law can ask (and get) their money back.

Okras also seem to carry significant sociocultural connotations that need to be mentioned here. Although okras are part of the famous Mediterranean diet, they are not very popular among Greeks and many Greek children or adults have been forced to eat them by their mothers, on the grounds that they are nutritious and delicious. Thus, okras are stereotypically perceived as an unpopular dish which Greeks are often forced to eat even if they do not like it. The husband's negative reaction to them is not incongruous in this context. On the contrary, many Greeks would find such a reaction expected or even justified.

Given the above, within a few days after the advertisement appeared on Greek television, the Greek General Secretariat for Gender Equality of the then Ministry of Internal Affairs, Decentralization, and E-Government filed an official complaint against the advertisement, asking the National Council for Radio and Television (NCRTV) to ban it. This is the official text of the complaint:

(2.30) Υπουργείο Εσωτερικών, Αποκέντρωσης και Ηλεκτρονικής Διακυβέρνησης
Γενική Γραμματεία Ισότητας των Φύλων
Αθήνα, 03 Μαρτίου 2011
ΔΕΛΤΙΟ ΤΥΠΟΥ
ΚΑΤΑΓΓΕΛΙΑ ΣΤΟ ΕΘΝΙΚΟ ΣΥΜΒΟΥΛΙΟ ΡΑΔΙΟΤΗΛΕΟΡΑΣΗΣ
Η Γενική Γραμματεία Ισότητας των Φύλων του υπουργείου Εσωτερικών, Αποκέντρωσης και Ηλεκτρονικής Διακυβέρνησης καταγγέλει τη νέα διαφήμιση της εταιρίας Γερμανός που προβάλλεται τις τελευταίες μέρες από όλα τα τηλεοπτικά δίκτυα.
Η εν λόγω διαφήμιση ουσιαστικά απογυμνώνει τη γυναίκα από την ανθρώπινη αξία της εξισώνοντάς την με αντικείμενο και εμπόρευμα, για την προώθηση του προϊόντος που διαφημίζεται.
Οι προβαλλόμενες απόψεις παραβιάζουν τα ανθρώπινα δικαιώματα, σύμφωνα με την παρ. 1 του άρθρου 2 του Συντάγματος που ορίζει ότι «ο σεβασμός και η προστασία της αξίας του ανθρώπου αποτελούν την πρωταρχική υποχρέωση της πολιτείας» και τις παρ. 1 και 2 του αρθρ. 25, είναι απαράδεκτες, συνιστούν και αναπαράγουν σεξιστικές στερεοτυπικές αντιλήψεις ως προς τους ρόλους, την αξία και τις ικανότητες γυναικών και ανδρών.
Η Γενική γραμματεία ισότητας των Φύλων προσέφυγε σήμερα στο ΕΣΡ, ζητώντας να αποσυρθεί άμεσα η εν λόγω διαφήμιση.
(General Secretariat for Gender Equality 2011)
Ministry of Internal Affairs, Decentralisation, and E–Government
General Secretariat for Gender Equality
Athens, March 3rd 2011
PRESS RELEASE
COMPLAINT TO THE NATIONAL COUNCIL FOR RADIO AND TELEVISION
The General Secretariat for Gender Equality of the Ministry of Internal Affairs, Decentralisation, and E–Government denounces the new advertisement of the Germanos company, which has recently been broadcast on all television networks.
The advertisement in question actually deprives the woman of her humanity by equating her with an object and merchandise, in order to promote the advertised product.
The projected views violate human rights, according to paragraph 1 of chapter 2 of the [Greek] Constitution which asserts that "the respect and protection of humanity constitute a primary obligation of the state" and [according to] paragraphs 1 and 2 of chapter 25, [they] are inadmissible, [they] constitute and reproduce sexist stereotypical perceptions of women's and men's roles, value, and abilities.

The General Secretariat for Gender Equality appealed to the NCRTV today, asking it to immediately withdraw the advertisement in question.

The request was granted and the advertisement was banned immediately from all television channels. However, it can still be found online (see *Germanos advertisement–mpamies [money back]* 2011).

The advertisement and its withdrawal triggered a significant number of official and unofficial reactions from journalists, politicians, activists, and citizens who agreed or disagreed with what had happened, and expressed their views on whether the advertisement was humorous or not, why, etc., thus revealing their metapragmatic stereotypes on (the advertisement) humor. The present discussion is based on a corpus compiled from March 23rd until June 29th, 2011, including metapragmatic comments and reactions which became available online. The corpus consists of 23 articles from newspapers, websites, and blogs, and 277 comments from websites and blogs where speakers talked about the advertisement and the subsequent events in relation to it. Humor is discussed in 11 out of the 23 articles referring to the advertisement (47.82%) and in 90 out of the 277 online comments (32.49%).

In what follows, I will analyze metapragmatic comments on humor coming from this corpus, so as to reconstruct the main two conflicting metapragmatic stereotypes of humor emerging during this public debate.

2.5.2.2 Two conflicting metapragmatic stereotypes on humor

The main humor–related topics discussed during the debate seem to be the following three: *the (non) humorous quality of the advertisement* (i.e. whether it is or is not considered funny), *the sociopragmatic functions of the advertisement humor* (in relation to the dissemination of bias), and *its limits* (i.e. whether or not some things should be joked about). Here, I analyze metapragmatic comments showing speakers' diverse opinions and positionings in relation to these three topics and hence revealing opposing metapragmatic stereotypes on humor.

2.5.2.2.1 The (non) humorous quality of the advertisement

Some speakers argue in favor of the advertisement and its humor, since they appear to believe that humor exists independently of whether all its recipients (are willing to) recognize it. In this context, those who do not understand it are more often than not negatively evaluated:

(2.31) Η διαφήμιση είναι χιουμοριστική. Αυτοί που δεν το καταλαβαίνουν μπορούν να κάνουν μήνυση (lunatic 9/3/2011 in Semfe.gr 2011).
The advertisement is humorous. Those who do not understand it can press charges [against the advertisers and the selling company].

This speaker has no doubt about the humorous quality of the advertisement and clearly states that there may be some recipients who do not get the humorous message. By suggesting that such recipients can actually sue the advertisers and the selling company, the speaker implicitly portrays them in a negative manner: lawsuits against humorists are rare in Greece and those who file them are considered humorless and/or very easily offended.

On the other end of the continuum, speakers who do not approve of the advertisement and its humor argue that not all people share the same sense of humor, hence they may not laugh with/at the same stimuli:

(2.32) Εφόσον γελάτε με την ανάλυση έχετε προφανώς πολύ περίεργη, για να μην πω προβληματική, αίσθηση του χιούμορ (Dimitris M. 28/2/2011 in Andriotakis 2011).
Given that you laugh with the [sexist] analysis [of the advertisement], you obviously have a very strange, not to say problematic, sense of humor.

This speaker alludes to the existence of multiple senses of humor and explicitly states that some of them may not be "normal", in the sense that they may put up with, or even promote, discriminating behaviors and values. It is therefore implied that a single text may be humorous to some recipients but not necessarily to all of them. In this sense, humorous intent is not enough to qualify a text as humorous, hence humor does not exist independently of its reception.

So far, the "universality vs. variability" of humor emerges as one of the main parameters differentiating the one metapragmatic stereotype from the other. Those who defend the advertisement suggest that humor exists no matter how its recipients may interpret it, while those who focus on the sexist dimension of the advertisement suggest that humor exhibits variation: people may not share the same preferences when it comes to producing, interpreting, and evaluating humor.

2.5.2.2.2 The sociopragmatic functions of the advertisement humor

The second point raised by the speakers involves the sociopragmatic functions of humor, in particular its effect on public opinion and social attitudes. The following examples are illustrative:

(2.33) Είναι πέρα από προφανές ότι η εν λόγω διαφήμιση σατιρίζει ακριβώς το εν λόγω σεξιστικό στερεότυπο για το οποίο «καταγγέλλεται». Όλη η δομή του διαφημιστικού σεναρίου κινείται γύρω από την πρόκληση γέλιου για την παρωχημένη συμπεριφορά του συζύγου, ο οποίος αντιλαμβάνεται εργαλειακά το ρόλο της συζύγου του.
Όλος ο λόγος που χρησιμοποιείται είναι χιουμοριστικός: η αναφορά σε αριθμό καφέδων, γευμάτων, περίεργων ταινιών (ο Έρωτας στη Ζουαζουλάνδη), δώρων γενεθλίων, εντάσσονται ξεκάθαρα σε μια κωμική στόχευση. (...)
Είναι δεδομένο ότι ο σκοπός του διαφημιστικού μηνύματος δεν είναι φυσικά η επικρότηση μιας ακραίας και καταδικαστέας αντίληψης, αλλά η διακωμώδησή της, μέσα από το κλασικό στρατήγημα της σάτιρας που είναι η απόδοση ιδιοτήτων «αντικειμένου» (ή ζώου) σε ανθρώπους. Μέσα από αυτή την ανάλυση είναι σαφέστατο ότι η Γενική Γραμματεία Ισότητας προέβη σε μια άκρως επιφανειακή ανάγνωση του εν λόγω διαφημιστικού, χωρίς να αναζητήσει το κωμικό context και την εφαρμογή συγκεκριμένων κανόνων της σάτιρας, η οποία προφανώς και αποτελεί μεταφορικό κι όχι κυριολεκτικό λόγο (Naked men on the beach 2011).
It is more than obvious that the advertisement in question satirizes exactly the same sexist stereotype for which it is "denounced" [by those who do not approve of the advertisement]. The whole structure of the advertisement script aims at eliciting laughter at the expense of the outdated behavior of the husband, who perceives his wife's role in a derogatory manner.
The whole discourse used [in the advertisement] is humorous: the reference to the number of coffees [drunk by the couple and paid by the husband], meals, strange films (Love in Swaziland), birthday gifts is clearly part of the advertisement's attempt at humor. (...)
It is given that the aim of the advertising message is not at all to applaud an extreme and condemnable view, but to ridicule it through the classic strategy of satire, that is, through attributing "object" (or animal) qualities to humans. This analysis makes clear that the General Secretariat for Gender Equality opted for a most superficial reading of the advertisement in question, without taking into consideration the comic context and the application of specific rules of satire, which obviously belongs to figurative and not literal discourse.

In this extract, a supporter of the advertisement and its humorous potential underlines its humorous and satirical purpose and its non literal meaning. His/her aim is to eventually put forward the claim that the advertisement does not foster sexist, etc. stereotypes, but ridicules them by satirizing the husband's incongruous behavior.

Those who accuse the advertisement of being sexist, on the other hand, highlight the particularities of the Greek sociocultural context where the advertisement is circulated and interpreted:

(2.34) Κατ' αρχήν ας συμφωνήσουμε: Πράγματι το σποτ είναι χαριτωμένο, ξεκαρδιστικό ίσως για κάποιους, ευρηματικό κ.λπ., κ.λπ. Πράγματι επίσης στην Ελλάδα του 21ου αιώνα πολλές οικογένειες μεγαλώνουν τα παιδιά τους αναπαράγοντας πολύ χειρότερα στερεότυπα απ' αυτό που αναπαράγει, χιουμοριστικά έστω, το σποτ. (...) Η αναπαραγωγή στερεοτύπων του παρελθόντος σε μια κοινωνία σαν την ελληνική, που εξακολουθεί όχι μόνο βάσει κοινής αίσθησης αλλά και βάσει στατιστικών στοιχείων να είναι δέσμια αρνητικών συνεπειών αυτού του παρελθόντος, δεν είναι χρήσιμη, είναι αντιθέτως εξαιρετικά άστοχη, θα πρόσθετα, και βαρετή. Όταν δε η ευρηματικότητα και η πλακίτσα έχουν μονομερώς και μονότονα το ίδιο περιεχόμενο τότε και η πλακίτσα χάνεται και το πράγμα αλλάζει (Apostolaki 2011).

First of all, let's agree [on something]: Indeed the [advertising] spot is cute, maybe hilarious to some [viewers], creative, etc., etc. And indeed in 21st century Greece, many families raise their children by reproducing much worse stereotypes than the one reproduced –even in a humorous manner– by the spot. (...) The reproduction of stereotypes of the past in a society such as the Greek one, which –it is not only common belief but a statistically confirmed finding– still suffers from the negative consequences of this past, is not useful, but, on the contrary, it is totally pointless, I would add, and boring. Moreover, when creativity and kidding have the same one-sided and monotonous content, then kidding is not funny anymore and the thing changes [i.e. the message of the advertisement is interpreted literally, thus favoring sexism].

Here, the speaker insists on the sexist potential of the advertisement humor. She considers such an interpretation more salient in the Greek context, thus she suggests that this kind of humor can reinforce and perpetuate sexist values and behaviors in a community where people (especially women) still suffer from sexist discriminations. In other words, in her view, such humor may have a negative effect on people's attitudes and views.

To sum up, two different sociopragmatic functions of the advertisement humor are mainly discussed during this debate: humor as a means of satirizing and challenging outdated sexist stereotypes and practices; and humor as a means of confirming and further disseminating already existing sexist stereotypes and practices. The first one is supported by those who argue for the advertisement and its humor, while the second by those who argue against them. Each function ascribes to a different metapragmatic stereotype of humor.

2.5.2.2.3 The limits of humor

Speakers also have diverse views concerning the limits of humor. Those who seem to enjoy the humor of the advertisement object to any attempt to set boundaries to the expression of humor:

(2.35) Το να υπάρχουν άνθρωποι που βλέπουν την διαφήμιση του «Γερμανού» με τον σύζυγο που αγανακτεί για τις μπάμιες και επιστρέφει τη γυναίκα του στη μάνα της και δεν καταλαβαίνουν ούτε την ειρωνία της ούτε το πόσο κοροϊδεύει τα στερεότυπα, είναι αναμενόμενο και θεμιτό. (...) Επειδή κάποιοι δεν πιάνουν (ή δεν θέλουν να πιάσουν) το αστείο με την καρικατούρα του φαλλοκράτη «μπάμια», απαιτούν να διακοπεί η μετάδοση της διαφήμισης! (Zachariadis 2011).

That there are people who watch the advertisement by "Germanos" with the husband who becomes angry over the okras and takes his wife back to her mother, and do not understand either its irony or how it mocks stereotypes, this is expected and fair. (...) Because some [people] do not get (or do not want to get) the joke with the caricature of the phallocrat "okra–man",[26] they demand that the airing of the advertisement be stopped!

(2.36) Εκνευρισμός από γυναικείες οργανώσεις από τη διαφήμιση της αλυσίδας κινητής τηλεφωνίας. ΡΕ ΤΙΣ ΦΕΜΙΝΙΣΤΡΙΕΣ ΟΥΤΕ ΤΗΝ ΠΛΑΚΑ ΔΕΝ ΕΠΙΤΡΕΠΟΥΝ (Ekdosi.com 2011).

Women's organizations irritated by the advertisement of the mobile phone seller company. WELL, THESE FEMINISTS, THEY DON'T EVEN ALLOW JOKING.

Both extracts (2.35) and (2.36) resist any attempt to censor humor. In the first one, the exclamation mark at the end indicates the speaker's disapproval of

---

26 *Μπάμιας* 'okra–man' is a pun evoking, on the one hand, the husband who hates okras in the advertisement script and, on the other, a swear word in Greek: *μπάμιας* is sometimes used to refer to stupid, naïve people. It may also allude to small male genitals, thus also constituting an insult.

people who demand the banning of the advertisement, while, in the second one, the speaker specifically refers to the reactions by the members of women's organizations (including the General Secretariat for Gender Equality; see example 2.30), which are also negatively evaluated. Both metapragmatic comments seem to be based on the premise that humor should have no boundaries, in other words, that everyone should be free to joke as s/he wishes.

Those who argue against the advertisement and its humor adopt the opposite view: there should be limits to the expression of humor, especially in public. The following extract is indicative of this stance:

(2.37) Προσθέτει [η γενική γραμματέας Ισότητας των Φύλων κυρία Μαρία Στρατηγάκη] ότι εν προκειμένω οι διαφημιστές έχουν υπερβεί τα όρια του χιούμορ, καθώς «το ιδιωτικώς εκφερόμενο χοντρό αστείο μπορεί απλώς να είναι κακόγουστο, το δημοσίως προβαλλόμενο όμως είναι απαράδεκτο, ειδικά όταν αναπαράγει ακραίες σεξιστικές συμπεριφορές» (Ismailidou 2011).
[The General Secretary for Gender Equality Mrs. Maria Stratigaki] adds that, in the present case, the advertisers have exceeded the limits of humor, since "the tactless joke told in private settings may just be untasteful, but the one circulated in public is inadmissible, especially when it reproduces extreme sexist behaviors".

In extract (2.37), it is suggested that not all jokes can be told in public, hence there should be limits to what one is allowed to say, if s/he does not want to be negatively evaluated. We have already seen (in example 2.32) that those who do not approve of the advertisement and its humor usually claim that there are different kinds and senses of humor. This line of thought is here taken a step further: some utterances intended to be humorous may not be (perceived as) humorous after all; in other words, they may not be considered funny by everybody independently of their sense of humor.

In sum, those who exhibit positive attitudes towards the advertisement and its humor suggest that humor should have no limits, hence they resist any kind of censorship that may be imposed. Those who expressed themselves negatively in their evaluation of the advertisement suggest that there are certain kinds of humor that need to be sanctioned, especially if they happen to be circulated in the public sphere and could be interpreted as disparaging and discriminating. Hence, the two emerging metapragmatic stereotypes differ as to whether there should or should not be restrictions on humor use, and when/where.

2.5.2.3 Comparing speakers' metapragmatic stereotypes with scholarly analyses of humor

So far, we have seen how the participants of the debate are divided into two groups on the basis of their divergent metapragmatic stereotypes on humor, as expressed in relation to this particular advertisement. These two metapragmatic stereotypes are summarized in Table 2.1:

Table 2.1: The two opposing metapragmatic stereotypes on humor, as expressed during the public debate concerning the Greek advertisement.

	Metapragmatic stereotype of those who approve of the advertisement and its humor	Metapragmatic stereotype of those who disapprove of the advertisement and its humor
The (non) humorous quality of the advertisement	An utterance/text intended as humorous is humorous independently of how its recipients may interpret it.	Speakers do not agree on what is humorous; they may not share the same sense of humor.
The sociopragmatic functions of the advertisement humor	Humor denounces and satirizes stereotypes.	Humor reinforces and perpetuates stereotypes.
The limits of humor	There should be no limits to the expression of humor.	There should be limits to the expression of humor, especially in the public sphere.

Thus, the participants in this online debate appear to form two opposing *normative communities of humor*, to use the terminology put forward by Kuipers (2008a). According to her definition,

> [e]very group or society has its (mostly implicit) rules and agreements about what can be joked about. People within such a community generally abide by such rules, even if they do not agree with them. (...) Normative communities also have such unwritten rules about, for instance, the propriety of jokes about sex or people in power, or situations where joking is or isn't allowed. (...) All social groups establish some sort of consensus on what can be laughed about (Kuipers 2008a: 8).

In other words, every normative community exhibits different habits and preferences concerning humor use (cf. the sociocultural assumptions of humor use in Table 1.1, column A).[27] It could therefore be suggested that the two opposing

---

[27] Kuipers' (2008a) *normative communities of humor* seem to resemble what Anderson (1991) and McBride (2005) call *imagined communities* whose members may never meet in person, but

2.5 The sociopragmatic functions of metapragmatic comments — 59

normative communities of humor identified here are shaped on the basis of the two above-mentioned metapragmatic stereotypes. Each of these communities defends their positions on the advertisement humor while simultaneously trying to discredit the others' positions (cf. Kramer 2011).

It is interesting to note here that these two opposing metapragmatic stereotypes on humor are reminiscent of two different traditions within humor research. More specifically, the premise that a text/utterance is humorous independently of its recipients' interpretations of it has been an important presupposition for a significant number of humor studies so far. Humor researchers traditionally tend to presuppose that humorous texts will normally be perceived as such, namely that both humor producers and recipients will find the same humorous content funny. On the other hand, it has been suggested that humor may be interpreted differently by different speakers. Even for canned jokes there is not a "single", "correct" interpretation, although they are usually repeated in more or less the same form in different contexts (Morreall 2009: 98–101).[28] Recent research has confirmed that different people may derive different (humorous and non-humorous) meanings from texts intended as humorous (see among others Lockyer and Pickering 2001; Lockyer 2006; El Refaie 2011; Kramer 2011; Laineste 2011; Stewart 2013; Constantinou 2019; Dynel and Poppi 2019).

The diverse sociopragmatic functions of humor, namely the second point dividing the informants in the data examined here, have also been debated when humorous texts involving discriminatory content (e.g. racist, sexist) are discussed within humor research. On the one hand, traditional approaches to humor (see among others Raskin 1985, 2008a; Davies 1998, 2008, 2018) argue that, since humor belongs to *non-bona-fide communication*, where nothing serious, sincere, relevant, or accurate is to be expected, it does neither reflect reality nor intend to cause offense. Instead, humor usually involves already existing fictitious scripts and false beliefs which have nothing to do with humorists' "true" beliefs and standpoints. As a result, humor, it is suggested, cannot be blamed, for example, for promoting racist, sexist, or other discriminatory views, although it may exploit them to make people laugh. Moreover, the *non-bona-fide* quality of humor seems to be directly related to its lack of limits: since humor does not convey "serious", "literal", "sincere", or "accurate" messages, anything can be said in a humorous manner without (caring if we are)

---

are connected via (among other things) written discourse – in the present case, online discussions and public media texts. Imagined communities enable individuals to connect themselves with others by highlighting the differences between different groups (see also Hale 2018a: 39).
28 See also Billig (2005a: 31–32), Pickering and Lockyer (2005: 2), Willis (2005: 135), El Refaie (2011: 87).

offending or attacking someone or something. Given the above, any attempt to restrain or ban humor constitutes an act of censorship.[29]

On the other hand, it has been claimed (see among others Billig 2011, 2005a, 2005b; Lockyer and Pickering 2005; Weaver 2016; Archakis and Tsakona 2019) that humor can create and be considered responsible for disseminating prejudicial and discriminatory views by ridiculing specific targets, such as ethnic groups, women (wives, blonds, mothers–in–law, etc.), minorities, migrants, lawyers, homosexuals, politicians, political institutions, etc. Both superiority and relief theories of humor attempt to capture, and account for, this dimension of humor: in the first case, humor attacks a supposedly inferior target, while, in the second, humor allows speakers to express themselves in socially unacceptable and condemnable (i.e. discriminatory) ways. Thus, humor can undermine the social status of the targeted individuals or entities, and significantly contribute to their negative representation and evaluation. Given the above, topics such as the limits of humor in specific contexts, the thin line between humor and offense, its sociopolitical repercussions, and its effects on social relations have nowadays become important foci of analysis (see among others Lockyer and Pickering 2001, 2005; Billig 2005a; Lewis 2008; Smith 2009; Tsakona and Popa 2011b; Chen 2013, Weaver 2016; Takovski 2016).

These two poles are interestingly described by Morreall (2009). On the one hand, humor can be considered an *aesthetic experience* which we can enjoy without worrying whether we are insulting or disparaging our humorous targets (Morreall 2009: 72). On the other, the same author (Morreall 2009: 102–106) recognizes the limits of the aesthetic quality of humor: humor can actually hurt people and damage their relationships, since it may stem from, and be a sign of, frivolous behavior, lack of empathy, and bias. Somewhere in between

---

29 As Raskin (2008a: 27) remarks, "the serious–message aspect of humor is marginal and uncommon".

Davies is ambiguous in his positioning towards the objects of his numerous studies. On the one hand, he strongly supports that jokes function as "thermometers" conveying truths about the sociopolitical system generating them (Davies 2011: 248). On the other, he characterizes jokes as "trivial uses of language", thus treating them as "non-serious" and "insignificant" texts (Davies 2018: 26). In relation to the offensive content of jokes, Davies maintains that "[w]e know that jokes are important to us and of no consequence to anyone else and we will have the jokes we want and on our terms whether you like them or not" (2004: 40), thus defending jokers' freedom to insult and resisting the idea of humor limits. He also claims that "[h]umor does not *give* offense; its recipients *take* offense" (2008: 6, emphasis in the original), implying that jokers do not have "serious" intentions of offending the joke targets; only some recipients may detect "serious" meanings in jokes and thus feel offended themselves or think that jokes are offensive for somebody else.

these two poles, Mulkay (1988) claims that it is not humor *per se* that is *pure*, namely without important social consequences, or *applied/impure*, namely bearing some serious impact on social relations and values; it is speakers who decide whether humor can influence or not social reality and how. Speakers' interpretations of, and negotiations over, humor can bring to the surface its "innocuous" and "amusing" character (pure humor) or can capitalize on its "serious", negative consequences (applied/impure humor). Table 2.2 provides a summary of the main suggestions by humor scholars:

Table 2.2: Humor researchers' positionings and findings concerning the (non) humorous quality of a text, the sociopragmatic functions of humor, and its limits.

	Traditional approaches to humor	More recent approaches to humor
The (non) humorous quality of the text	Humorous texts have a single interpretation which is reached at and accepted by all recipients.	Humorous texts do not have a single "correct" interpretation; recipients may extract different meanings from them.
The sociopragmatic functions of humor	Humor does not reflect or influence reality and does not offend.	Humor may reflect, and have an effect on, people's social attitudes and beliefs, hence it can cause offense.
The limits of humor	Anything can be said in a humorous manner without any sanctions.	There may/can be limits to humorous expression.

The comparison between the Tables 2.1 and 2.2 reveals that the similarities between speakers' metapragmatic stereotypes on humor and researchers' interpretations and findings are by far more significant and intriguing than their differences. A possible interpretation of such similarities would once again (see also Section 2.5.1.3) involve the fact that humor scholars are *de facto* members of specific normative communities of humor and have their own metapragmatic stereotypes, which may influence not only their own research interests but also their research questions, hypotheses, analyses, and eventually results. In other words, research findings can be more or less influenced by researchers' ideologies concerning humor as well as by the reasons and ways they themselves use humor in their everyday interactions. Furthermore, it is important to underline here that speakers' metapragmatic statements and insights could eventually prove a valuable resource for researchers who wish to formulate hypotheses or confirm their own interpretations and analyses (see Section 2.3).

In addition, the metapragmatic data under scrutiny seems to confirm Mulkay's (1988) observation that it is speakers and their values that set the boundaries between *pure* (i.e. harmless) and *applied/impure* (i.e. harmful) humor. Their assessments and negotiations may highlight or downplay its positive or negative aspects in each context. Viewing humor as "innocuous" and "mere fun" without taking into consideration the specific context a humorous text is produced, circulated, and interpreted, may be an attractive option underlining humor's *positive* attributes and functions. Nevertheless, such a decontextualized view of humor overlooks the fact that its repercussions in real interactions among real people are unpredictable and may actually be *negative* (e.g. damaging) for social relations (see among others Billig 2005b; Lockyer 2006: 44; Smith 2009; Weaver 2016; Hale 2018a: 37). Moreover, it does not help researchers account for the fact that public debates over (the metapragmatics of) humor such as the one examined here do take place around the world due to recipients' diverse perceptions of humorous phenomena.

2.5.3 Summarizing the sociopragmatic functions of metapragmatic comments and stereotypes

Both cases examined here have confirmed earlier metapragmatic research on pragmatic phenomena other than humor. In particular, the metapragmatic comments offered on humor (and the emerging metapragmatic stereotypes) exhibit significant sociopragmatic functions in interaction (on the sociopragmatic functions of metapragmatic indicators, see Section 2.2 and references therein):

1. metapragmatic comments evaluate language use (see e.g. the "amusing", "clever", "wise", "timely", etc. character of crisis jokes; or the " sexist" or "innocuous" advertisement humor) and speakers, especially when "their" perceptions of humor are different from "ours" (e.g. "humorless", "easily offended", or "sexist" individuals);
2. metapragmatic comments may be conflictual, thus dividing speakers in two (or more) opposing normative communities of humor;
3. they defend specific communicative norms, while rejecting others (e.g. it is "permitted" or "funny" to denigrate politicians through political jokes; sexist humor "should" be banished at least from public contexts);
4. they enable speakers to construct specific identities for themselves (e.g. we are the victims of the debt crisis and/or we are responsible for the same crisis; we defend gender equality by resisting sexist humor), for their interlocutors (e.g. they abuse freedom of speech to insult and denigrate women;

they are humorless individuals), and for the targets of humor (e.g. politicians are corrupt and deceitful individuals and incapable of fulfilling the institutional role properly); hence, metapragmatic comments foster ingroup/outgroup distinctions;
5. metapragmatic comments (or other indicators) are employed more frequently when speakers disagree with each other or their expectations are violated, hence they feel the need to monitor the interpretation of discourse and to explicitly point to certain meanings, while simultaneously rejecting those meanings they disagree with (e.g. in the Greek advertisement case). In other words, metapragmatic comments help members of normative communities of humor to promote their own positions and interpretations of a specific text as the only "appropriate" or "correct" ones.

In addition, our discussion so far has underlined the significance of analyzing speakers' metapragmatic/emic comments (or other kinds of metapragmatic indicators, after all) to confirm, enrich, or even refute scholarly/etic analyses of humor. This is an important step towards a theoretical model for humor which will not limit itself to the analysts' (etic) criteria for identifying and interpreting humor and its sociopragmatic functions, but will also take into serious consideration real (emic) interpretations and views on humor offered by participants in communicative settings and speech events where humor is produced and processed.

2.6 Summary

Speakers' perceptions of, and comments on, humor and related phenomena are considered to be a significant part of the context of humor (as we have seen in Chapter 1). Drawing on recent research on the area of metapragmatics, this Chapter set out to explore the main concepts, goals, methodologies, and analytical tools that could prove relevant to, and useful for, the investigation of the metapragmatics of humor. By conceptualizing speakers' comments as metapragmatic indicators of humor reflecting speakers' metapragmatic stereotypes on humor, I have tried to demonstrate how the latter may either bring speakers closer together or divide them in opposing groups. More specifically, it seems that, when speakers share the same views on what humor is and how it works in a specific text or communicative setting, humor and its interpretations create or reinforce the solidarity bonds among speakers. On the contrary, diverging opinions on what humor is, how it works, and on whether a text is humorous or not, usually create controversies among speakers that cannot be easily resolved. Furthermore, I have argued that metapragmatic stereotypes on humor appear to influence scholarly analyses of humor as they often converge with the diverse characteristics, sociopragmatic functions, and goals assigned to humor.

In the following Chapter, the context of humor is further explored by focusing on the genres where humor occurs and their transformations.

3 Genres with/and humor

3.1 Introductory remarks

As already discussed in Chapter (1), one of the most important parameters of context that is directly related to the forms, meanings, and sociopragmatic functions of humorous discourse, is *genre*. Two seemingly contradictory, but in fact complementary to each other, statements seem to describe the importance of genre for producing and interpreting humor. On the one hand, Chiaro (1992: 117) points out that "[i]n real life, jokes may, of course, occur anywhere and at any moment", thus underlining the variability and omnipresence of humor in contemporary societies. On the other, Goatly (2012: 146) reminds us that "[c]ertainly cultures are selective about the genres where jokes are embedded", thus compromising the omnipresence of humor: humor may not occur in each and every genre in a linguocultural community, as there may be restrictions concerning its use in certain communicative settings. Speakers' knowledge concerning how, when, and why humor may be employed in a given genre, or when and why it is not expected to appear, is part of their metapragmatic stereotypes on humor (see Sections 1.3 and 2.2). Based on their linguocultural experience, speakers gradually become familiar with when, where, and how they may/should (or may not/should not) resort to humor to achieve their interactional goals.

The significance of genre for the study of humor is highlighted by the fact that, in the framework of the General Theory of Verbal Humor (Attardo 1994, 2001), one of knowledge resources introduced for accounting for the similarities and differences among humorous texts is the so-called *narrative strategy*. Narrative strategy "is in fact a rephrasing of what is known (...) as 'genre'" (Attardo 1994: 224; see also Attardo 2011: 137–138). However, as Attardo points out (2001: 23), "[l]ittle work has gone towards this KR [i.e. knowledge resource]", as humor scholars usually focus on different aspects of humor, such as its topics, its targets, its linguistic and logical mechanisms.

This Chapter is dedicated to issues related to the genres of humor. After a brief theoretical overview on genres and humor (Section 3.2), First, I offer a taxonomy of humorous genres depending on whether, and to what extent, humor is an indispensable ingredient in them (Section 3.3); and then I discuss how humorous genres may be transformed in time, mostly due to the new needs arising in online communication and the new media. New genres may emerge, while old ones may transform to adjust to the new environments of (humorous) communication (Sections 3.4–3.4.3). It will therefore be confirmed that genre is indeed one of the key features affecting humor production and interpretation.[30]

3.2 On the interplay between genres and humor

It is common knowledge among (at least) humor scholars that humor surfaces in most genres. For instance, Pickering and Lockyer (2005: 3) observe that

> [h]umor is not confined to any particular genre or form of narrative, even though certain genres and narrative forms are defined by their mode of being funny, regardless of whether they achieve this. Nor is it by any means exclusive to conventional occasions or locations. Humor infiltrates every area of social life and interaction, even rearing its head in situations where it is not normally regarded as appropriate.

In line with both Chiaro's (1992: 117) and Goatly's (2012: 146) quotations (see Section 3.1), Pickering and Lockyer point not only to the ubiquity of humor but also to the sociocultural restrictions imposed on its use: in some contexts, they claim, the use of humor "is not normally regarded as appropriate". They also refer to the fact that humor is indispensible to some genres but not to all the genres it may occur in. Humor scholars indeed investigate the use and function of humor in a wide range of texts and contexts: from casual interactions among intimates to parliamentary debates, from business meetings and service encounters to informal online chat between strangers, and from educational settings to most kinds of media texts. So, first, let's see how the concept of *genre* may help us describe the variability and the ubiquity of humor, but also its absence from some communicative settings.

Although we may not always realize it, every time we communicate we use discourse in more or less conventionalized ways. Growing up in a specific sociocultural community we gradually yet constantly become familiar with conventions concerning not only our lexico–grammatical choices, but also the "appropriate" associations between such choices, on the one hand, and the communicative settings and activities we engage in, on the other. By "appropriate" we usually mean those conventions that will allow us to use discourse in an effective way, so as to achieve our communicative or, more generally, social goals. Moreover, communicative settings and social activities do not occur *hapax* but more often than not constitute recurring experiences in our lives, as we tend to look for, and eventually perceive, similarities across various occasions. Hence, as

---

[30] This Chapter draws from Tsakona (2015, 2017d, 2018c) with appropriate modifications to adjust to the purposes of the present book.

we resort to specific discoursal choices and strategies in similar contexts, discourse becomes more or less conventionalized therein. This is how *genres* are created.[31]

It should be underlined here that it is we as speakers who create such associations and become immersed in them, as we spontaneously or systematically (e.g. via education) learn to use discourse in specific ways so as to be able to participate in specific activities. At the same time, we encounter discoursal choices and strategies that are considered "unconventional", "inappropriate", and eventually less effective in achieving certain goals or in completing certain tasks. By both avoiding such choices and opting for more "conventional" ones, we tend to reproduce specific patterns of language use in specific contexts, thus establishing certain generic features or conventions.

On the other hand, convention does not necessarily entail rigidness and lack of adjustment. We are capable of, and permitted to, modify generic conventions according to the specific circumstances at hand and our own personal goals and needs. The impact of such modifications varies: either adjustments are minimal and local, hence the text produced is easily recognized as belonging to the genre typically associated with a specific kind of context; or they become widespread and may eventually contribute to transforming the genre, thus having a more or less lasting effect on its particularities. This is how genres are *renewed* and *recreated*. Still, we do not always go along with genre modifications: we may consider them "strange", disapprove of them, or even resist them, as they seem to come into conflict with our perceptions and expectations about how discourse "should" be used in a particular communicative setting or by which discoursal choices the relevant social goals are "best" fulfilled.

Both processes of genre creation and recreation show that it is us, speakers, who exert control over generic conventions via our communicative and social practices, while at the same time we are responsible for adjusting them to the current conditions and our own private goals and needs, thus operating in what Coogan (2012: 205) succinctly calls "the convention/invention balance": "[t]his balance connects to two primal needs – the need for familiarity and the need for novelty. (...) Familiar treatments of [generic] conventions help the reader know what they are getting into. Novelty emerges from invention (...). Readers want a certain amount of change and newness in what they read, but not too much" (Coogan 2012: 207; see also Solin 2011).

---

31 On genre, see Bakhtin (1986: 60–102), Briggs and Bauman (1992), Bauman (2004) as well as more recent approaches such as Freedman and Medway (1994), Miller (1994), Bhatia (1997), Johns (2002), van Leeuwen (2005: 117–138), Bawarshi and Reiff (2010), Solin (2011), Coogan (2012).

In contemporary postmodern societies, the adapting and transformative potential of genres seems to gain prominence. Generic conventions are creatively violated and genre–mixing or –hybridization is common practice among speakers (Fairclough 1992b: 221; Bhatia 1997: 363–364; Solin 2011: 130–131; Jones 2012: 7–10). Discoursal choices are reappropriated and acquire new social meanings as they emerge in new contexts. The notion of *intertextuality* is most relevant here. Intertextuality highlights the relations between different texts, given that texts are shaped by prior ones and may resemble each other in terms of content, structure, and/or function. Hence, intertextuality, like genre hybridity, attests to speakers' creativity: they have the ability to transform prior texts or genres to "new", "novel" ones by modifying their generic structure and conventions and/or by reproducing their content (cf. Bakhtin 1981, 1986; Fairclough 1992b: 101–136).[32]

Such a tendency for recontextualization of generic conventions appears to relate to humor in (at least) two ways: first, humor as a discoursal strategy becomes more widespread and surfaces in more contexts nowadays; second, diverse and "incompatible" generic features are combined to create humorous texts and genres. More specifically, this tendency for recontextualization of generic conventions first results in the transference and hence appearance of humor in an increasingly wider variety of texts and contexts, where it may not be normally or conventionally expected. In this sense, humor is a discoursal strategy typical of, or indispensable to, some genres, but severely restricted in others; generic conventions may include or discourage the use of humor respectively. In between these two categories there seem to be genres where humor is not obligatory but may occur whenever speakers think that its use serves their situated communicative goals. Furthermore, humor may result from the fact that the boundaries between different genres are often blurred as speakers deliberately and more or less playfully combine discoursal features coming from different genres. This "generic crossing in a text" (Coutinho and Miranda 2009: 44) has been shown to form one of the most common strategies for the production of humor.[33]

In both cases, speakers' metapragmatic stereotypes (see Sections 1.3, 2.2–2.4) seem to play a significant role in using, recognizing, and interpreting humor. In

---

[32] On humor and intertextuality, see also Tsakona (2018a, 2018b) and references therein.
[33] This often results in stylistic humor, satire, and/or parody. See among others Attardo (1994: 230–253, 262–268, 2001: 104–110, 2009: 315), Antonopoulou (2003), Simpson (2003), Coutinho and Miranda (2009), Antonopoulou and Nikiforidou (2011), Tsiplakou and Ioannidou (2012), Archakis et al. (2014, 2015), Tsami et al. (2014), Antonopoulou, Nikiforidou, and Tsakona (2015), Tsami (2018), Piata (to appear).

the first case, the presence of humor in, or its absence from, specific genres depends on participants' opinions and assessments on whether humor constitutes an "appropriate" or "inappropriate" discoursal means for attaining generic goals. In this process, the evoked metapragmatic stereotypes refer not only to where, when, how, and why humor may be used, but also to what may be included in the genre at hand. In the second case, humorists also rely on their own and their addressees' metapragmatic stereotypes on humor and on the genre(s) involved: such mental models are expected to help them recognize the recontextualized generic features as well as to grasp the new meanings such features acquire in their new environments and via their combinations with other, "incompatible" ones. They are also expected to enable them to assess whether humor is "appropriately" used or whether its presence is a more or less "successful novelty".

To sum up, humor seems to relate to genre in, at least, two ways: first, *humor may constitute a more or less indispensable ingredient of a genre*, thus enabling participants to fulfill specific (generic) goals; second, *humor may function as a genre–renewal mechanism*, as new genres or creative texts may be produced through the recontextualization of generic conventions for humorous purposes. The following classification of genres will be based on the premise that the presence or absence of humor seems to play a significant role for the materialization of genres (see Section 3.3). Then, I will focus on humor as a means of genre renewal resulting in the recontextualization of generic conventions and in the transformation of genres (Sections 3.4–3.4.3).

3.3 Classifying the genres of humor

Several taxonomies of humor have been proposed, each of them based on different criteria of classification. Some of them are based on the levels of linguistic analysis, so jokes are divided into graphological, phonological, morphological, syntactic, lexical/semantic, and pragmatic or discourse ones (see among others Chiaro 1992; Alexander 1997; Ross 1998; Goatly 2012). Another common type of taxonomy of humor begins with the distinction between canned jokes, which are reproduced more or less verbatim in different contexts, and conversational humor, which is spontaneous, emerges from the interaction it appears in, and can hardly be reproduced and understood in other contexts (see among others Norrick 1993; Dynel 2009). Less often, the content of humor (ethnic, sexist, political, etc.) becomes the classificatory criterion (see Raskin 1985: 148–264). Within the framework of the General Theory of Verbal Humor, Attardo (2001) puts forward a taxonomy based on the position of humorous lines (i.e. punch lines and/

or jab lines),[34] that is, on the distribution and function of humor along the text (see also Tsakona 2004, 2007; for a detailed and critical discussion of different taxonomies, see Tsakona 2017d: 490–492).

Trying to take into consideration speakers' metapragmatic stereotypes on humor, and in particular when and where speakers think humor may/should (or may not/should not) appear (see Section 2.2), the main criterion for the proposed classification of humorous genres is the centrality of humor in them, namely how expected or unexpected its presence seems to be in each one of them. In other words, speakers' practices concerning humor use and the respective underlying perceptions of its "(in)appropriateness" in a given communicative setting become the main criteria for this classification of humorous genres. Four categories can therefore be identified:[35]

A. Genres produced predominantly for the amusement of the audience, such as (canned) jokes, comedies (films, plays), cartoons, sitcoms, TV satire, standup comedy, and internet memes. Such genres would not be the same and, most importantly, would not even exist as such without the presence of humor in them; humor is the *sine qua non* condition for them. In contrast to all the following categories, these genres are produced exclusively in a humorous form and primarily for a humorous purpose.

Canned jokes are the first genre that comes to mind for this category. Canned jokes include subgenres such as narrative jokes, riddle–jokes, and one–liners (see also Section 3.4.1). They end in a punch line causing a surprise effect but may also include one or more jab lines, as does the following one (where the humorous lines are italicized):

---

34 On the distinction between a jab line and a punch line, Attardo (2001: 82) proposes the following:

> The concept of *jab line* was introduced (...) to distinguish between punch lines, which have been found (...) to occur virtually exclusively in a final position in jokes, from a type of humorous trigger which occurs in the body of the text. Jab lines differ from punch lines in that they may occur in any other position in the text. Semantically speaking they are identical objects. Their only difference lies in the textual position in which they occur and in their textual function (emphasis in the original; see also Tsakona 2003a, 2007; Attardo 2017a: 130, and Section 4.2 in the present book).

35 Only two examples are provided here for each category; the list of genres in each category is obviously not exhaustive.

(3.1) At four o'clock in the morning, a hotel receptionist receives a phone call from *a guy who sounds drunk and asks him at what time the bar opens*. "The hotel bar opens at noon, sir", replies the receptionist. An hour later, the receptionist receives another phone call from *the same guy who sounds even more drunk:* "At what time does the bar open?" "As I told you, sir, the bar opens at noon", answers the receptionist. After one hour, *the guy calls again and sounds even more drunk than before:* "At what time did you say the bar opens?" The receptionist replies: "The hotel bar opens at noon, but, if you cannot wait, you can ask from the room service to bring you something to drink in your room." *"No, I don't want to get into the bar" says the man. "I want to get out of it"*.

The jab lines of the joke setup evolve around the unexpected events of drinking alcohol as a matter of the utmost urgency (and not just a pleasure) and of pestering (rather than asking) for information. The final punch line (*"No, I don't want to get into the bar" says the man. "I want to get out of it"*) constitutes the punch line causing the script opposition, so the audience realize that the man on the phone is not eager to enter the bar and start drinking (initial script), but is anxious to get out of it (final script; for a more detailed analysis, see Tsakona 2003a: 323). Such fictional stories are circulated to amuse addressees, usually in informal contexts (see also Section 2.5.1.1).

Howlers are similar to jokes (especially to one–liners) in that they are more or less verbatim reproduced in order to produce a humorous effect via the mistake they are based on:

(3.2) My friend's three–year–old son recently made us laugh by pointing out various mistakes of car, and then asking if ours was a Ford FIASCO! (H. Gullen, Twickenham; *Woman*, February 14th, 1989; cited in Chiaro 1992: 21).

This extract shows how spontaneous mistakes become howlers when they are recontextualized –here narrated in a letter to the magazine *Woman*– thus entering public circulation. Instead of *Ford Fiesta*, the boy said "Ford Fiasco", thus creating a pun pointing to the problematic features of the family car. Like canned jokes, howlers predominantly aim at entertaining the audience via the creation of a humorous effect (see also Tsakona 2005).

B. Genres that may often include humor and may aim, among other things, at creating a humorous effect. For example, everyday interactions among peers, conversational narratives (or personal anecdotes; see Norrick 1993), most kinds of literary texts (novels, short stories, poems; see Attardo 2001; Tsakona 2004,

2007), animation films, aphorisms, epigrams, online posts and interactions, proverbs, advertisements, birthday cards, graffiti, and bumper stickers belong here. The presence of humor in these genres is not obligatory (as was the case with category A): humorous texts belonging here constitute "humorous *realizations* (...) that modify a serious genre" (Kotthoff 2007: 292; emphasis mine).

Oral conversational narratives can be either serious or humorous (see Archakis and Tsakona 2012 and references therein). Example (3.3) is a humorous one including (italicized) jab lines:

(3.3) Γιάννης: Πρόσεξε έγραφα Βιολογία εγώ τη Δευτέρα πρώτη ώρα, εγώ, ο Φίλιππος και η Άννα και μας βάζει και τους τρεις στα πίσω–πίσω θρανία τώρα, ένα – ένα – κι ένα//
Ερευνήτρια 1: Α:::
Γιάννης: Κάθομ' εγώ μπροστά η Μαρία//
Νίκος: Όχι ρε πούστη (   )//
Γιάννης: Δεν είχα διαβάσει τίποτα. Με το που με βάζει εμένα να γράφω, βλέπω την κόλλα, ελλειπτικός κύκλος τη σκουντάω, Μαρία τι είναι ελλειπτικός κύκλος; *Άντε Μαρία άντε, άντε Μαρία.* Κι όπως γράφω τώρα εγώ, μόνο μια κόλλα πάνω στο θρανίο κι ένα στυλό τίποτ' άλλο, με το τετράδιο. *Αντίγραψε μου λέει και μου το χώνει πάνω στο θρανίο και φεύγει {γέλια} Γυρνάει μπροστά και μένει το τετράδιο ανοιχτό τώρα//*
Ερευνήτρια 2: Ι:://
Γιάννης: *Της το πετάω πάρτο μωρή γαμημένη της λέω τι 'ναι αυτά που κάνεις; Μετά//*
Ερευνήτρια 1: Γιατί ρε δε το 'παιρνες; Δε σε 'παιρνε μπροστά το θρανίο;
Γιάννης: Δε μ' έπαιρνε. Θα μ' έβλεπε. Ολόκληρο το τετράδιο, πού να το βάλω; Ένα χαρτάκι μωρέ, σκονάκι τώρα, *λες και θα 'τανε σωστά τώρα//*
Ερευνήτρια 1: *Λες και θα 'τανε σωστά*
Γιάννης: Καλά, μπορεί να 'χε γράψει τίποτ' άλλο.
Ερευνήτρια 1: (   )
Γιάννης: Μαρία, Μαρία τι 'ναι ελλειπτικός κύκλος; Μου στέλνει ένα χαρτάκι πίσω και τι μου γράφει; *Τι μου λες μου λέει γιατί μ' ενοχλείς;* Σε παρακαλώ, μην το παρακάνεις. Είσαι βλαμμένη της γράφω γράψε μου τι 'ναι ελλειπτικός κύκλος. Και τι μου λέει; *Θα σου πω μετά.*
Νίκος: {γέλια} *Θα σου μετά λέει* {γέλια}
Γιάννης: Χτυπάει το κουδούνι. Έρχεται η καθηγήτρια//
Νίκος: {γέλια}//
Γιάννης: Πίσω απ' το κεφάλι μου ρε μόνο πίσω απ' το κεφάλι μου, κανένας άλλος μες στην τάξη. Εγώ και η Μαρία τώρα. Η Μαρία καθόταν μες στην τάξη. Καθόταν η Μαρία μπροστά, πίσω μου η καθηγήτρια. Γυρνάει και τι

μου λέει; Ελλειπτικός κύκλος είναι. *Και να την ακούει ρε η άλλη* {γέλια} *Την κοιτάει έτσι η άλλη και να μην έχει πάρει χαμπάρια.*
Ερευνήτρια 2: ( )
Γιάννης: Εγώ σου λέω έγραφα, πετάω το στυλό και να κάθομαι έτσι/ ασ' την να λέει και να 'χει γυρίσει πίσω χωρίς να τη βλέπει η καθηγήτρια και να λέει. *Ελλειπτικός κύκλος είναι τα κύτταρα που προκαλούν αυτήν την εε: ε: και να λέει, να λέει, να λέει και την κοιτάει η καθηγήτρια, καλά βλαμμένη είναι αυτή.*
Ερευνήτρια 2: {γέλια} A:μάν.
Yannis: Now see, I was taking a biology test on Monday, it was my first class, there were me, Filippos and Anna and the teacher puts the three of us at the very back desks, one by one//
Researcher 1: Ahaa.
Yannis: I sit down and in front of me was Maria//
Nikos: Oh, fuck ( )//
Yannis: I was absolutely unprepared. As the teacher asks me to start writing, I see the questions on the paper, elliptical circle, I push her, Maria what is an elliptical circle? *Hurry up Maria, hurry up, hurry up Maria.* And as I am writing now, on my desk there is only a piece of paper and a pen, nothing else, she gives me her whole notebook. *Copy, she says to me and she puts it on my desk and she leaves* {everybody laughs} *She turns her back on me putting the notebook open on my desk now*//
Researcher 2: Oooh//
Yannis: *I throw it back at her, take it* fucking asshole I tell her, *what are you doing?* Then//
Researcher 1: Why didn't you take it? Couldn't you do that in view of everyone?
Yannis: I couldn't do it. {The teacher} would see me. It was the whole notebook, I couldn't hide it. A very small piece of paper {was all I needed} now, *not to mention that the answer wouldn't be right anyway*//
Researcher 1: *The answer wouldn't be right anyway*
Yannis: Sure, she might have written down something else.
Researcher 1: ( )
Yannis: Maria, Maria what is the elliptical circle? She passes back to me a small piece of paper and what does she write on it? *What do you want, she says to me, why are you bothering me*? Please stop overdoing it. Are you out of your mind, I write to her, write down what is the elliptical circle. And what does she say to me? *I'll tell you later.*
Nikos: {laughter} *She will {tell} you later she says* {laughter}
Yannis: The bell rings. The teacher comes//

Nikos: {laughter}//
Yannis: She {the teacher} was behind my back, only behind my back, nobody else was in the classroom. Me and Maria now. Maria was sitting in the classroom. Maria was sitting in front of me, the teacher was behind my back. Maria turns back to me and what does she say to me? *Elliptical circle is. And the teacher can hear her* {everybody laughs} *And the teacher has her eyes on her, while Maria hasn't realized what is going on.*
Researcher 2: (   )
Yannis: {Though} I was trying to write, I throw the pen and I sit like this/ {and I say to myself} let her talk *and she had turned behind without the teacher seeing her and she keeps on saying. Elliptical circle is the cells which cause this ee:: e: and she keeps on talking, talking, talking and the teacher is watching her*, well she is absolutely mad.
Researcher 2: {laughter} Oh God.

In this oral narrative Yannis represents an incident involving his classmate Maria and himself: during a written exam, he asks for her assistance and, instead of communicating quickly and quietly, they end up throwing each other a notebook and talking louder than expected, so the teacher could actually see what was going on (yet she did not react; see the italicized jab lines). Another humorous detail involves Yannis asking Maria's help even though he does not trust her skills (*λες και θα 'τανε σωστά τώρα* 'not to mention that the answer wouldn't be right anyway'), while Maria takes her time in giving him the answer he urgently needs (*θα σου πω μετά* 'I'll tell you later'). Via narrating this incident in a humorous manner, Yannis evaluates Maria's uncooperative and careless behavior as "incongruous" and hence laughable, while he projects his own as "normal" (for a more detailed analysis, see Archakis and Tsakona 2005: 52–54). Such personal narratives can emerge without humor in casual interactions and without causing laughter reactions to the audience. Actually we could imagine a more or less different version of the same sequence of narrated events if, for example, Yannis was sad and disappointed and was blaming himself for his failure at the exam, when not even Maria could effectively help him.

Aphorisms can also be serious or humorous. The following humorous one is attributed to Oscar Wilde:

(3.4) Examinations consist of the foolish asking questions the wise cannot answer.

Wilde here employs a role reversal to create humor: the teachers would be (stereotypically) expected to be characterized as "wise" and the students as "foolish" (especially if they do not want to become "wise" like their teachers). Instead, the teachers are represented as ignorant who ask questions to students who seem to know much more (see Antonopoulou and Tsakona 2006: 13).

C. Genres where humor may occasionally occur but it is not normally or always expected. In contrast to the genres belonging in category B, where the presence of humor is quite common, and those belonging in category D, where humor seems unexpected, here the occurrence of humorous utterances is neither very common nor severely restricted. For example, business negotiations, service encounters, news reports, newspaper articles, political speeches, parliamentary debates, school textbooks, classroom interactions are included here.

First, let's consider the genre of live text commentary. As Chovanec (2012: 143) suggests, "[s]ports reporting is a genre that is not –per se– associated with humor, although humor may be present, sometimes to significant degree, in particular sports commentaries". The following extract is illustrative. It comes from the live text commentary of the football match between Greece and Sweden at the European Football Championship in 2008 in Salzburg, Austria. The online commentary was hosted by the online version of *The Guardian*:

(3.5) **22 min:** Gekas as a central striker is supposed to be an improvement on Greece's 2004 version, but he's been anonymous thus far. Karagounis's poor cross is cleared.
25 min: "At the risk of taking us into Carry On territory," writes Mr Burke. "I am somewhat duty bound to advise that even in event of a Larsson hat–trick it may require the use of the telescope at Jodrell Bank to notice any movement in my strides. Mrs Burke enjoys knitting and needle point." It's "Carry On Giving the Ball Away" in Salzburg now.
27 min: The Greeks are lacking width, with Karagounis (a central midfielder) on one side and Charisteas (a center forward by trade) on the other. Sweden are lacking a spark in the final third and Ibrahimovic has got little change out of three giant centre–halves (Chovanec 2012: 139).

In general, the match is evaluated as boring and tedious, hence the journalist and his audience found time to engage in humorous exchanges. More specifically, humor is here used as "time filler" (Chovanec 2012: 142) when the match is uneventful and the journalist wishes to keep the communication channel open for his audience and maintain their attention. Hence, he inserts a humorous comment sent by a member of the audience, Mr. Burke, who contributes to an ongoing (humorous) discussion: Mr. Burke's words are quoted verbatim in the "25 min" post (for a more detailed analysis, see Chovanec 2012: 151–152).

The classroom could also be considered a context where humor would not be easily and frequently produced by the majority of teachers (see also Sections 5.2 and 5.6). In the following extract, however, both a student, Jeff, and the teacher use humor. The teacher has just asked the whole class to say the numbers together and Jeff shouts the numbers showing an "over-eager participation" (Norrick and Klein 2008: 100):[36]

(3.6) Class: [seventy-seven]
Jeff: [SEVENTY-SEVEN]
Class: [eight-six]
Jeff: [SE- ((even more loudly)) EIGHTY-SIX]¨
Class: [ninety-nine]
Amy: [ninety-nine]
Jeff: [NINETY-NI:NE]=
Teacher: ((laughingly)): =Jeff had his Wheaties this morning.
((several pupils laughing))
(Norrick and Klein 2008: 100)

At the end of this sequence of turns, the teacher humorously remarks on Jeff's incongruous behavior by implying that Jeff has had an energy breakfast that morning, thus relaxing an "otherwise rigid classroom situation" (Norrick and Klein 2008: 100). At the same time, he underlines Jeff's humorous acts.

D. Genres where humor hardly ever (or never) occurs, such as religious genres (Geybels and Van Herck 2011), funeral speeches (de Jongste 2013), laws, and court decisions (Capelotti 2016; Milner Davis and Roach Anleu 2018). Humorous utterances in such genres are rather unexpected than expected.

Humor scarcity can be attested, first, in legal and judicial contexts. In a case discussed in Hobbs (2007), however, the plaintiff sued a driver who lost

---

[36] In this example, the transcription conventions of the authors (see Norrick and Klein 2008: 104–105) are maintained:

[...]	overlapping talk
CAPITALS	heavy stress, speech louder than the surrounding discourse
((...))	aspects of the utterance such as whispers, coughing, and laughter
xx-	cut-off with a glottal stop
x:	prolonging of the sound
=	latching between turns
..	pauses of one second or less

control of her car and struck an oak in front of his house, for the "injuries" sustained by the tree. Although the trial court dismissed the suit, the plaintiff brought the case before a Court of Appeals, which also dismissed the case giving a unanimous opinion in the form of a humorous poem:

(3.7) We thought that we would never see
    A suit to compensate a tree.
    A suit whose claim in tort is prest
    Upon a mangled tree's behest;
    A tree whose battered trunk was prest
    Against a Chevy's crumpled crest;
    A tree that faces each new day
    With bark and limb in disarray;
    A tree that may forever bear
    A lasting need for tender care.
    Flora lovers though we three,
    We must uphold the court's decree.
    Affirmed.
    (Hobbs 2007: 54–55)

The judges wrote a parodic version of a schoolchildren's poem, thus highlighting the incongruity of the suit itself (for a more detailed analysis, see Hobbs 2007: 54–57).

Finally, although most religious genres (e.g. sacred books, Biblical tales, masses, hymns, sermons) would not be considered suitable for humorous incongruities, humor and religious discourse are not always incompatible. This is illustrated in Bell, Crossley, and Hempelmann's (2011) study on church marquees in the USA, whose content may sometimes be humorous:

(3.8) We're all the in the gutter but some of us are looking up to Jesus (Bell, Crossley, and Hempelmann 2011: 196).

This marquee text creatively plays with Oscar Wilde's famous quotation "We are all in the gutter but some of us are looking at the stars", thus producing humor. As Bell, Crossley, and Hempelmann (2011: 187) suggest, via such advertising marquees, churches may be "seeking to attract attention and perhaps get sinners to reconsider their ways through the messages they read on [them]".

The categories identified here seem to form a continuum with the obligatory presence of humor on its one end and the absence of humor on the other. Genres are placed at different points along this continuum according to how (un)typical the presence of humor is considered in them. In other words, in some genres, speakers appear to think that humor is an indispensable discoursal strategy (category A), while in others they deem its use most unconventional and irrelevant (category D). In between these two poles, speakers may opt for humorous realizations of "serious" genres (category B) or may occasionally embed humorous utterances in activities usually perceived and constructed as "serious". Humor can therefore be perceived as a discoursal strategy available to speakers wishing to modify genres or to adjust them to their own private goals and needs. This is mostly attested in those genres which may be realized with or without humor (categories B–D).

This taxonomy tries to account for speakers' metapragmatic stereotypes of humor, in particular their implicit ideas about when and where humor is expected to be used or not. Such stereotypes emerge from speakers' practices concerning humor use and from their views about when, where, and for what purposes the use of humor is deemed "appropriate" and potentially "effective". Nevertheless, no classification is without limitations. Here, some genres could be inserted in more than one (adjacent) categories. For example, aphorisms/quotations have been included in category B, together with other genres which may have serious or humorous realizations. Aphorisms/quotations, however, are often classified as a kind of one-liners (see among others Dynel 2009), which would be placed in category A, as a subgenre of canned jokes. Moreover, the inclusion of a specific genre in a specific category does not have universal value: the same genre may be classified in a different category in different sociocultural communities, as metapragmatic stereotypes on humor are culture-specific (see Section 2.2). For example, humor may surface in religious sermons in certain religious communities in the USA (thus this genre could be classified in category C), but is not at all expected –and would be considered most inappropriate or even blasphemous– in Greek Orthodox masses (thus it would be placed under category D). The notion of the *normative communities of humor* (Kuipers 2008a) could obviously account for such variation: different communities establish and abide by different rules of humor use (see also Section 2.5.2.3). Finally, this classification could not *de facto* refer to all the genres of/with humor, as many of them are either less common and culture-specific (cf. Oring 2008: 191–192) and/or they have not (yet?) attracted the attention of scholarly research. So, further research is required to confirm or refine the categories identified here.

Finally, by bringing to the surface the variety of genres where humor is attested, the present taxonomy underscores the significance of genre as a contextual parameter of humor and of genre-recontextualization practices, which seem to be a common means for the creation of humor in postmodern societies, especially in the new media. To such practices we turn our attention in the following Sections.

3.4 Humor and the recontextualization of generic conventions

One of the most salient characteristics of genres is their fluidity: genres may exhibit differences from one realization to the other and may even change with time to adjust to speakers' new communicative needs and purposes (see Section 3.2). The following Sections involve different aspects of genre fluidity, concentrating specifically on how such fluidity may lead to the emergence of new humorous (sub)genres (Section 3.4.1), to the transformation of already existing ones (Section 3.4.2), as well as to the manipulation or recontextualization of generic conventions to create a humorous effect (Section 3.4.3). Even though all the cases examined here involve some kind of modification or recontextualization of generic norms, the latter case is different from the other two because it shows that the changes in generic conventions and norms may not necessarily result in the emergence of a new humorous genre, but may merely lead to the *ad hoc* production of a humorous effect.

3.4.1 The emergence of new humorous (sub)genres

The dynamic and fluid character of genres as well as their tendency to develop intertextual links with each other is most clearly demonstrated in the emergence of new subgenres belonging to the broader generic category of canned jokes including humorous texts considered to be self-contained and circulated in a more or less fixed form. It is usually suggested that canned jokes traditionally contain three main subgenres evolving around an incongruity, entertaining interlocutors, and creating solidarity among them (see Attardo and Chabanne 1992; also Attardo 1994: 295–299, 2001: 61–62, and the data examined in Raskin 1985):
1. *narrative jokes*, namely short fictional stories located in the "past" with a surprise ending in their (final) punch line. They often represent a brief dialogue between two or more characters;
2. *riddle-jokes*, which include a question and an answer, the latter forming the punch line with the unexpected, incongruous content; and
3. *one-liners*, namely very brief texts including an incongruous piece of information and offering an unconventional comment on a topic.

Canned jokes, however, appear to undergo changes due to intertextual influences and hybridization, hence new joking (sub)genres emerge, especially online (see among others Boxman-Shabtai and Shifman 2015; Chen 2013; Moalla 2013). This means that speakers explore innovative ways of constructing and communicating their humorous messages without necessarily abandoning more "traditional" forms of humor. For instance, Moalla (2013: 2, 4–6) discusses jokes "creating an alternate reality", namely referring to potential future contexts, and allowing humorists to shift perspective and distance themselves from their problems and the stressful circumstances they find themselves in.

In order to illustrate some new subgenres of canned jokes, I rely on the corpus of Greek political jokes on the current debt crisis (see Sections 2.5.1–2.5.1.3). As already mentioned, canned jokes are usually categorized in three groups: *narrative jokes*, *riddle–jokes*, and *one–liners*. Let's see some examples for these "traditional" categories first:

(3.9) Πάει ένας τύπος σε ένα μπαρ στεναχωρημένος και λέει στον μπάρμαν «βάλε μου ρε φίλε 5–6 ποτάκια, να σου πω τι έχω».
Τα βάζει ο μπάρμαν και τον ρωτάει «τι έχεις ρε άνθρωπε...».
–«Βάλε ρε φίλε άλλα 5–6 ποτάκια να σου πω...».
Τα ξαναβάζει ο μπάρμαν, «θα μου πεις τώρα;».
–«Μόνο 5 ευρώ».
A guy walks into a bar looking upset and says to the bartender: "Pour me 5–6 drinks, pal, and I'll tell you what's wrong with me".
The bartender pours the drinks and asks him: "What's wrong with you, man?..."
"Pour 5–6 more drinks, pal, and I'll tell you..."
The bartender pours again: "Are you going to tell me now?"
"[I have] only 5 euro".

Example (3.9) narrates a brief story including a dialogue between two Greeks and commenting on the lack of money currently experienced by the Greek people, which does not allow them to pay for their drinks (or, more accurately, to pay for drinking as much as they would like to). The final utterance *Μόνο 5 ευρώ* 'only 5 euro' constitutes the punch line of the joke revealing the unexpected twist of the story: even though the set up creates expectations that the customer faces some serious problems, it turns out that his "serious" problem is that he does not have enough money to pay for all his drinks (which is actually the bartender's problem as well, as he will not be paid for his services). Example (2.9) is also a narrative joke representing a brief conversation between a mother and a son in Uganda. Although for Greeks Uganda has for decades been considered more underprivileged than Greece, the punch line of this brief story reveals a humorous reversal: in "poor" Uganda children have school textbooks, while in Greece they do not (see also example 3.1).

In riddle–jokes, the initial utterance, namely the question, prepares the ground for the second utterance, which constitutes the answer to the question and simultaneously the punch line of the joke causing the humorous effect:

(3.10) Τί κοινό έχουν οι Έλληνες με τις γαλοπούλες;
Τη βγάζουν δεν τη βγάζουν μέχρι τα Χριστούγεννα. . .
What do Greeks and turkeys have in common?
They may not survive until Christmas. . .

In example (3.10), humor is based on an analogy between Greeks and Christmas turkeys, implying that both turkeys and Greek people may not manage to survive until next Christmas: turkeys will be slaughtered to be eaten on Christmas day, while Greeks will be exhausted or even eliminated due to the austerity measures imposed on them during the financial crisis. Example (2.7) is also a riddle–joke humorously comparing the (sinking) Greek economy to the Titanic.

In one–liners, humorists offer (or are represented as offering) brief, unconventional comments on various aspects of social reality, in the present case on the repercussions of the financial crisis on their lives and/or the inefficacy of the austerity measures imposed on Greek people:

(3.11) Είμαστε η γενιά που πρόλαβε τα καλοριφέρ αναμένα.
We belong to the generation that lived with house heating on.

One–liners humorously comment on Greek people's inability to pay for house heating (example 3.11). Examples (2.3–2.6) also constitute one–liners humorously commenting on the increased rates of unemployment in Greece and its consequences (examples 2.3–2.4) as well as on Greek people's responsibility for their current financial and political state (examples 2.5–2.6).

Two subgenres of canned jokes appear to be added to the already existing ones: *monological fictionalization jokes* and *intertextual jokes*. First, the term *fictionalization* is borrowed from Kotthoff (1999) who explores the fictional scenarios speakers construct in their oral interactions, in order, among other things, to amuse themselves and to enhance their solidarity bonds. Fictionalization involves future narratives constructed by speakers and describing how a situation or event could potentially evolve in the future. In Kotthoff's (1999) study, such narratives are jointly constructed by more than one speaker (see also Georgakopoulou 2007; Archakis and Tsakona 2012),[37] but, in the present case, the joker alone builds an incongruous, unrealistic future scenario. Hence, it could be suggested that canned jokes involving fictional scenarios constitute *monological fictionalizations*. The following joke is indicative:

(3.12) Οι νέοι λογαριασμοί της ΔΕΗ θα έχουν φωσφορούχα γράμματα για να διαβάζονται στο σκοτάδι....
The new electricity bills will be written in fluorescent letters, so that they can be read in the dark...

The humorist in example (3.12) creates a fictional scenario concerning the new format of the electricity bills which will have to be read by all people, including those who could not afford to pay their bills and now live without electricity in crisis-ridden Greece. Such future narratives are created for a variety of topics (see Section 2.5.1.1): what people will do at the super markets where they will not be able to buy anything (example 2.1), how their pets will have to survive in houses without heating (example 2.2), or how the German Chancellor Angela Merkel will deliver pre-election speeches in open rallies around Greece (example 2.13). In general, such scenarios allow jokers to be creative and imagine circumstances and actions that are incongruous and not necessarily plausible.

The second emergent subgenre of canned jokes involves *intertextual jokes*, which draw on non-humorous genres to convey their humorous messages. Intertextuality here is employed to create content or structural similarities between jokes and non-humorous genres. The following examples are illustrative of this category:

(3.13) Κρίση είναι να σε ταΐζουν τα περιστέρια στο Σύνταγμα.
Crisis is to have pigeons feed you at Syntagma Square.[38]

---

[37] Other terms that have been used to refer to this genre are the following: *joint fictionalization* (Kotthoff 1999, 2007: 278–283; Archakis and Tsakona 2012: 99–105), *joint fantasizing* (Kotthoff 2006: 293–299; Priego-Valverde 2006; Chovanec 2012), *humorous fantasy* (Kotthoff 2006: 297, 2007: 282; Vandergriff and Fuchs 2012: 446–448), *fantasy humor* (Hay 2001: 62, 65), *comical hypothetical* (Winchatz and Kozin 2008), and *fantasizing* (Stallone and Haugh 2017).
[38] Syntagma Square is the central square in Athens, the Greek capital, right in front of the Greek parliament. The square attracts not only tourists but also Greek families, whose children very often feed the pigeons crowding the square. Here this image is reversed for humorous purposes: the pigeons feed the humans.

(3.14) Κύριος που διαθέτει πετρέλαιο κίνησης, ζητά γνωριμία με κυρία που διαθέτει πετρέλαιο θέρμανσης.
Gentleman with car fuel wants to meet lady with heating fuel.

(3.15) Μόλις άναψα το καλοριφέρ. Γενική είσοδος 10 ευρώ με ποτό!!!
I just turned house heating on. 10 euro for entry and a drink!!!

(3.16) Υπάρχουν και ευχάριστα: Στο φεστιβάλ των Καννών πήραμε σήμερα το βραβείο μισθού μικρού μήκους.
There is also good news: at the Cannes [International Film] Festival today we received the award for the shortest [i.e. smallest] salary.[39]

(3.17) ΜΕΡΙΚΟΙ ΛΟΓΟΙ ΠΟΥ ΜΑΣ ΑΡΕΣΕΙ Η ΟΙΚΟΝΟΜΙΚΗ ΚΡΙΣΗ ΣΤΗΝ ΕΛΛΑΔΑ
Μου αρέσει που όταν λέω για αύξηση στο αφεντικό μου δε με αγριοκοιτάζει αλλά λιώνει στα γέλια. Άσε που έδιωξε κανα δυο που δε μου άρεσε η μούρη τους..
Μου αρέσει που τα καφενεία έχουν γεμίσει άνεργους επιστήμονες με 2 μεταπτυχιακά. Πλέον πας για ουζάκι και αντί για μπάλα συζητάς για μαύρες τρύπες τουλάχιστον. (...)
Μου αρέσει που το μέλλον της χώρας είναι αβέβαιο, γιατί σε όλους μας έλειπε λίγο πολύ η περιπέτεια στη ζωή μας.
Μου αρέσει που μπορώ να έχω κατάθλιψη ελεύθερα. Παλιά μου τα είχαν πρήξει όλοι «Τι σου λείπει ρε; Τη δουλειά σου την έχεις, το αμαξάκι σου, τι άλλο θες;» (...)
Μου αρέσει που αν πω ότι δουλεύω 2 φορές τη βδομάδα με κοιτούν με συμπάθεια και μου λένε κουράγιο, ενώ πιο παλιά σκεφτόντουσαν «Ρε τον τεμπέλη»..
Μου αρέσει που θα έχω και εγω μία ιστορία πόνου και δυστυχίας να λέω στα εγγόνια μου, όπως εμείς ακούγαμε για χούντα και κατοχή. Αλλιώς θα με πέρναγαν για πολύ φλώρο.
SOME REASONS WHY WE LIKE THE FINANCIAL CRISIS IN GREECE
I like it when I ask my boss for a raise and he does not frown on me but bursts into laughter. Not to mention that he fired a couple of guys whose faces I didn't like...

---

39 An untranslatable pun is involved here. Based on the phrase *ταινία μικρού μήκους* 'short film', the humorist constructs the phrase *μισθός μικρού μήκους* 'short salary' actually meaning 'small salary'.

> I like that the coffee shops are full of unemployed scholars with 2 post-graduate degrees each. Now you go out to drink ouzo [i.e. a traditional Greek alcoholic beverage] and instead of football you talk about black holes to say the least. (...)
> I like that the future of the country is uncertain, because we all more or less lacked a sense of adventure in our lives.
> I like that I can be depressed without feeling guilty. Previously everybody would attack me "What's your problem, pal? You've got your job, your car, what more do you want?" (...)
> I like it when I say I work 2 times per week and people look at me with sympathy and they try to encourage me, while in the past they would think "What a lazy dude"...
> I like that I too will have a story of pain and misery to tell my grandchildren, like the ones we used to listen about the [Greek military] junta [i.e. 1967–1974] and the [Nazi] occupation [i.e. 1941–1944]. Otherwise, they would think that I am totally uncool.

In the case of intertextual jokes, humorists borrow conventions from non-humorous genres to create jokes, in the present case about the Greek debt crisis and its repercussions: a dictionary definition is used to humorously represent the fact that some Greek people cannot afford to feed themselves due to salary/pension cut-offs or unemployment in crisis-ridden Greece (example 3.13); a fictional personal ad comments on the incongruously high fuel prices (example 3.14); another ad creates an incongruous analogy between a night club and a house with heating whose owner tries to gain some money to pay the heating bill by charging his/her guests (example 3.15); a short news report criticizes the incongruously low salaries in Greece (example 3.16); and a list like the ones appearing in fashion magazines includes a variety of unexpected reasons why Greek people seem to (ironically) enjoy certain negative aspects of the financial crisis (example 3.17). In particular, they enjoy the bad working conditions and relations, going out for coffee with highly educated yet unemployed people, living in insecurity, feeling depressed, working part-time, and narrating tragic stories from the hard times of the crisis.

Interestingly, there do not seem to be any restrictions as to the genres that will be exploited to create intertextual jokes: in the corpus discussed here, genres such as popular sayings, songs, politicians' statements, religious texts (e.g. prophecies, prayers), letters, grammar books, public announcements, games, etc. are exploited to create intertextual jokes.

To sum up, the jokes examined here demonstrate that (at least) two new categories (i.e. monological fictionalizations and intertextual jokes) are added to more traditional ones (i.e. narrative jokes, riddle–jokes, one–liners). Generic creativity plays a significant role in this process. Finally, it should be noted that the subgenres of canned jokes discussed here may not always be clear-cut categories but may occasionally overlap. This can be illustrated in example (3.12) which could be considered a monological fictionalization and/or a one–liner. Overlapping is attested in example (3.16) as well, which was analyzed as an intertextual joke based on a news report, but could also be considered a narrative one, as it includes the representation of a (fictional) past event (πήραμε το βραβείο ... 'we received the award ... ') that happened in a specific place and time (στο φεστιβάλ των Καννών 'at the Cannes Festival', σήμερα 'today').

3.4.2 The transformation of humorous genres

Genre transformations are often triggered (or sped up) by the new technologies, especially the digital media and the social networks developed therein: "media may play a role in genre form, and the introduction of new media may occasion genre evolution" (Yates and Orlikowski 1992: 299).[40] The present Section explores the particularities of a quite recent genre of humor, which is here dubbed *online joint fictionalization*. The case study discussed here is intended to reveal significant similarities between the new genre and what Kotthoff (1999) calls *joint fictionalization*, which involves the construction of humorous fictional scenarios in informal face-to-face interactions among peers (see Section 3.4.1). Concurrently, the new genre incorporates other (humorous) genres which are typical of online communication and, in this new context, contribute to the construction of the fictional scenario at hand. In other words, the new digital genre of online joint fictionalization emerges from the modification of a previous oral one and exploits the affordances offered by online communication.

3.4.2.1 The generic structure and sociopragmatic goals of oral joint fictionalization

Let's begin with a brief description of oral joint fictionalization as a genre. The construction of such a text is based on speakers' use of their turns to depart from the ongoing topic and turn–taking system in order to build a fictional story or setting by adding details to it. Such details are more often than not humorous, that is, they are in contrast with what would normally be expected in

---

[40] See also Thurlow, Lengel, and Tomic (2004), North (2006: 229), Shifman (2014b), Boxman–Shabtai and Shifman (2015: 522–523), Chovanec and Dynel (2015: 6–10).

the specific context, and result in the creation of absurd, incongruous representations or perceptions of the narrated (fictional) events or the described (fictional) settings. In Winchatz and Kozin's (2008: 383) terms, this "speech phenomenon (...) forms at the juncture of storytelling, humor, and imagination". Participants thus get the opportunity to come closer by laughing with/at the same things. It should be noted here that, even if a single speaker in a group builds the scenario via his/her turn(s), it is still considered a "joint" achievement as long as the others offer signs of acknowledgment and entertainment (e.g. phatic signals, laughter; Winchatz and Kozin 2008).

Previous research on joint fictionalization has shown that such constructions are based on shared knowledge among participants which often involves mass culture (con)texts, such as TV shows, media registers, and individuals or events that have become popular via the entertainment media.[41] Such intertextual connections enable participants not only to display and share their knowledge on such topics, but also to position themselves towards them, that is, to display their positive or negative stance towards the person, event, register, etc. alluded to. Furthermore, as Kotthoff (1999: 145) observes, "humorous fictionalizations establish *unusual* perspectives on concrete images and scenes" (emphasis mine). Participants thus get the opportunity to express their evaluations that would not probably be as easily expressed and/or accepted in "serious" discussions on the same topic.

Even though the overall effect of such scenarios is humorous, not all contributions need to be humorous: "the topic of joking remarks can also be seriously pursued" (Kotthoff 1999: 136; see also Vandergriff and Fuchs 2009, 2012; Archakis and Tsakona 2012: 99–105). The non–humorous utterances of a fictionalization may also contribute to the fictional scenario (and the evaluation of its content) and do not necessarily suspend or cancel the humorous tone and goal of the interaction. In general, humorous or serious turns adding to the scenario at hand are more often than not supportive of the humorous effect of this kind of interaction (Hay 2001; Vandergriff and Fuchs 2009: 35–36, 38–39, 2012), unless, of course, speakers clearly express their disagreement with the content of the previous contribution(s).

Winchatz and Kozin (2008) suggest that joint fictionalizations are clearly set off from the surrounding talk and sequentially structured, and they identify four phases constituting the genre:

---

[41] See Baym (1995), Kotthoff (1999: 134–135, 144, 2006: 293–299, 2007: 282–283), Winchatz and Kozin (2008: 395–396, 401–402), Archakis and Tsakona (2012: 99–105), Chovanec (2012).

1. *Initiation*: A speaker decides to suspend the ongoing talk and at the same time requests permission to "move the conversation from the realm of the real and the concrete (...) to the realm of the imaginary or hypothetical" (Winchatz and Kozin 2008: 392). This is usually achieved via an utterance which introduces the hypothetical scenario, often based on preceding talk.
2. *Acknowledgment*: One or more recipients show their approval of the initiator's move by offering an appreciation signal (e.g. phatic signals, laughter, evaluative comments) or a creative addition to the scenario introduced by the initiator. Lack of reaction, that is, recipients' silence, can also be considered a kind of acknowledgment allowing the initiator or a third party to proceed with building the scenario.
3. *Creating the imaginary*: The fictional scenario is built by the initiator with or without the help of other participants. They contribute to the ongoing interaction by adding details to the imaginary script, by laughing, and sometimes by leading the fictionalization to what Winchatz and Kozin (2008: 396) call "an absurd extreme, that is, something completely and utterly unbelievable, highly unlikely, and at times almost cartoon–like". Intertextual references to various cultural, historical, relational, etc. contexts are often exploited to construct the scenario.
4. *Termination*: The fictionalization is led to an end when a participant suggests that they (seriously) ponder on the imaginary scenario, or decides to cause a sudden switch back to reality. It may also fade out through participants' shared laughter. After the termination phase, interlocutors continue the previous topic of interaction or begin a new one.

In what follows, I will try to demonstrate how this generic form has been transformed in online interactions and practices, and how online participants form a group whose main aim is the construction of the fictionalization *per se*. Although speakers have kept specific generic characteristics intact (i.e. the absurd, fictional content, the mass culture intertextual allusions, the collaborative and supportive participation, the humorous tone and effect), they have enriched the genre with other practices which are common in online humorous communication such as online posts and memes.

Memes in particular will be discussed here as an integral part of the online joint fictionalization genre, since participants produce and circulate them as their contributions to the construction of a fictional scenario. Hence, a few words on their content and sociopragmatic functions are deemed relevant at this point. Memes employ "script and sound, static pictures and moving images" (Shifman 2007: 190) and rely on intertextual allusions to convey playful and often complex or unconventional messages. They are considered prototypical instances of contemporary internet culture reflecting and enhancing speaker involvement and everyday creativity. Although it would be "unwise to characterize all emergent memes as being humorous" (Wiggins and Bowers 2015: 1899), humor is identified as the *sine qua non* for the production of most memes as well as an important reason for their continuous circulation and success. In addition, memes are more often than not perceived and investigated as autonomous texts whose meaning(s) point to various events, ideologies, stereotypes, texts, etc.[42] Here, however, I will concentrate on their potential to be part of a broader online discussion of a topic of mutual concern and to coexist with other genres, such as Facebook posts, news articles, etc.

3.4.2.2 The data of the online fictionalization case study

The fictionalization discussed here relates to the unexpected discovery of a crocodile on the Greek island of Crete. From July 4th, 2014 until April 3rd, 2015, I collected over 1,000 posts and 59 memes coming from 5 different Facebook communities supporting the crocodile and his right to stay in Crete. These communities were created a few days after the crocodile was spotted and, until April 3rd, 2015, had acquired 19,598 followers. The participants in these communities jointly created an online humorous fictionalization according to which the crocodile originated in Crete and exhibited local cultural and linguistic features. The following account of the events concerning the crocodile of Crete is based on a corpus of 100 news articles collected in the same period and on the same event (for a more detailed presentation, see Tsakona 2017b, 2018c).

According to news reports of July 4th, 2014 (e.g. Κροκόδειλος περίπου δύο μέτρων σε φράγμα στην Κρήτη 2014), a crocodile was accidentally discovered by two firemen who passed by the Potami Dam Lake in Amari, near the town of Rethymno in Crete. The event was immediately reported to the authorities, as crocodiles do not live free in any part of Greece. The issue was evaluated as an important one, as the safety of the inhabitants and the tourists was considered in jeopardy. Hence authorities set out to find and arrest not only the crocodile but also the person who abandoned the reptile in the lake. They also placed fences in several parts around the lake to prevent the crocodile from escaping, as well as traps with dead chickens as baits to entice the animal. By July 10th, the crocodile was already given the name *Sifis* (Μένει Κρήτη ο «Σήφης» ο κροκόδειλος (;), που μπορεί να μην είναι μόνος 2014), thus acquiring a local identity and a gender one:

---

[42] On memes, see among others Shifman (2007, 2013, 2014a, 2014b), Ramoz–Leslie (2011), Milner (2013), Ekdale and Tully (2014), Miltner (2014), Peck (2014), Wiggins and Bowers (2015), Laineste and Voolaid (2016), Piata (2018, to appear).

Sifis is one of the most common male names in Crete. The choice of name was indicative of the locals' wish to consider the crocodile "one of their own" and to keep him in the area. While the police could not find the owner of the animal, local people suggested that Sifis should remain in the lake because he caused no harm (provided he was restricted in a specific area by fences). In addition, the animal had already become a tourist attraction: hundreds of tourists (and locals) visited the lake daily hoping they could take a glance at Sifis and feed him. The emerging Facebook communities fervently supported Sifis' right to live in Crete, and resisted any idea of capturing and removing him from the lake.

In the meantime, Olivier Behra, a famous herpetologist, was summoned to help capture Sifis, but without any lack ("World's greatest crocodile hunter" fails to catch "Sifis" – Crete's fugitive reptile 2014). Interestingly, his first attempt was sabotaged by locals who tried to warn Sifis and scare him away from the traps and the herpetologist (Κρήτη: Ο «Σήφης» κατάγεται από το Νείλο και είναι ... καλοταϊσμένος 2014). After more than 10 unsuccessful attempts to capture Sifis, the reptile remained on the loose, but locals seemed not to be afraid of him. The final act was written at the end of March 2015, when Sifis was found dead at the shore of the lake. His death was attributed by the authorities to the particularly long and heavy winter in Crete.

The above summary of the news articles of the corpus brings to the surface (at least) the following unexpected events/situations:
1. A crocodile was found in a lake in Crete. Although the animal does not originate in Greece, it has been assigned a local (Cretan/Greek) identity as well as a gender one (male) by being named *Sifis*.
2. Local people disagree with the authorities' proposition to capture and remove the reptile from the lake; even though crocodiles are not endemic to Greece, local people consider him to be a local and want to keep him there.
3. The crocodile has proven difficult to arrest even for an experienced herpetologist.

These events could be rephrased as the following humorous incongruities/ script oppositions attested in the set of data under scrutiny:

Incongruity/script opposition 1: *exotic dangerous animal/local pet with human qualities*
The crocodile is an exotic dangerous animal brought to Crete, Greece from abroad/Sifis the crocodile has male human attributes and originates in Crete.

Incongruity/script opposition 2: *remove from/keep in the lake*
The best and safest solution (suggested by the authorities) is to remove the crocodile from the lake/the best solution (proposed by citizens) is to leave the crocodile in the lake.

Incongruity/script opposition 3: *captivity/freedom*
The crocodile should be captured/should not be –and has not been– captured, in spite of several attempts by experienced specialists.

In the following Section, I discuss how participants in Facebook communities build their online humorous fictionalization and simultaneously refer to and reframe these incongruous events through creating humorous verbal posts, images, and memes, among other things.

3.4.2.3 Jointly constructing the online fictionalization

The following analysis of the data concentrates on two interrelated topics: the structure of the genre and its content (e.g. the humorous reframing of, and elaboration on, Sifis' story as narrated by newspapers and other media). Both aspects of the analysis are intended to show the similarities between the online genre and the initial oral one, as well as the adaptation of the genre to practices which are already popular among internet users.

In order to describe the generic structure of online joint fictionalization, I draw on Winchatz and Kozin's (2008) four-phase model emerging from oral data (see Section 3.4.2.1). The first phase of *initiation* involves someone beginning an imaginary scenario related to something mentioned earlier in interaction. Here, the imaginary scenario is introduced by the anonymous administrators of the examined Facebook pages, who presuppose that at least some Facebook participants are familiar with news reports on the discovery of the crocodile. So, by launching these pages they called for audience attention and simultaneously created spaces for speaker participation and involvement. Furthermore, by naming the crocodile *Sifis* and posting the first photos, cartoons, status updates, links to newspaper articles, etc., they started the construction of the humorous scenario, where a personified, male reptile living in Crete and acquiring local features became the protagonist (see Figure 3.1).

The second *acknowledgment* phase was enacted by those Facebook users who "liked" the relevant pages, "shared" their content, and responded to administrators' posts. Thus, the online interaction quickly entered the third *creating the imaginary* phase, where participants contributed in various ways.

Let's explore in more detail how the third *creating the imaginary* phase is materialized. First of all, it should be noted that *all* relevant Facebook pages

Figure 3.1: Cover photo and profile photo of the Facebook page *The Crocodile of Amari Should Remain in the Potami Dam*.

are administered by people pretending[43] to be Sifis the crocodile. Thus, the crocodile is not only personified as a local male individual, but also participates in online social networks and interacts with his fans. Sifis speaks Greek (and sometimes the Cretan dialect) and refers to himself mostly using the first person singular (and less often the third person singular). The following list includes the most common types of Sifis' posts, whether humorous or serious:

1. hyperlinks to news articles, videoclips, or images related to the story of Sifis – or framed so as to become relevant to it (see Figures 3.2a, 3.3–3.5);
2. texts (e.g. poems, memes), images (e.g. children's drawings), and comments sent to Sifis by his fans; they are often responded to with a thank-you-for-your-support note from Sifis (see Figures 3.3–3.5);
3. phatic comments such as greetings, wishes, advice on various topics (e.g. *καλημερα!!!!!!!!!* 'good morning!!!!!!!!!!', *Σας έλειψα καθόλου;* 'Did you miss me?', *Μην τρομάζετε τα παιδιά. Την αλήθεια να τους λέτε, πάντα* ... 'Do not scare children. Tell them the truth, always ... ', *Χρόνια Πολλά σε όλα τα κροκοδειλάκια της παρέας* ... *Καλά Χριστούγεννα* 'Season's greetings to all the little crocodiles of the group ... Merry Christmas');

---

[43] On overt pretense as a source of humor, see Dynel (2018).

Figure 3.2a: Sifis' post on the arrival of the herpetologist.

4. comments on Sifis' story as well as on other issues (e.g. politics, sports – *Όχι άλλα κροκοδείλια δάκρυα από τους πολιτικούς που οδήγησαν την Ελλάδα στο χείλος του γκρεμού* ... 'No more crocodile tears for the politicians who led Greece on the verge of disaster ... ').

Such activities are indicative of Sifis' effort to inform the audience on recent developments concerning his case as well as to maintain the interest of his supporters via discussing a variety of topics with them. Needless to say, such actions are not typical of a crocodile but of a real person, who seeks to communicate with other people and, most importantly, to sustain the fictional scenario according to which the crocodile originates in Crete, is an "authentic" Cretan figure, and hence should be allowed to live free on the island.

Figure 3.2b: Comments (3.18–3.26).

On the other hand, Sifis' fans respond to his posts via:
1. sending their own comments on the relevant events as reported by the media, or on the other topics Sifis initiates (e.g. politics, sports);
2. sending greetings, expressing their support, affection, admiration, and offering advice on how to escape captivity (see Figures 3.2b–3.2d);
3. uploading memes, hyperlinks (e.g. news articles concerning Sifis, videoclips with crocodiles or other animals from YouTube), photos with crocodiles, poems inspired by him, cartoons, jokes, and other humorous texts.

Interestingly, Sifis' fans address him using the second person singular, as if the crocodile could actually read and reply to their contributions. They refer to him using the third person singular only when an answer is not expected from him but from the other participants.

Some illustrative examples are provided here. Figures (3.2b–3.2d) come from the same thread of comments initiated by Sifis by posting a news article on his status update (Ήρθε ο ερπετολόγος Ολιβιέ Μπεχρά για τον Σήφη τον κροκόδειλο

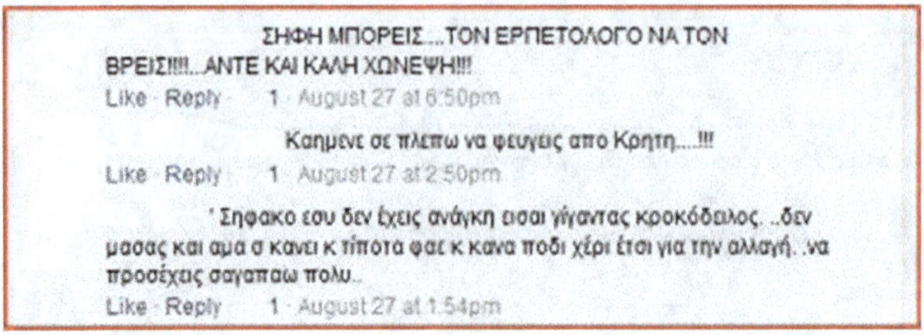

> ΣΗΦΗ ΜΠΟΡΕΙΣ....ΤΟΝ ΕΡΠΕΤΟΛΟΓΟ ΝΑ ΤΟΝ
> ΒΡΕΙΣ!!!!...ΑΝΤΕ ΚΑΙ ΚΑΛΗ ΧΩΝΕΨΗ!!!
> Like · Reply · 1 · August 27 at 6:50pm
>
> > Καημενε σε πλεπω να φευγεις απο Κρητη....!!!
> > Like · Reply · 1 · August 27 at 2:50pm
>
> > ' Σηφακο εσυ δεν έχεις ανάγκη εισαι γίγαντας κροκόδειλος...δεν μασάς και αμα ο κανει κ τίποτα φας κ κανα ποδι χέρι έτσι για την αλλαγή..να προσέχεις σαγαπαω πολυ..
> > Like · Reply · 1 · August 27 at 1:54pm

Figure 3.2c: Comments (3.27–3.29).

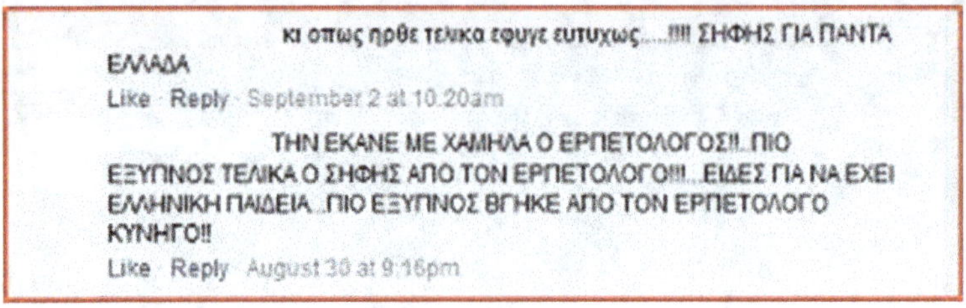

> κι οπως ηρθε τελικα εφυγε ευτυχως......!!!! ΣΗΦΗΣ ΓΙΑ ΠΑΝΤΑ ΕΛΛΑΔΑ
> Like · Reply · September 2 at 10.20am
>
> > ΤΗΝ ΕΚΑΝΕ ΜΕ ΧΑΜΗΛΑ Ο ΕΡΠΕΤΟΛΟΓΟΣ!!..ΠΙΟ ΕΞΥΠΝΟΣ ΤΕΛΙΚΑ Ο ΣΗΦΗΣ ΑΠΟ ΤΟΝ ΕΡΠΕΤΟΛΟΓΟ!!!...ΕΙΔΕΣ ΓΙΑ ΝΑ ΕΧΕΙ ΕΛΛΗΝΙΚΗ ΠΑΙΔΕΙΑ...ΠΙΟ ΕΞΥΠΝΟΣ ΒΓΗΚΕ ΑΠΟ ΤΟΝ ΕΡΠΕΤΟΛΟΓΟ ΚΥΝΗΓΟ!!
> > Like · Reply · August 30 at 9:16pm

Figure 3.2d: Comments (3.30–3.31).

2014; see Figure 3.2a) and referring to the arrival of the herpetologist and his collaboration with the local authorities in order to capture Sifis. Sifis offers a first comment wondering: *Ήρθε ο ερπετολόγος ... Και τώρα;* 'The herpetologist is here ... What now?'. This thread of comments includes 48 responses from Sifis' fans. Here we will concentrate on 14 of them (Figures 3.2b–3.2d) which give us a representative snapshot of fans' reactions to the news. Their analysis will attempt to show how such comments (re)produce and sustain the above-mentioned humorous incongruities (see Section 3.4.2.2).[44]

Translation of comments (3.18–3.31):

(3.18) Hang on Sifis.

(3.19) what did the poor pet do to them???? it made the area famous!!! they should take advantage of this [i.e. the fame] and leave it [i.e. the poor pet] alone!!!!

---

[44] The names and personal photos of commentators have been erased to protect their anonymity.

(3.20) THE HERPETOLOGIST WILL EAT THE CHICKEN [chickens were used as baits to entice Sifis]

(3.21) SIFIS IS NOT GOING ANYWHERE

(3.22) poor Sifis what do they do to you dear... since the pet does not do any harm why do you torture it! hang on

(3.23) the herpetologist will get what he deserves!!!!!

(3.24) rather Sifis will get... an exquisite meal: a famous herpetologist...

(3.25) what could the herpetologist do [?] Sifis is an important figure and did it again [i.e. he managed to escape]

(3.26) go hide Sifis...

(3.27) SIFIS YOU CAN DO IT... YOU CAN FIND THE HERPETOLOGIST!!!!...[45] GO ON AND ENJOY YOUR MEAL!!![46]

(3.28) Poor [Sifis] I see you leaving Crete...!!!

(3.29) Sifis dear you don't need anybody you are a super crocodile... you are not afraid of anything and if he [i.e. the herpetologist] gets to you, eat a leg or a hand just for a change [i.e. instead of eating ducks and chickens all the time]... take care... I love you very much...

(3.30) he [i.e. the herpetologist] left as he came [i.e. without taking Sifis with him] thank God...!!!! SIFIS FOREVER IN GREECE

(3.31) THE HERPETOLOGIST RUN OFF!!... SIFIS [TURNED OUT TO BE] SMARTER THAN THE HERPETOLOGIST!!!... HE DID IT BECAUSE HE HAS BEEN RAISED [lit. educated] IN GREECE... HE OUTSMARTED THE HERPETOLOGIST HUNTER!!

---

[45] Σήφη μπορείς ... τον ερπετολόγο να τον βρεις, here translated as 'Sifis you can do it ... you can find the herpetologist', is a rhyming slogan with intertextual links to Greek football ones.
[46] Καλή χώνεψη, here translated as 'enjoy your meal', could be glossed as '[have a] good digestion'; it is a common wish among Greeks after an enjoyable meal.

All the comments are in favor of the crocodile and against the herpetologist and his effort to arrest Sifis. Some of them (comments 3.18, 3.22, 3.25–3.29) are encouraging Sifis to resist arrest and expressing sympathy and positive feelings towards him. Other comments constitute (more or less direct) threats against the herpetologist (comments 3.20, 3.23, 3.24, 3.27, 3.29) suggesting that Sifis could instead attack his adversary. Comments (3.30–3.31) expressly indicate participants' satisfaction after the herpetologist' failure to capture Sifis. All these comments revolve around the *captivity/freedom* script opposition.

Participants in the community also suggest that the crocodile is harmless, hence it should be kept in the lake (comments 3.19, 3.22, 3.28). It is interesting to note here that, in order to highlight the benign nature of Sifis, participants use expressions such as *(το κακόμοιρο) το ζωάκι* '(the poor) pet' (comments 3.19, 3.22), *καημένε* 'poor' (comment 3.28), and the diminutive *Σηφάκο* 'Sifis dear, little Sifis' (comment 3.29). Other participants directly object to Sifis' removal from the lake (comments 3.21, 3.30). All such comments reproduce the *remove from/stay in the lake* incongruity, supporting the crocodile's right to remain where it currently lives despite fears for the safety of the inhabitants and the tourists in the area.

Finally, via addressing the crocodile in the second person singular (comments 3.18, 3.22, 3.26–3.29), via using address terms typical of human addressees (*Σήφη(ς)* 'Sifis' in comments 3.18, 3.22, 3.26; *αρε Σήφη* 'poor Sifis' and *παιδάκι μου* 'dear [lit. my little child]' in comment 3.22; *καημένε* 'poor' in comment 3.28), and generally via referring to him using his Cretan name (comments 3.18, 3.21–3.22, 3.24–3.27, 3.29–3.31), participants contribute to the personification of the crocodile by attributing it human qualities it does not really have. They also employ various expressions which are typically used for humans such as *μεγάλη μορφή* 'important figure' (comment 3.25) and *γίγαντας* 'super [lit. giant]', *να προσέχεις* 'take care', *σαγαπάω πολύ* 'I love you very much' (comment 3.29), *έξυπνος* 'smart', and *έχει ελληνική παιδεία* 'has been raised [lit. educated] in Greece' (comment 3.31). Comment (3.31) also highlights the local Greek identity assigned to the crocodile even though crocodiles are not endemic to Greece. Thus, the *exotic dangerous animal/local pet with human qualities* script opposition becomes salient in these examples.

Figures (3.3–3.5) are memes referring to Sifis and built around the same humorous incongruities. In Figure (3.3), Sifis says: *16.440 Ρεθυμνάρα σου'ρχομαι!* '16,400 points, wonderful Rethymno, here I come!'. The crocodile is portrayed as a Greek student who has succeeded in his university entry exams and is checking the results together with other students. His grades (i.e. 16,400 points) allowed him to be accepted at the University of Crete in Rethymo, hence now he lives in the nearby lake. A talking and studying (hard) crocodile accepted at the local university evokes the *exotic dangerous animal/local pet with human*

Figure 3.3: '16,400 points, wonderful Rethymno, here I come!'.

qualities script opposition and enriches it with more (humorous) details as to why Sifis has moved to Rethymno.

Figure (3.4) is a map of Greece featuring Sifis in the place where Crete should have been. Such a replacement implies that the crocodile is undoubtedly Cretan and an indispensable part of Greece. This comes in sharp contrast to the fact that crocodiles have never been endemic to Greece. Hence, this meme could be considered as a humorous argument in support of the wish expressed by the local people to keep Sifis in the lake, and hence is associated with the *remove from/ stay in the lake* script opposition.

Finally, in Figure (3.5), Sifis is once again personified (see also Figure 3.3): he is pictured together with well-known and wanted Greek terrorists, Nikos Maziotis and Christodoulos Xiros, the first of them already captured, while the second one still wanted at that time. Sifis is represented as still wanted, too, since the numerous attempts to catch him were unsuccessful; the crocodile proved hard to get. The third script opposition, that is, *captivity/freedom*, is particularly salient in this meme, as Sifis remained free despite the authorities' efforts to capture him.

Finally, the fourth *termination* phase of the online fictionalization was not as abrupt or clearcut as it seems to be in oral fictionalizations. It could rather be suggested that the specific online fictionalization faded away, as no news about Sifis was reported in the media, hence participants lost interest in the subject. After the failed attempts to capture the animal, the media stopped publishing reports on Sifis, as there was nothing tellable to report: Sifis spent his days quietly, swimming and eating in the lake. A few months later, a limited

98 — 3 Genres with/and humor

Figure 3.4: Map of Greece with crocodile instead of Crete.

Figure 3.5: 'Sifis the crocodile wanted'.

3.4 Humor and the recontextualization of generic conventions — 99

number of posts appeared when the media reported that the animal passed away because of the harsh weather.

This difference from the oral genre could be accounted for in terms of the connection between the ongoing fictionalization and the surrounding talk, and of the relationships among participants. Oral fictionalizations are typically part of extended face-to-face interactions among interlocutors who as a group move from one conversational activity (e.g. casual, informal conversation) to another (i.e. joint fictionalization) and back (see Section 3.4.2.1). On the contrary, participants in online fictionalizations such as the one presented here are often brought together *for/by this particular activity*: they did not necessarily interact and/or belong to the same group before launching the fictionalization and/or after its termination. As a result, when the material used to build the scenario at hand (e.g. media reports) seems to run out, the online fictionalization gradually fades away and the relevant webpages become inactive.

In sum, the analysis of all these examples illustrates how participants in Facebook communities reproduce and enrich the incongruities/script oppositions originating in the news articles concerning Sifis, the Cretan crocodile, so as to construct their online joint fictionalization. In their contributions, whether verbal comments, images, or memes, they enact a fictional and humorous scenario involving the male, Cretan/Greek identity of the crocodile; his innocuous character, and hence participants' preference for keeping him in the lake; the crocodile's resistance against any attempts to capture him and simultaneously participants' expressed support for the animal's right to freedom.

The present analysis shows that humor underlies most of participants' contributions and keeps their interaction going even though participants may not necessarily be in the same place or may never meet offline. I have also attempted to show how an oral genre, namely joint fictionalization, occurring in face-to-face interactions among peers mostly for entertainment purposes, has been transferred to online contexts and has subsequently been modified to adjust to the restrictions and affordances of the new medium (e.g. through the use of posts and humorous memes instead of conversational turns). A modified, parallel genre has thus emerged, which maintains the four-part sequential structure of the original oral one and brings together participants whose main aim seems to be to contribute to the humorous fantasy under construction. In its new, online form, joint fictionalization appears to maintain its humorous and fictional quality, the open floor for any participant to contribute to the scenario, and the intertextual allusions to other media or cultural texts, which are reframed in the new environment. However, while in oral fictionalizations participants are brought together by interactional activities from which the fictionalization emerges, in online ones they appear to be brought together by the fictionalization itself.

3.4.3 Recontextualizing generic conventions to create humor

The blending of generic conventions does not solely aim at creating new genres or newer versions of older genres (as we have seen so far in this Chapter), but may also involve the creation of a humorous effect *per se*. Generic structures and/or lexico–grammatical features typical of a specific genre may be reframed, thus resulting in a humorous incongruity.[47]

The following extract comes from an everyday interaction among teenager friends which was recorded for research purposes. Interlocutors start by commenting on the recording process as they are not familiar and comfortable with it, yet. Soon their everyday interaction is colonized by the discourse of (Greek) televised matchmaking programs and/or that of beauty contests:

(3.32) Δημήτρης: Χειρότερα, κομπλάρω κάπως μ' αυτό να με γράφει ( ) {δείχνει το μαγνητόφωνο}
Κατερίνα: (   )//
Δημήτρης: //*Την επόμενη φορά θα έχουμε και μια κάμερα για να δουν ότι εκτός των άλλων είναι και ωραίο παιδί. Όχι όποιος ενδιαφέρεται* {γέλια} *να* ( ) *με τη Μάρθα και να της πάρω και τη δουλειά* {γέλια}
Κατερίνα: {γέλια}
Δημήτρης: *Λέγομαι Δημήτρης.*
Κατερίνα και Δημήτρης: {γέλια}
Δημήτρης: *Το επώνυμο (   ) είμαι ένα ογδόντα πέντε*//
Κατερίνα: //*Ένα ενενήντα*//
Δημήτρης: //*Ψηλός, ξανθός γεροδεμένος* {γέλια} *ακριβώς όπως τα λέω όμως, με τρομερό πρόσωπο, τρομερή προσωπικότητα*//
Κατερίνα: //(   ) *τελείως*//
Δημήτρης: //*Με πάρα πολύ* {γέλια}. *Δε γίνεται*//
Κατερίνα: //*Κοιλιακούς το κάτι άλλο* (   )//
Dimitris: Worse, I'm rather inhibited by this thing recording me (   ) {he points at the tape recorder}
Katerina: (   )//
Dimitris: //*Next time we'll have a camera too so that they can see that apart from everything else he's also a good looking guy. No, anyone who*

---

[47] Such humorous incongruities are accounted for in terms of stylistic humor, parody, or satire. See among others Attardo (1994: 230–253, 262–268, 2001: 104–110, 2009: 315), Antonopoulou (2003), Simpson (2003), Kotthoff (2007), Coutinho and Miranda (2009), Antonopoulou and Nikiforidou (2011), Tsiplakou and Ioannidou (2012), Archakis et al. (2014, 2015), Tsami et al. (2014), Antonopoulou, Nikiforidou, and Tsakona (2015), Tsami (2018), Piata (to appear).

3.4 Humor and the recontextualization of generic conventions

is interested {laughter} to (   ) with Martha and I'll take her job too {laughter}
Katerina: {laughter}
Dimitris: *My name is Dimitris.*
Katerina and Dimitris: {laughter}
Dimitris: *My surname is (   ) I'm one point eighty five* {meter} *tall*//
Katerina: //*One ninety*//
Dimitris: //*Tall, blond well built* {laughter} *but exactly as I am saying it, with a wonderful face, a wonderful personality*//
Katerina: //(   ) *exactly*//
Dimitris: //*With many*/ {laughter}. *I can't*//
Katerina: //*With great six packs* (   ) //

Dimitris humorously presents himself as a candidate for marriage or for a title in a beauty competition (see his jab lines appearing in italics). Katerina plays along with his humorous scenario (see her jab lines also in italics), thus also contributing to the hybridization of discourse: informal interaction to be recorded for research purposes and TV matchmaking/beauty contest discourses are mixed in an effort to produce humor and entertain the participants. The laughter particles dispersed along the interaction confirm the humorous effect attained (for a more detailed analysis, see Archakis and Tsakona 2012: 99–105).[48]

A second example involves the mixing of the dog-training genre and the advertisement one:

(3.33) A man loses his dog so he puts an ad in the paper. And the ad says, 'Here, boy' (Spike Milligan, in Carr and Greeves 2006: 12; cited in Goatly 2012: 154).

Humor results from the incongruous (and eventually ineffective) recontextualization of an oral order to the dog in the personal advertisement text, which the dog cannot possibly read. Hybridization of generic conventions is also attested in example (3.7), where the discourse of the decisions of the Court of Appeals is

---

48 It should also be noted here that this example is a clear case of oral joint fictionalization, as participants create and sustain a fictional scenario involving features belonging to mass media genres (see Section 3.4.2.1). The fictionalization is initiated by Dimitris' jab lines (*την επόμενη φορά* ... 'the next time ... '; *initiation* phase) and becomes accepted through Katerina's laughter (*acknowledgment* phase), and then both of them foster the absurdity with comments and more laughter (*creating the imaginary* phase). The fictionalization comes to an end when they find nothing else to add to the scenario (*termination* phase).

mixed with the children's poem, and in example (3.8), where elements from an aphorism are recontextualized in a church marquee (see Section 3.3).

3.5 Summary

It has often been pointed out within humor research that humor surfaces in an increasingly high number of communicative settings and genres, even though there remain some occasions where its use is restricted. This Chapter has tried to address issues concerning the relationship between humor and genres, which is not often discussed in the relevant literature, but seems to be significant for building a theory of humor placing emphasis on context. More specifically, first, I have attempted to classify genres according to the compulsory, more or less frequent, or limited presence of humor therein. Then, the discussion moved on to how new humorous genres can be created; how existing humorous genres can be transformed in time and across media (specifically from oral to online communicative settings), thus enriching the list of genres where humor is attested; and how blending generic conventions can result in the creation of humor.

It therefore seems that the investigation of the interplay of humor and genre (or generic conventions) is significant for humor research and theory, as it brings to the surface widespread genre–related mechanisms of humor production and simultaneously underlines the dynamic, jointly negotiated construction of humor. Genre participants seem to manipulate generic conventions and derive (humorous or other) meaning(s) out of this manipulation. All this will be further discussed and exploited to develop a theory accounting for humor performance in the following Chapter.

4 Towards a "contextualized" theory of humor

4.1 Introductory remarks

So far, I have elaborated on the importance of context for producing and interpreting humor. Special emphasis has been placed, first, on the metapragmatics of humor including utterances and reactions reflecting speakers' beliefs and practices about what humor is and how it is to be used (Chapter 2); and, second, on the genres where humor is more or less expected to surface, which also reflect speakers' views on when, how, and why humor is to be used in human communication (Chapter 3). As already mentioned (in Chapter 1), these are not the only aspects of context relevant to humor and its analysis.

Despite the importance of context for processing humor, the two most influential linguistic theories of humor, namely the Semantic Script Theory of Humor (SSTH; Raskin 1985) and the General Theory of Verbal Humor (GTVH; Attardo and Raskin 1991; Attardo 1994, 2001), programmatically declare that context will be left out of their account of humor. The following discussion pertains to the reasons for such an exclusion (Section 4.2) and then moves on to recent developments which have tried to expand the General Theory of Verbal Humor, so as to include aspects of context which were left out of its initial version (Section 4.3). This discussion will also propose a performance theory of humor, here dubbed the *Discourse Theory of Humor* (DTH),[49] which attempts to encompass most (if not all) aspects of context that are significant for the creation and interpretation of humor (Section 4.4). It should be noted here that the present discussion of the Semantic Script Theory of Humor, the General Theory of Verbal Humor, and the criticism leveled against them is not meant to elaborate on every topic covered by them. Drawing on some basic works (Raskin 1985, 2017a, 2017b; Attardo and Raskin 1991, 2017; Attardo 1994, 2001, 2008, 2017a, 2017b), here I refer to those aspects of the theories and their criticism that seem to be most relevant to the goals and scope of my study.

A performance theory of humor such as the one put forward here cannot but account for humor failure and humor quality issues, so I also try to address these topics (Section 4.5). The present discussion is rounded up with a tentative application of the Discourse Theory of Humor to the controversial humorous/sexist advertisement examined in Sections (2.5.2–2.5.2.3). In the same Section (4.6), the theory's scope and limitations are also explored.

---

[49] The name is attributed to Attardo (2017b: 104).

4.2 The Semantic Script Theory of Humor and the General Theory of Verbal Humor: The competence theories of humor

"Theories are there to structure our knowledge by informing us what is what and how it all fits together" (Attardo and Raskin 2017: 53). Based on this premise, Raskin (1985) comes up with a combination of generative linguistics theory (Chomsky 1965), semantic scripts theory (see among others Schank and Abelson 1977), and pragmatics (among others, Grice's 1975 cooperative principle) to explain the linguistic mechanisms of humor. He draws on a corpus of *single–joke–carrying texts* (Raskin 1985: 99), namely short canned jokes where humor is attested in their final punch line and which are usually circulated from one context to another to amuse the audience (see Sections 2.5.1.1, 3.3, 3.4.1). While building his theory, Raskin assumes that the meaning of such jokes is identical each time they are repeated, and that their audiences will find them funny independently of the context of their appearance. In particular, using Chomsky's (1965) terminology, Raskin (1985: 58) states that "[t]he semantic theory of humor is (...) designed to model the native speaker's intuition with regard to humor, or in other words, his [sic] *humor competence*. (...) [T]he theory is formulated for an ideal speaker–hearer community, i.e., for people whose senses of humor are exactly identical" (emphasis in the original). Attardo (1994: 197) elaborates on the humor competence of the ideal speaker/hearer assumed by the Semantic Script Theory of Humor as follows:

> The SSTH models the humorous competence of an idealized speaker/hearer who is *unaffected by racial or gender biases, undisturbed by scatological, obscene or disgusting materials, not subject to boredom, and, most importantly, who has never "heard it before" when presented with a joke*. (...) This idealization is similar to the one adopted by most generative linguistics, which assume an idealized homogeneous speaker–hearer community (emphasis mine).

Thus, Raskin's theory follows Chomsky's (1965) distinction between *competence* and *performance* modeled on Saussure's ([1916] 1959) dichotomy between *langue* and *parole*. Raskin's emphasis on the ideal speaker–hearer is a clear reflection of Chomsky's (1965) focus on competence. And just like him, what Raskin also leaves out of the theory is performance – that is, the processing of discourse in actual settings.[50]

---

[50] Raskin (1985: xiv, 59–98), however, does not actually ignore or underestimate the significance of performance/parole and context for the analysis of humor (see Section 1.2).

The main hypothesis of the Semantic Script Theory of Humor is the following:

> A text can be characterized as a single–joke–carrying text if both of the conditions (...) are satisfied.
> (i) The text is compatible, fully or in part, with two different scripts
> (ii) The two scripts with which the text is compatible are opposite (Raskin 1985: 99).

Script overlap and opposition are thus used to describe incongruity in semantico-pragmatic terms (on the Semantic Script Theory of Humor as an incongruity theory, see among others Attardo and Raskin 1991: 331, 2017: 54–56; Attardo 1997: 403, 2008: 107–109; Larkin-Galiñanes 2017: 15). It is also implied that, in Raskin's world of the ideal speaker-hearer, humor recipients will identify the same scripts in a humorous text and the same script oppositions, independently of their own sociocultural characteristics and the contexts they may participate in.

In Attardo and Raskin (1991), the Semantic Script Theory of Humor turned into the General Theory of Verbal Humor.[51] This first presentation of the General Theory of Verbal Humor also pertained to single–joke–carrying texts or canned jokes and tried to identify the factors that render such texts dis/similar. Those factors were named *knowledge resources* – here's their list:

1. *Script Opposition*, see above;
2. *Logical Mechanism*, namely the distorted, playful logic the script opposition is based on. This knowledge resource accounts for the partial and non–serious resolution of the script opposition, hence it is an optional one, as some script oppositions may not be resolved (e.g. in absurd humor). Several logical mechanisms have been identified (analogy, role reversal, parallelism, missing link, juxtaposition, etc.; see Attardo 2001: 27; Attardo, Hempelmann, and Di Maio 2002), but the lists proposed are not exhaustive;
3. *Situation*, namely the objects, participants, settings, activities, etc. of the humorous text. This must be the less studied knowledge resource of all. In an effort to highlight its significance, recently Attardo (2017a: 131) observes that it involves "the overall macroscript that describes the background in which the events of the text (...) take place", thus relating it to the initial script of the script opposition;
4. *Target*, namely the persons, groups, ideas, institutions, etc. ridiculed in the humorous text. Humorous targets may have stereotypes attached to them, due

---

51 The General Theory of Verbal Humor has not been the only effort to expand the Semantic Script Theory of Humor: the *Ontological Semantic Theory of Humor* (OSTH) has been another effort to further develop the Semantic Script Theory of Humor (see Raskin 2008b, 2012b, 2017b; Raskin, Hempelmann, and Taylor 2009; Taylor Rayz 2017, and references therein).

to which they are perceived as inferior or deviating from social norms and expectations (see e.g. blonde jokes). The addition of this knowledge resource to the General Theory of Verbal Humor has resulted in the combination of incongruity and superiority/aggression theories of humor in a single analytical model, thus underscoring the complementarity of the two (Attardo and Raskin 2017: 55; see also Archakis and Tsakona 2005).

5. *Narrative Strategy*, namely the genre which includes humor and/or the speech act performed by the humorist. Given that this knowledge resource involves the organization of humorous texts, it is also responsible for the distribution of humor throughout them and for whether the humorous utterances will be considered jab or punch lines (for this distinction, see below). Attardo (2017a: 130) admits that the term *Narrative Strategy* "was a misnomer, as it might have given the impression that the GTVH was trying to handle narratological concerns, which are mostly beyond its scope" (see also Tsakona 2007: 37).

6. *Language*, namely the actual wording of the humorous text, the verbal encoding of humor. Originally, this knowledge resource was meant to highlight the distinction between verbal and referential humor, namely the difference between humor caused through wordplay/punning and humor which could be paraphrased and maintain its funny content/meaning. Later applications of the theory demonstrated that this knowledge resource is also suitable for accounting for humor produced by non-verbal means (e.g. visual ones)[52] as well as for stylistic humor.[53]

Such an expansion through the addition of knowledge resources gives the General Theory of Verbal Humor a broader scope. Attardo (2001: 22) claims that "[w]hereas the SSTH was a 'semantic' theory of humor, the GTVH is a linguistic theory 'at large' – that is, it includes other areas of linguistics as well, including, most notably, textual linguistics, the theory of narrativity, and pragmatics broadly conceived". Furthermore, it seems that "[t]he adjective 'general' referred to the fact that, unlike the purely semantic SSTH, the GTVH incorporated phonological, morphological, etc. information (in the Language knowledge resource), text-level organization (in the Narrative Strategy knowledge resource), sociological information (in the Target knowledge resource),

---

[52] See Balirano and Corduas (2008), Tsakona (2009), Manteli (2011), Gérin (2013), Dore (2018a).
[53] See Archakis et al. (2014, 2015), Tsami et al. (2014), Tsami (2018); Piata (to appear).

cognitive information (in the Logical Mechanism knowledge resource), etc." (Attardo 2017a: 126).⁵⁴

Nevertheless, one of the most significant points of criticism raised against the Semantic Script Theory of Humor and the initial version of the General Theory of Verbal Humor is their limited scope concerning humorous texts: they could only account for single-joke-carrying texts or canned jokes ending with a punch line. Even though subsequent research has tried to address this (see among others Chłopicki 1987; Ermida 2008), it was not before the application of the General Theory of Verbal Humor to texts larger than canned jokes (Attardo 2001) that researchers were offered usable tools to analyze longer humorous texts or humorous texts with different structure from canned jokes. Such an application was made possible with the introduction of, among other things, the distinction between *jab lines* and *punch lines*:

> A jab line and a punch line differ in their placement within the text: a punch line occurs at the end of the text, whereas a jab line occurs anywhere else. They also differ in terms of their function: jab lines are not disruptive of the development of the main interpretation of the texts, whereas punch lines often force a reinterpretation of said interpretation. Semantically, they are indistinguishable, as they both involve a script opposition (Attardo 2017a: 130).⁵⁵

Equally significant was the classification of humorous texts into two broad categories: "those texts that are structurally similar to jokes (i.e., they end in a punch line) and those which (...) happen to be much more numerous, [and which] can be most profitably analyzed as consisting of two elements: a non-humorous narrative and a humorous component" (Attardo 2001: 29). Both the jab/punch line distinction and this text classification allow for "the analysis of the text as vector, with each humorous instance coded as per the GTVH" (Attardo 2008: 110). In other words, they allow for the in-depth investigation of texts where humor does not exclusively occur at their final utterance, but may include humorous utterances at several points before their ending.

Besides script opposition as their common core, the Semantic Script Theory of Humor and the General Theory of Verbal Humor share another common feature: they are both intended to work as competence, not performance theories (on this distinction, see above). Attardo (2001: 30) programmatically states the following:

> I am proposing a theory of the speakers' *competence* at producing/interpreting longer humorous texts, not a theory of their performance doing so. (...) I will thus propose a (partial) theory of the speakers' potential production/interpretation on the basis of their

---

54 See also Attardo and Raskin (1991: 330).
55 See also Attardo (2001: 29), Tsakona (2003a, 2004, 2007), and Section (3.3) in this book.

knowledge and skills and not a theory of the actual, concrete interpretation/production of a given text. (...) When interested in the structure of a humorous text (mainly, what makes it funny) one can and must abstract away from the reception of said text by any given audience. Their reactions are essentially irrelevant, since what is being investigated is an abstract "ideal" reader's analysis of the text (emphasis in the original).

So, even though Attardo explicitly recognizes the existence of different interpretations of, and reactions to, humor offered by different people, he admits that he "will say virtually nothing about the role of the audience" (Attardo 2001: 31).

It is also interesting to note here that Attardo (2001: 100) briefly addresses the possibility of multiple interpretations of a single humorous utterance when he discusses what he calls the *hyperdetermination of humor*: "hyperdetermined humor [involves] the presence of more than one active source of humor at the same time, or (...) the simultaneous activity of a given source of humor in different contexts". In both cases, more than one script opposition, and hence interpretation, can be proposed for a single humorous utterance. However, Attardo (2001: 100–101) insists that such cases cannot be effectively handled by the General Theory of Verbal Humor and the Semantic Script Theory of Humor.

Such theoretical perspectives and limitations come as no surprise if we consider, on the one hand, the significant influence of Chomsky's (1965) proposal on linguistics since the 1960s and, on the other, the fact that both theories were originally built on decontextualized canned jokes which were considered as humorous irrespectively of their context of delivery. Such an approach implicitly framed the multiple perceptions of, and reactions to, humor as "problematic" and enabled scholars to solve (or, more accurately, bypass) the "problem" of humor identification. As Attardo (2017a: 136) observes,"[g]enerally speaking, the identification of humor has not been a central problem in humor studies. This was due to the fact that researchers often used jokes or other texts that are clearly identified as humorous, or when they used conversational data they were often participant observers and therefore could rely on their inside status to identify the humorous turns". In other words, the identification of humor was exclusively based on *etic*, namely analyst–oriented, criteria (e.g. the generic label "joke" assigned to humorous texts by them and/or their assessment of a given situation) rather than *emic*, namely participant–oriented, ones (i.e. actual participants' framings and perceptions of a text as humorous or not; see Attardo and Raskin 2017: 58).[56]

All this is most compatible with a competence theoretical approach to the analysis of humor. However, the analytical expansion to texts other than canned jokes as well as the increasing focus on cases where humor fails called

---

56 On the *emic/etic* distinction, see Pike ([1954] 1967) and Section (2.4) in this book.

for a linguistic theory that could account for humor performance (as well). This is clearly indicated by the fact that 27 years after his seminal work on the linguistic mechanisms of humor, Raskin (2012a) still insists that a major theory of humor is expected to explain "what is funny, why it is funny, how it is funny, when it is funny, and to whom it is funny" (see also Norrick 1993: 4, in Section 1.2). It is exactly in this context that some attempts have been made to expand the General Theory of Verbal Humor.

4.3 Expanding the General Theory of Verbal Humor

As already mentioned, the General Theory of Verbal Humor was programmatically intended for application to all humorous texts and genres (Attardo 2001: 28). Despite its broader scope, the application of the General Theory of Verbal Humor was relatively limited, especially for analyzing texts and genres different from canned jokes.[57] It appears that the General Theory of Verbal Humor may have been perceived as a rather "static" model as it focuses mostly on the semantic/pragmatic content of humorous texts and does not account for indispensable features of discourse such as prosody, intonation, gestures, laughter, smiling, the relationships between interlocutors, the sociopragmatic goals they wish to attain through humor, and their pragmatic, ideological, etc. presuppositions (see among others Norrick 2004). In addition, it seems difficult for the General Theory of Verbal Humor to account for different interpretations and reactions (whether humorous or not) to the same humorous utterance/text emerging in real settings and offered by real speakers (and not "ideal" ones; see Section 4.2). The theory could not accommodate the ambiguity of humor which "opens up the possibility that the social purpose of the joker could be interpreted differentially by members of the same audience" (Davies 2017: 482).[58]

A small step in this direction was made with the application of the General Theory of Verbal Humor to oral narratives coming from spontaneous interactions among peers. Archakis and Tsakona (2005, 2006, 2012) show that, in their interactions, speakers negotiate and often co-construct the script oppositions and the targets of their humor based on commonly accepted assumptions and values (see also Antonopoulou and Sifianou 2003). These studies have also

---

[57] See Antonopoulou and Sifianou (2003), Tsakona (2004, 2007, 2009), Archakis and Tsakona (2005, 2006, 2012), Corduas, Attardo, and Eggleston (2008), Corduas and Balirano (2008), Manteli (2011), Ruiz-Gurillo (2012, 2013, 2016c), Gérin (2013), Dore (2018a), Tsami (2018).
[58] The following five paragraphs draw on Tsakona (2013a: 28–29, 2017e: 184–185) with appropriate modifications to suit the purposes of the present study.

underlined the function of laughter as an important contextualization cue for framing script oppositions as humorous, thus providing guidelines to the audience as to how to interpret script oppositions.

The significance of contextualization cues for humor reception is also highlighted in another effort to expand the scope and analytical tools of the General Theory of Verbal Humor. Canestrari (2010) argues for the addition of a seventh knowledge resource, the *Meta-Knowledge Resource*, which involves "the signals that refer to the speaker's intention of being humorous and to the hearer's recognition of such intention" (Canestrari 2010: 330; see also Canestrari 2010: 339, 341, 343). Such signals may be:

1. *verbal*, namely explicit comments on (the presence of) humor, such as "I'll tell you a joke", "That was funny";[59]
2. *non-verbal*, such as gestures, smiling, winking, blank face;
3. *para-verbal*, such as intonation patterns, voice tone, laughter (Canestrari 2010: 339).[60]

As Canestrari (2010: 343) points out, "[t]he definition of the Meta-Knowledge Resource grew from the need to analyze humorous performance which, as such, involves real spectators". Still, Canestrari's analysis of the verbal and visual humor of a comic film does not take into consideration any reactions coming from the audience. Her discussion is limited to the metalinguistic and paralinguistic signals occurring within the film, and hence this application of the General Theory of Verbal Humor in a sense confirms the fact that the theory is speaker- and not audience-oriented.

Furthermore, although the signals included in the Meta-Knowledge Resource (see above) could lead recipients to opt for a humorous interpretation of a text (Canestrari 2010: 344), some questions remained: What if such signals do not eventually lead to a humorous uptake of a text?[61] What if the audience chose to ignore the meta- and paralinguistic cues as well as the script opposition, the logical mechanism, etc., all used to create a humorous effect? How could a theory of humor account for a non-humorous interpretation of a (potentially) humorous text? And, most importantly, how could a theory of humor benefit from non-humorous interpretations of humorous texts to enhance its analytical scope and tools?

---

59 See also Tsakona (2003b), Shilikhina (2017, 2018).
60 See also Archakis et al. (2010), Attardo and Pickering (2011), Attardo, Wagner, and Urios-Aparisi (2013), and references therein.
61 See also the relevant discussion in Dynel (2011).

In this context, and based on speakers' negotiations over humor providing useful information regarding not only if, how, and why a text is funny, but, most importantly, when and to whom it is funny (see Raskin 2012a in Section 4.2), a new, eighth knowledge resource pertaining to the sociocultural context of humor has been proposed (Tsakona 2013a, 2017e). In particular, it has been claimed that a revised version of the General Theory of Verbal Humor could enable researchers to analyze not only the content, the linguistic form, and the textual organization of a humorous text, but also its reception in the form of multiple and even competing interpretations by different recipients. This eighth knowledge resource has been called *Context* and attempts at further expanding the scope of the General Theory of Verbal Humor by accounting for the sociocultural context of the humorous text. It involves two different but interrelated kinds of information:

1. the *sociocultural presuppositions* for the production and interpretation of script oppositions, logical mechanisms, and humorous targets, namely the (presumed as) shared background knowledge speakers are expected to rely on when processing humor, or what participants need to know about the sociocultural context of the text to derive meaning from a humorous text;
2. speakers' *metapragmatic stereotypes* on humor, namely their internalized models including ideological assumptions and stances on whether a specific text can be considered humorous or not, why, how, when, and to whom. Speakers' metapragmatic models of humor pertain to the ways they use humor, their social goals, and their evaluations of humorous utterances and texts (see also Sections 1.3, 2.2–2.3).

The Context knowledge resource is based on the premise that humor reception depends on the degree to which humor recipients are familiar with specific sociocultural presuppositions as well as on their metapragmatic stereotypes on humor. Both kinds of information are part of the sociocultural context where a humorous text occurs. In this sense, speakers with different (or even competing) metapragmatic stereotypes on humor and sociocultural presuppositions tend to belong to different normative communities of humor, since they would more or less disagree on what is (or can be) humorous, why, how, etc. (see Kuipers 2008a in Section 2.5.2.3).

Taking into consideration these developments, Attardo (2017b) revisits his earlier proposal (in Attardo 2002; see also Attardo 2008: 116) connecting humor performance with *humor delivery* and *humor repertoire*. On the one hand, humor delivery includes all the linguistic and paralinguistic choices made by the speakers as they produce the humorous utterance (ranging from pitch and volume with which the syllables are uttered, to the font choice of the text, for example). (...) Delivery may be part of the Language knowledge resource, which depending on how one classifies prosodic phenomena, is clearly part of the context (Attardo 2017b: 96–97).

On the other hand, humor repertoire includes the following potential reactions to humor:
a) not get the joke and laugh;
b) get the joke but not react;
c) get the joke and smile;
d) get the joke and laugh;
e) get the joke and comment metalinguistically;
f) get the joke and change the subject;
g) not get the joke and ask for clarification, etc. (Attardo 2017b: 95).

Viewing performance as the combination of humor delivery and humor repertoire is compatible with, and confirms the significance of, Canestrari's (2010) proposal for a Meta–Knowledge Resource including the contextualization cues that could be used to sway the audience towards a humorous uptake of the utterance/text.

In addition, Attardo (2017b: 96) tries to determine other (con)textual factors which should be taken into consideration by a performance theory of humor. In order to explain the relations among these factors and with the General Theory of Verbal Humor, he provides Figure (4.1). The rationale behind this representation as well as its limits (mostly stemming from the inevitable overlap of these factors and the fact that context –in its broad sense– could subsume all the others) are discussed by Attardo himself (2017b: 96):

> [this figure] is a gross over–simplification. For example, speakers have beliefs (opinions) about texts, contexts, and repertoires, hence the speakers' beliefs are represented here as a larger circle than the inner three. However, *some* speakers' beliefs are also part of the context in which the text is produced and in fact are "represented" within it, primarily in the presuppositional basis of the text. Consider that any details that are not included in the text, but are somehow relevant to it, are assumed to be shared known information. Finally, the interplay of ideologies, systems of belief, societal beliefs, etc. and the other layers are complex and largely unexplored (emphasis in the original).

One cannot help but notice that the factors discussed here are not only compatible with aspects of context discussed by other humor scholars (see Section 1.2), but also with the content of the Context knowledge resource including the assumed

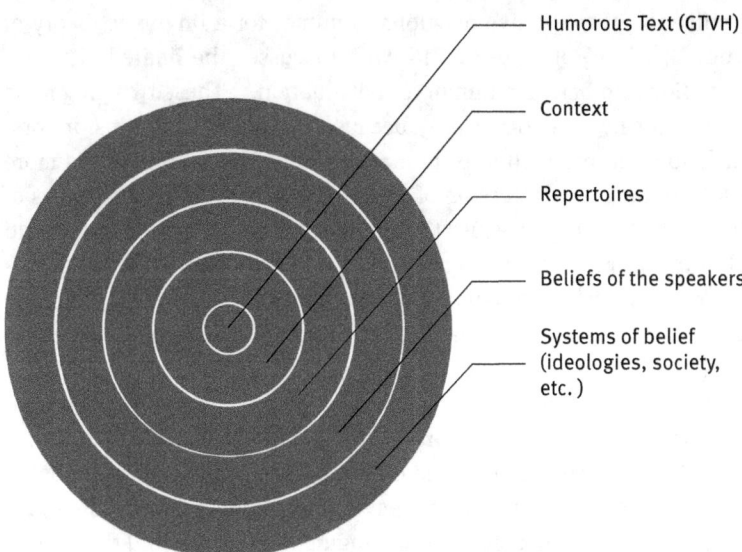

Figure 4.1: The interplay of factors in a theory of humor performance (Attardo 2017b: 96).

background knowledge on which humor is built, and speakers' metapragmatic stereotypes on humor (see above).

Eventually, as implied in Figure (4.1), Attardo (2017b: 97–104) argues for building a *separate* theory of humor performance rather than trying to complement the competence-oriented General Theory of Verbal Humor, without however strongly insisting on such a separation (see also Attardo 2017a: 137–139).

Without adding more knowledge resources, but instead by trying to elaborate their content and scope, some other interesting proposals for the expansion of the General Theory of Verbal Humor have also been put forward. In the *Revised General Theory of Verbal Humor* Ruiz-Gurillo (2012, 2013, 2016c) enriches and clarifies certain aspects of the initial version of the General Theory of Verbal Humor. In particular, she further specifies the Logical Mechanism knowledge resource by adding reasoning and syntagmatic relationships to the list of logical mechanisms; and the Narrative Strategy one by including register, genre, and text type in it. She also adds metapragmatic markers, inferences, and conversational principles (in particular those of manner and quantity; see Grice 1975) to the Language knowledge resource. Finally, she connects this knowledge resource with Verschueren's metapragmatic awareness (see Section 2.2): "language is understood as a reflection of speakers'/writers' variability, negotiability and adaptability" (Ruiz-Gurillo 2016c: 86).

The significance of evaluative reactions to humor for a linguistic theory of humor is underlined by Alba-Juez (2016) who discusses the limited attention paid to the relationship between humor and evaluation.[62] These two pragmatic phenomena are closely related not only because evaluative reactions or comments often follow the production of humor, but also because humor is more often than not used for the expression of values and stances towards aspects of social reality. In this sense, Alba-Juez (2016: 14) argues that "evaluation should be included or taken into account as one or as part of the knowledge resources of humor". Indeed, humor is inherently evaluative as it is based on assessing and framing certain events, ideas, people, acts, etc. as incongruous, namely as violating our expectations and deviating from specific values perceived as commonly accepted or widespread. The target of humor further attests to its evaluative character as it captures the person, idea, institution, etc. responsible for the incongruity/violation humor is based on. Moreover, evaluation could be related to the Language and Narrative Strategy knowledge resources (Alba-Juez 2016: 16), since these are responsible for the linguistic encoding and the generic structure of humor. Thus, Alba-Juez elaborates on the inherently evaluative nature of humor rather than tries to accommodate the evaluative reactions to humor within the General Theory of Verbal Humor.

So far, we have seen that most efforts to expand the General Theory of Verbal Humor have stemmed from the fact that it has been designed and practically meant to work as a competence theory of humor. In the following Section, I will try to show that, even in its initial form with only six knowledge resources, the General Theory of Verbal Humor includes aspects of context, which render it a suitable basis for building a performance theory of humor.

4.4 Building a performance theory of humor

Even though Attardo (2011) has clearly demonstrated that the General Theory of Verbal Humor can be applied to texts of various kinds and lengths, very few researchers coming from discourse analysis and sociolinguistics have tried to expand the scope of the theory in practice. The fact that the General Theory of Verbal Humor could not handle or account for aspects of context that are central to discourse analytic or sociolinguistic approaches to humor could be considered as one of the main reasons for this development (see Section 4.3). Here

---

[62] On evaluation, see among others Labov (1972), Georgakopoulou and Goutsos (2004), Hunston and Thompson (1999), Thompson and Alba-Juez (2014).

I will try to propose a theoretical model that takes into consideration previous expanding approaches and tries to restructure the parameters that are deemed significant for the analysis of humor. It should be underlined in advance that this proposal does not try to explain what humor is: the Semantic Script Theory of Humor and the General Theory of Verbal Humor have already done this. Moving further than this, the proposed theoretical schema tries to account for the parameters that are negotiated between humor producers and recipients in their effort to jointly construct humorous discourse. Rather than identifying the points of convergence or divergence among canned jokes, I will try to map those aspects of humorous discourse that appear to be significant for its production, interpretation and, eventually, analysis.

To this end, in what follows, I will discuss two main premises for a performance theory of humor: a conceptualization of humorous discourse as jointly constructed and negotiated among participants (Section 4.4.1); and an emphasis on the contextual parameters presented in Section (1.2), some of which have already been taken into consideration by the General Theory of Verbal Humor (Section 4.4.2). Then, I will try to describe the Analytical Foci that could help researchers investigate humorous discourse as a dynamic and jointly constructed activity (Section 4.4.3).

4.4.1 Humorous discourse as dynamically constructed and negotiated

I would like to begin this discussion by assuming that humorous discourse is *always* dynamically constructed and negotiated by interlocutors (Chovanec and Tsakona 2018: 8–11; see also Attardo 2017b: 94). A significant amount of humorous texts is jointly constructed in face-to-face or digital interactions and circulated in the electronic media and online social networks (even if originally produced in the oral or written medium). Humor and its multiple meanings are not negotiated exclusively in face-to-face interactions, but also in online or written exchanges even among people who are (more or less) strangers to each other. Individuals have acquired easy access to humorous texts as well as to platforms or public spaces where they can comment on such texts and express their opinions. In other words, all forms/genres of humor (even written ones) may (and do) become the object of public negotiations and their meanings are interactively (re)constructed by participants in online social media, journalists, commentators, scholars, etc.[63]

---

[63] See among others Baym (1993, 1995), Lewis (2008), Kramer (2011), Laineste (2011), Stewart (2013), Marone (2015), Tsakona and Chovanec (2018), Constantinou (2019), Dynel and Poppi

This further suggests that the analysis of humorous discourse needs to take into consideration the meanings or interpretations offered by interlocutors. Humor recipients may have different perceptions not only of oral forms of humor (e.g. in everyday encounters among intimates) and mediated texts (e.g. sitcoms, ads; see Baym 1993, 1995, and Sections 2.5.2–2.5.2.3 in this book), but also of written ones (e.g. written canned jokes, novels, cartoons; see Lewis 2008; Laineste 2011; Stewart 2013; Constantinou 2019). In this sense, all kinds of exchanges where interlocutors discuss the different meanings of humor and offer their own perceptions on what humor is, how it is (or should be) used, when, by whom, against whom, etc. are expected to become the focus of interest when investigating humorous discourse. For instance, it is difficult to imagine how humor could be created in texts such as stand-up comedy or oral anecdotes, if the stand-up comedian or the narrator did not try to elicit or did not receive any kind of feedback from their audience. Audience participation is therefore an indispensable part of some humorous genres, even if humor production appears to emanate from a single individual in a seemingly monological manner.[64] The fact that research has often concentrated on the text produced by the stand-up comedian or the narrator of the oral anecdote does not necessarily mean that audience reactions and contributions are not equally (if not more, sometimes) important for the unfolding of discourse and the continuation of the interaction in real time.

Another quite common example nowadays comes from mediated humorous genres such as memes, humorous status updates on Facebook, or humorous tweets, which are more often than not meant to generate interaction among participants in the social media. This is achieved either via responding to previous texts using intertextual references, or via explicitly or implicitly inviting the addressees to comment on them, share, forward, or re-create and recontextualize them (see among others Shifman 2014a; Piata 2018, and Sections 3.4.2–3.4.2.3 in this book). Something similar could be suggested even for written genres such as cartoons or humorous literature. Even though the cartoonist or the author/writer may not always receive immediate feedback from the readership or may not have access to all the reactions or comments offered on their work, they often have their work reviewed (e.g. book reviews) or commented upon (e.g. online or TV discussions of cartoons or books) by readers often proposing diverse interpretations and evaluations of the humorous meanings emerging from such humorous

---

(2019), and Sections (2.5–2.5.3) in this book. For a detailed discussion of the relationship between this conceptualization of humor and relevant concepts such as *conversational humor*, *interactional humor*, and *humor in interaction*, see Chovanec and Tsakona (2018: 8–11).

64 See Rutter (2001), Dore (2018b), Karachaliou and Archakis (2018), Seewoester Cain (2018), and references therein.

texts. Even though such activities may not be considered indispensable for the creation of such written texts/genres, they still become increasingly accessible and popular nowadays thanks to the digital media, and are most relevant when investigating the social meanings and sociopragmatic functions of humorous texts.

To sum up, the present theoretical proposal is based on the assumption that, when analyzing humorous discourse, emphasis should be placed on how interlocutors negotiate and eventually agree to entering the humorous mode;[65] on the processes of humor production; on the step–by–step co–construction of humorous sequences; and on the diverse reactions to, and interpretations of, an utterance/text intended as humorous. In this sense, any form or genre of humor can be considered as jointly constructed as long as there is empirical evidence demonstrating that its production and/or interpretation are the outcome of the effort of, and the interaction between, more than one individual. Even texts or genres traditionally perceived as monological (e.g. written canned jokes, cartoons, short stories) could be analyzed as negotiated among participants when research shows that they do not have a "single" meaning/interpretation (usually the one intended by, or ascribed to, their original producer), but instead may acquire multiple meanings suggested by more than one interlocutor. In such cases, the analysis of humorous discourse within a performance theory of humor is expected to consider all the attested different interpretations of humor and not to limit itself to the one "intended" by the humorist or "ascribed" to him/her. In this conception, humor is always a dialogical phenomenon (in Bakhtin's 1986 sense; for a more extensive discussion, see Chovanec and Tsakona 2018).

4.4.2 Contextual parameters within the General Theory of Verbal Humor

Such a perspective on humor calls for a theoretical model placing emphasis on contextual factors. Although the General Theory of Verbal Humor is said to have been designed as a competence theory of humor overlooking context (see Section 4.2), here I intend to argue that this theory did incorporate elements of context within its knowledge resources even before Canestrari's (2010) or Tsakona's (2013a, 2017e) additions (see Section 4.3). This will allow me to explain later on how the proposed theoretical schema builds and further develops analytical concepts already present within the General Theory of Verbal Humor.

---

65 See Shilikhina (2017, 2018).

To this end, let's recall which aspects of context are deemed significant for the analysis of humor by scholars working on it: Table (4.1) is a reproduction of Table (1.1) with the addition of those contextual factors Attardo (2017b) considers important for a performance theory of humor (see Section 4.3 and Figure 4.1).

The first thing that comes to mind when looking at Table (4.1) is that genres (column B) have always been part of the General Theory of Verbal Humor subsumed under the Narrative Strategy knowledge resource. Genres or the Narrative Strategy could be complemented with more detailed descriptions of the specific communicative setting where a humorous utterance/text occurs, included in column C (see also Ruiz-Gurillo's 2016c suggestions in Section 4.3).

The Language knowledge resource of the General Theory of Verbal Humor pertains to the exact wording of the humorous text, hence columns D and E including text, co-text, and the contextualization cues are most relevant to this knowledge resource. Contextualization cues, whether coming from the humorist or from his/her audience, are a significant part of the negotiation and joint construction of humor, hence they would rather be examined in combination with, and not separately from, the semantic/pragmatic content of the text. The same holds for the explicit reactions to, and comments on, humor (column G). The importance of such cues has also been highlighted by Canestrari's (2010) Meta-Knowledge Resource as well as by Attardo's (2002, 2017b) humor repertoire (see Section 4.3). Within a dynamic, contextualized approach to humor (such as the one described in Section 4.4.1), it would be a contradiction to separate the semantic/pragmatic content of the humorous text from its contextualization cues and from its recipients' contributions to the construction of meaning. Furthermore, it should be noted that dissonance or lack of consensus concerning the interpretation of the contextualization cues and/or the textual elements will result in humor failure.

The characters of a humorous text, their actions and speech as part of the context of humor (column F) are also part of the General Theory of Verbal Humor in the form of the Situation knowledge resource.

So far, we have seen that half of the knowledge resources of the initial version of the General Theory of Verbal Humor are closely related to most aspects of context. The only aspects of context that seem to be left outside the General Theory of Verbal Humor are the sociocultural assumptions on humor use (column A), and the preferences and differences in humor use among different speakers/hearers (column H). In my view, the Context knowledge resource (Tsakona 2013a, 2017e; see Section 4.3) has tried to account for such aspects of context as it involves the sociocultural presuppositions of humor as well as participants' metapragmatic stereotypes on it.

Table 4.1: Accounts of context within humor research (also including Attardo 2017b).

	A	B	C	D	E	F	G	H
	Sociocultural assumptions on humor use	Genres of humor	The specific communicative setting where a certain humorous utterance/text occurs	Text and co-text	Contextualization cues	The characters of the humorous text, their actions and speech	Reactions to and comments on humor	Preferences and differences in humor use among different speakers/hearers
Raskin (1985)	(6) social and cultural background			(2) stimulus				(3) participants' life experiences (4) participants' dispositions to humor
Norrick (1993)	(1) cultural lore about places, customs, interactions, and stereotypes	(2) a community's habits concerning the use of humor or its avoidance or prohibition		(3) co-text	(4) contextualization cues			
Oring (2008)[66]	(1) cultural context	(2) social context: nature of their interaction and functions of humor	(2) social context: time, setting, participants and their relationships					(3) individual context

(continued)

[66] Oring's (2008) *comparative context* is omitted here as it mostly refers to humor research methodology and tradition rather than to participants' real-life circumstances, practices, and concerns.

Table 4.1 (continued)

	A	B	C	D	E	F	G	H
	Sociocultural assumptions on humor use	Genres of humor	The specific communicative setting where a certain humorous utterance/text occurs	Text and co–text	Contextualization cues	The characters of the humorous text, their actions and speech	Reactions to and comments on humor	Preferences and differences in humor use among different speakers/hearers
Canestrari (2010)					(1) contextualization cues		(2) reactions to humor	
Tsakona (2013a)	(1) sociocultural presuppositions of humor						(2) reactions to humor	
Attardo (2017b)	(4) beliefs of speakers (5) systems of beliefs		(2) context	(1) humorous text			(3) humor repertoires	(4) beliefs of speakers

4.4 Building a performance theory of humor

Filani (2017)	(1.2) shared cultural knowledge	(1.1) shared situational knowledge	(1.3) shared knowledge of code, (2.1) joke utterance	(2.4) conversational joke cues (2.5) nonverbal cues	(2.2) participants-in-the-joke (2.3) activity-in-the-joke (2.6) voicing	(3) sociocultural parameters of humor: participants' social characteristics
Chovanec and Tsakona (2018)	(3) sociocultural parameters of humor: community characteristics	(4) reasons and goals/functions of humor (5) genres of humor		(1) framing devices of humor	(2) reactions to humor	

At this point, I would also like to underscore the fact that these contextual factors are related to two other knowledge resources: the Script Opposition and the Target. The first one is necessarily built on participants' background knowledge about the world (column A) including, among other things, their beliefs and assumptions on the topics that can or cannot be humorously represented and negotiated in discourse (columns A and H). Otherwise, humor has limited chances of being effectively communicated. We should not forget here that the very definitions of *script* and, hence, *script opposition* are premised on context (see Raskin 1985: 59–98 and Section 1.2 in this book). The same could be suggested for the targets of humor and the stereotypes attached to them: they are part of interlocutors' contextual knowledge and sociocultural assumptions for humor, while interlocutors may not always agree on who or what can be targeted and denigrated through humor.

All this can be summarized in Table (4.2) showing the contextual aspects taken into account by the General Theory of Verbal Humor.

Table 4.2: Aspects of context associated with the knowledge resources of the General Theory of Verbal Humor.

Knowledge Resources	Aspects of context (see the columns in Table 4.1)
Script Opposition	– Sociocultural assumptions on humor use (A) – Preferences and differences in humor use among different speakers/hearers (H)
Logical Mechanism	
Situation	– The characters of the humorous text, their actions and speech (F)
Target	– Sociocultural assumptions on humor use (A) – Preferences and differences in humor use among different speakers/hearers (H)
Narrative Strategy	– Genres of humor (B) – The specific communicative setting where a certain humorous utterance/text occurs (C)
Language	– Text and co-text (D) – Contextualization cues (E)
Meta-Knowledge Resource	– Contextualization cues (E) – Reactions to and comments on humor (G)
Context	– Sociocultural assumptions on humor use (A) – Preferences and differences in humor use among different speakers/hearers (H)

4.4.3 The Analytical Foci of the Discourse Theory of Humor

After demonstrating that, in a sense, context has already been taken into account by the General Theory of Verbal Humor in the form of knowledge resources, my next step would be to re-arrange the knowledge resources so as to come up with a more cohesive and usable theoretical and analytical model for analyzing humorous discourse and for understanding how humor works in context. Thus, I would like to propose three main *Analytical Foci* for humor and summarize their content, namely what researchers are expected to investigate and analyze in depth through each one of them, as follows:

Analytical Focus 1: Sociocultural assumptions
Sociocultural assumptions include the background knowledge that is deemed necessary for processing humor and is co-constructed as shared. Such knowledge may differ from one community to the other and does shape individual preferences and differences in humor use. Participants' background knowledge determines what is considered expected, conventional, or normal in a specific community, and simultaneously what is considered unexpected, unconventional, and abnormal therein (i.e. the script opposition), and eventually defines who is held responsible for potential deviations (i.e. the target of humor). In other words, sociocultural assumptions form the basis for framing specific actions or people as incongruous and for representing them in a humorous manner. Furthermore, sociocultural assumptions include participants' metapragmatic stereotypes on what humor is, how it works, how it should or should not be used, where its limits should be set, what/who can or cannot be ridiculed through humor, etc. (see columns A and H in Table 4.1). In this way, this Analytical Focus combines the broader group-based norms on humor that are shared across the community and more personal preferences of humor producers and recipients. Hence, this Analytical Focus incorporates three knowledge resources: Context, Script Opposition, and Target.

Analytical Focus 2: Genre
Genre pertains to the types of texts where humor appears. As already mentioned (in Section 3.3), humor may be indispensable to certain genres (e.g. canned jokes, stand-up comedy), more or less common in others (e.g. informal conversation among peers, advertisements), and usually absent from some (e.g. legal or religious texts). The presence or absence of humor from specific genres is culture-specific (e.g. humor in classroom settings may be frequently attested in some sociocultural communities or may be banned in some others).

Genre also determines (or may be determined by) the sociopragmatic goals and functions of humor: each genre constitutes or serves a social activity through which participants attain specific social goals (e.g. humor may contribute to highlighting ingroup/outgroup boundaries, creating solidarity and reinforcing intimacy, establishing a pleasant atmosphere, expressing criticism, mitigating aggressive or face-threatening moves/acts, disparaging the "Other", breaking social relationships, attracting the attention of the audience, enhancing the popularity of the humorist, building gender, ethnic, political or other identities). This Analytical Focus is also closely related to the communicative setting a text/genre with humor occurs as well as to the roles participants assume in the negotiation or co-construction of humor (producer, recipient, etc.; see columns B and C in Table 4.1). Hence, this Analytical Focus could be perceived as an elaborated version of the Narrative Strategy knowledge resource.

Analytical Focus 3: Text
Text involves the semantic content and the stylistic choices of a stretch of discourse (e.g. wordplay, registers, dialects), the placement of humorous utterances (e.g. punch or jab lines), and the visual, slapstick, acoustic/musical elements, etc. therein. It also involves the contextualization cues that accompany this stretch of discourse as well as the various, perhaps also multimodal, reactions offered by the recipients. Given that this analytical model is based on the premise that humor is dynamically negotiated and jointly constructed by the participants in a specific communicative setting, the meaning/s derived from a humorous text do/es not stem exclusively from the (assumed) intentions of its producer/s but is/are shaped by the interpretations of its recipient/s. In other words, recipients' reactions and interpretations of humor are not examined separately from the humorous text but become part of it, so as to potentially account for all the meanings actually derived from it. Such meanings pertain to the characters, actions, views, etc. included in the text (see columns D, E, F, and G in Table 4.1). In this sense, this Analytical Focus incorporates the Language and Situation knowledge resources as well as the Meta-Knowledge Resource.

The three Analytical Foci put forward here seem to be closely related to one another: the genres and communicative settings where humor is attested (Analytical Focus 2) are directly related to interlocutors' sociocultural assumptions about when and why to use humor, about which topics or targets, etc. (Analytical Focus 1). For instance, different background knowledge will be presupposed and different script oppositions and targets will be constructed or chosen for designing a political cartoon, and different ones will be part of the

4.4 Building a performance theory of humor — 125

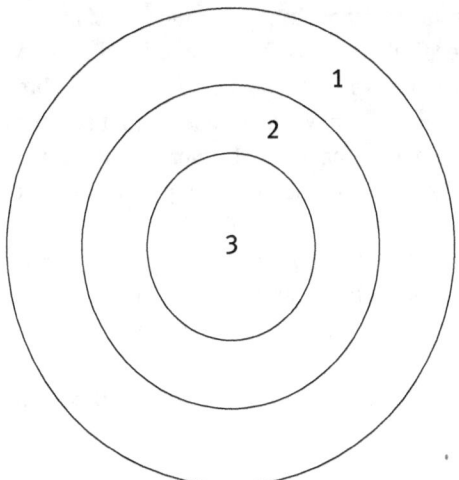

Analytical focus **1**:
Sociocultural assumptions
(Context, Script Opposition, and Target knowledge resources)

Analytical focus **2**:
Genre
(Narrative Strategy knowledge resource)

Analytical focus **3**:
Text
(Language, Situation, and Meta- Knowledge resources)

Figure 4.2: The Analytical Foci of the Discourse Theory of Humor.

humor produced during peer interaction concerning the division of labor for a school project. On the other hand, texts resulting from participants' choices at the performance level (Analytical Focus 3) are shaped by both the generic conventions of humorous texts (Analytical Focus 2) and the sociocultural assumptions on humor use (Analytical Focus 1). For instance, different contextualization cues will be employed in oral negotiations of humor (e.g. laughter, smile, intonation, gestures) and different in digital ones (e.g. unconventional punctuation or spelling, emojis). Figure (4.2) depicts the interplay between the three Analytical Foci.

To sum up, this theoretical model is meant to assist researchers in analyzing humorous discourse by taking into consideration various aspects of context that have been considered as significant by humor scholars so far. My aim here has been to offer a first version of the Discourse Theory of Humor, which could be employed for the analysis of what has so far been called *humor performance* (see Section 4.2). This potentially opens the door for applications not only in various areas of linguistics, but also in media studies, folklore, sociology, anthropology, literary studies, etc., which place particular emphasis on the overall situation, the participants, and other contextual factors affecting humorous communication. Needless to say, not every analysis of humor can account for all the aspects of (con)text mentioned here. Within pragmatics, discourse analysis, and sociolinguistics in particular, studies on humorous phenomena usually place emphasis on specific factors that contribute to the co-construction and negotiation of humor.

The Discourse Theory of Humor has been built on concepts and analytical tools from the Semantic Script Theory of Humor and the General Theory of Verbal

Humor, but has tried to develop them so as to better account for the role of context in humorous communication. More specifically, the six (and later on eight) knowledge resources have been revisited and rearranged so as to form the three Analytical Foci of the proposed model. The only knowledge resource that seems to be left out in this version of the Discourse Theory of Humor is the Logical Mechanism, so further elaboration on this model in the future may allow us to account for purely cognitive aspects of humor resolution as well.

In the following Sections, I will explore why and how the Discourse Theory of Humor could be used to analyze failed humor and to account for humor quality as well. I will also demonstrate how it can work in practice, thus showing that other analytical tools of the General Theory of Verbal Humor (mostly the punch lines and the jab lines) can also be useful within the Discourse Theory of Humor.

4.5 Accounting for humor failure and humor quality

A performance theory of humor such as the Discourse Theory of Humor is expected to be able to account for humor failure as well. After all, humor fails for various reasons *in context*. So, in this Section, I will try to offer a preliminary discussion of this topic, which, in my view, also pertains to the so-called *quality* of humor.[67] A comprehensive account of humor failure and relevant literature is included in Bell (2015; see also Bell 2017), hence I will begin with some of her suggestions as the basis for my discussion.

Failed humor involves "any utterance that is intended to amuse, but that, due to interlocutor, environmental or other factors, is not negotiated 'perfectly'" (Bell 2015: 4; see also Bell 2017: 356). It seems that previous (linguistic or other) theories of humor have not systematically, but only occasionally and often superficially, addressed humor failure (Bell 2015, 2017: 356–357; see also Hale 2018a: 37). This results from the fact that humor failure is admittedly a complex phenomenon: there can be diverse reasons why humor may fail. Relevant research reminds us that just like in cases when humor is "effectively" communicated and "properly" responded to, when humor fails, there are also significant social repercussions. Failed humor brings to the limelight (often in a painful, face-threatening, even disparaging manner) who belongs to the ingroup, who is attributed outgroup status, and where the limits of acceptable

---

[67] Even though the term *quality* is not only too vague but also too evaluative when referring to humor, I will reproduce it here because it is sometimes mentioned in humor research literature.

behavior are set each time; in a nutshell, how far humorous texts/utterances can go before they are perceived as aggressive or offensive in a given context. Thus, humor failure constitutes a "socially imposed limit on linguistic creativity, acting as a check to keep language use within certain boundaries" (Bell 2015: 12) and eventually as a "powerful reminder of group norms" (Bell 2017: 365; see also Bell 2015: 162, 167; Hale 2018a: 39). A competence theory of humor premised on the analysis of decontextualized texts would not be able to account for such cases, as is clearly stated by both Raskin (1985: 58, 2017a: 17) and Attardo (1994: 197, 2001: 30–32; see also Attardo and Raskin 2017: 58). Such considerations seem to be safely left for a theory of humor performance, such as the one proposed here (see also Bell 2015: 21, 29).

Drawing on Hay's (2001) discussion of humor support, Bell (2015, 2017) elaborates on three main parameters for negotiating and jointly constructing humor success or failure: the *recognition* of humor, its *comprehension*, and its *appreciation*. More specifically (see Bell 2017: 358–359):

1. the *recognition* of humor depends on its framing through appropriate contextualization cues. Inadequate framing may result in failure, because humor may remain unnoticed;
2. the *comprehension* of humor presupposes that recipients succeed in decoding the language used and identifying the sociocultural information alluded to and eventually the script opposition humor is based on. In this sense, humor failure may be caused by not taking into consideration or by miscalculating recipients' background knowledge;
3. the *appreciation* of humor results from misjudging what may be considered funny or may cause mirth to the audience:

    The causes for this type of failure can (…) be many. For instance, the attempt at humor may simply be weak, obvious, unoriginal, or overused. It might also be aggressive or offensive in some way. (…) [E]ither the speaker or hearer might be at fault here. Failures of appreciation occur because the speaker did not consider the hearer's background or personal proclivities, delivered the humorous line inadequately, or simply selected a poor joke. The hearer, on the other hand, might be chronically serious or very easily offended (Bell 2017: 359).

The investigation of failed humor, in my view, goes hand in hand with the discussion about the *quality* of humor. Humor quality is directly related to its success or failure: "good" humor is the one which is successfully negotiated by participants, while "bad" (or "weak", "poor", etc.) humor fails at least some of them.[68]

---

[68] The category of "sophisticated" (Raskin 1985: 46, 136) or "intellectual" humor (Hlynka and Knupfer 1997: 405; Kuipers 2009: 228) lies somewhere between these two poles/categories, in my view. Although it is considered well-formed and draws on background knowledge assumed as shared (and hence it could be "good"/successful), at the same time at least some

Although not the focus of systematic attention by scholars either, humor quality has been associated with the well-formedness of humorous texts in terms not only of generic structure but also of the degree of overlap and oppositeness of the scripts causing the script opposition(s) as well as of the availability of the scripts as part of participants' background knowledge. It has also been related to the brevity of humorous utterances, their dissemination throughout the humorous text, the timing of humor especially in oral performances, as well as the appropriateness of the communicative setting for its delivery and participants' psychological or emotional state.[69] Humor quality has also been discussed in view of the fact that there usually are some scripts, namely topics, persons, institutions, actions, etc., that are not deemed suitable for joking among the members of a specific community, as, for instance, the Danish cartoons case has clearly shown (see among others Lewis 2008; Boespflug 2011). Humor referring to such "unsuitable" or "forbidden" topics or targets may quite easily fail.

The discussion so far seems to indicate that the factors determining the high or low quality of humor and its success or failure are most relevant to the Analytical Foci proposed within the Discourse Theory of Humor. Table 4.3 attempts to map various causes of humor failure or low quality, and connect them not only with humor recognition, comprehension, and appreciation, but also, and most importantly in the present context, with the three Analytical Foci of the Discourse Theory of Humor. It therefore seems that the Analytical Foci of the Discourse Theory of Humor could assist humor analysts in identifying and accounting for the sources or reasons for humor failure or for evaluating some utterances or texts as "low quality" humor.

A final note should be made here concerning humor quality and success/failure. All such effects have often been attributed to interlocutors' *individual* and *personal* moods, preferences, or inclinations. Here, as Tables (4.1–4.3) have also shown,[70] I agree with Bell (2015) that all these factors are actually socially determined:

> despite the common understanding of a sense of humor as a deeply personal, often idiosyncratic character trait, our humor preferences are socially constructed. The strong

---

recipients may not get it because they may not share the necessary information (so, humor will be "bad"/failed for them; see also Tsakona 2018a, 2018b).

69 See among others Kolek (1985), Raskin (1985: 145–146), Attardo (1994: 214–216, 2017b: 98–103), Norrick (2001), Chłopicki (1987, 2002), Tsakona (2002, 2004: 105–107), Antonopoulou and Tsakona (2006), Kuipers (2006), Corduas, Attardo, and Eggleston (2008), Hale (2018b).

70 See also the discussions of metapragmatic stereotypes in Sections (1.3, 2.2) and of Analytical Focus 1 in Section (4.4.3).

Table 4.3: Accounting for humor failure or low quality within the Discourse Theory of Humor.

Analytical Foci	Factors for humor success/failure, high/low quality
1. *Sociocultural assumptions*	Humor recognition, comprehension, appreciation, and quality depend to a considerable extent on the availability of scripts, topics, targets, intertextual allusions, etc. employed for humor. *Humor may fail or be considered of low quality if interlocutors do not share the necessary background knowledge to recognize, comprehend, and appreciate it.*
2. *Genre*	Humor recognition, comprehension, appreciation, and quality correlate with the communicative setting where humor occurs. *Humor may fail or be considered of low quality if interlocutors assess its use in a specific communicative setting as inappropriate and/or ineffective.*
3. *Text*	Humor recognition, comprehension, appreciation, and quality are based on the well-formedness of each humorous text and the contextualization cues employed therein. *Humor may fail or be considered of low quality if it appears in the "wrong" parts of a text, its scripts oppositions are not comprehensible as such, and/or its contextualization cues are inadequate or ambiguous.*

influence that others exert on our humor tastes helps to delineate and maintain group boundaries. The failure of humor, perhaps even more so, contributes to the drawing of these lines between what are considered in- and out-group members. (...) Our judgments about what counts as "good" humor are shaped by our peers and others we identify with, and the boundaries of what is seen as acceptable humor are expressed in the reactions of the audience (Bell 2015: 162, 167).[71]

In other words, by recognizing, comprehending, and/or appreciating an utterance/text as humorous, we align ourselves with specific groups whose values and views we find acceptable, and distance ourselves from other groups whose views and values we disagree with. Furthermore, by attributing "low" quality or failure to an utterance/text intended as humorous, we develop or opt for "resistant readings" (Fairclough 1992b: 136), thus withdrawing ourselves from the joint construction of humor. Resistant readings have often been ignored or even resisted by earlier approaches to humor, but seem to become an increasingly significant focus of humor research nowadays.[72] The Discourse Theory of

---

[71] See also Kuipers (2006), Smith (2009), Hale (2018a).
[72] See among others Billig (2001, 2005a), Kramer (2011), Laineste (2011), Stewart (2013), Constantinou (2019), Dynel and Poppi (2019), and Sections (2.5.2.–2.5.2.3) in this book.

Humor is therefore designed to assist humor scholars in investigating both resistant and non-resistant readings of humor.

It is exactly these issues that I would like to address in the following Section by revisiting the case study of the advertisement that has been assessed as both humorous and sexist (see Sections 2.5.2–2.5.2.3).

4.6 An example of analysis using the Discourse Theory of Humor

To illustrate how the Discourse Theory of Humor could work as an analytical tool, I would like to return to the case study presented in Sections (2.5.2–2.5.2.3) concerning the contradictory reactions to the Greek TV advertisement of Germanos stores. As extensively discussed in the above-mentioned Sections, two main interpretations emerge from this advertisement, where the husband dreams of returning his wife to her mother because the former has cooked okras, a dish he does not appreciate. This fantasy serves as a metaphorical representation of what Germanos' customers can do if they do not like the mobile phone they bought from the store: they can take it back to the store and ask for their money back.

Taking into consideration both the advertisement text and the reactions to it, I would like to demonstrate that both the success and the failure of humor could be accounted for using the Discourse Theory of Humor. Let's start with that interpretation which found the text humorous and laughed at the incongruous image of the husband who fantasizes returning his wife to his mother-in-law:

Analytical Focus 1: Sociocultural assumptions
One reading of the advertisement and some recipients' reactions suggest that it is incongruous to consider treating one's wife like the husband dreams of doing, because patriarchal/sexist views and practices belong to the past and are not typical of contemporary Greek husbands (Script Opposition: real Greek husbands would not consider returning their wives to their mothers/the husband in the advertisement considers returning his wife to her mother; Target: the husband in the advertisement and the male chauvinist, sexist stereotype). In other words, the husband's behavior is perceived as incongruous, because such things may have happened in the past, but would be evaluated as outdated and worth-laughing at in contemporary Greece. The following comment on the advertisement humor is illustrative:

4.6 An example of analysis using the Discourse Theory of Humor

(4.1) Είναι πέρα από προφανές ότι η εν λόγω διαφήμηση σατιρίζει ακριβώς το εν λόγω σεξιστικό στερεότυπο για το οποίο «καταγγέλλεται». Όλη η δομή του διαφημιστικού σεναρίου κινείται γύρω από την πρόκληση *γέλιου για την παρωχημένη συμπεριφορά του συζύγου, ο οποίος αντιλαμβάνεται εργαλειακά το ρόλο της συζύγου του.*
Όλος ο λόγος που χρησιμοποιείται είναι χιουμοριστικός: η αναφορά σε αριθμό καφέδων, γευμάτων, περίεργων ταινιών (ο Έρωτας στη Ζουαζουλάνδη), δώρων γενεθλίων, εντάσσονται ξεκάθαρα σε μια κωμική στόχευση. (...)
Είναι δεδομένο ότι *ο σκοπός του διαφημιστικού μηνύματος δεν είναι φυσικά η επικρότηση μιας ακραίας και καταδικαστέας αντίληψης, αλλά η διακωμώδησή της, μέσα από το κλασικό στρατήγημα της σάτιρας* (...).
It is more than obvious that *the advertisement in question satirizes exactly the same sexist stereotype* for which it is "denounced" [by those who do not approve of the advertisement]. The whole structure of the advertisement script aims at eliciting *laughter at the expense of the outdated behavior of the husband, who perceives his wife's role in a derogatory manner.*
The whole discourse used [in the advertisement] is humorous: the reference to the number of coffees [drunk by the couple and paid by the husband], meals, strange films (Love in Swaziland), birthday gifts is clearly part of the advertisement's attempt at humor. (...)
It is given that *the aim of the advertising message is not at all to applaud an extreme and condemnable view, but to ridicule it through the classic strategy of satire* (...) (Naked men on the beach 2011, emphasis mine; see also example 2.33).

It therefore seems that the humorous uptake of this advertisement presupposes male chauvinist views on the social position and roles of women especially in the context of marriage, which used to prevail in the Greek society, but are considered as outdated and sexist nowadays. As already mentioned, male chauvinist phrases such as *Θα σε γυρίσω στη μάνα σου* 'I will return you to your mother' or *Αν δε σ' αρέσει, να γυρίσεις στη μάνα σου* 'If you don't like [it], go back to your mother' are reminiscent of the patriarchal structure of the Greek society and were used as threats by husbands who were not satisfied with their wives' behavior or who wanted to respond to their wives' complaints. A few decades ago, women (together with their dowries) were part of a financial transaction between the woman's parents and the future son-in-law; women could not have a say in such transactions, and thus they were incapable of defending themselves. Such practices are represented in, and/or evoked by, the advertisement text and some of the comments on it. The humorous interpretation of the advertisement highlights the fact that the situation has changed nowadays: such patriarchal/sexist practices and norms are not at all common (Context knowledge resource).

For sustaining a humorous interpretation of the advertisement, one also has to be familiar with the fact that, stereotypically speaking, many Greek people are not particularly fond of okras. Although okras are part of the famous Mediterranean diet, they are not very popular among Greeks and many Greek children or adults have been forced to eat them by their mothers, on the grounds that they are nutritious and delicious (Context knowledge resource).

Analytical Focus 2: Genre
In terms of generic category, the humorous text is a TV advertisement (Narrative Strategy knowledge resource). Advertisements are often deliberately entertaining in order to attract audience attention (see among others Simpson 2001; Hatzithomas 2008; Politis and Kakavoulia 2010; Archakis, Lampropoulou, and Tsakona 2018; Dore 2018a), hence the presence of humor in the one examined here comes as no surprise to the members of audience watching the advertisement on TV and discussing it online. From a sociopragmatic perspective, humor here aims at rendering memorable the advertisement message concerning the possibility of returning a mobile phone to the store if the buyer is not satisfied. According to recipients' reactions, it is also meant to satirize or ridicule the husband's incongruous behavior, thus criticizing his exaggerated and outdated sexist reaction to the okras dish (see example 4.1 above).

Analytical Focus 3: Text
Humor is produced during a lunch scene in the kitchen of a recently married couple and then at the doorstep of the wife's mother in front of the latter (Situation knowledge resource). The husband's words (see the jab lines in example 2.29: *Wha::::t's that?, Okras! {with fake enthusiasm} Okras again, Get up! Get up you! {in an angry tone}, So dear mother–in–law do you see her? Well, I am bringing her back [exactly] as I took her [from you]. Untouched, unworn, and in her packaging, She has cost me 650 coffees, 152 meals, 1 birthday present and 2 nameday ones, Maria dear {he addresses his wife}, can you tell me, did we watch it together that great movie "Love in Swaziland"? Well, plus 39 movie tickets*) including the accompanying paralinguistic features (intonation, prosody, gestures, facial expressions, body movements), as well as the wife's and her mother's facial expressions (mostly of surprise and indignation), all contribute to portraying him as exaggerating and hence incongruous (see the Script

Opposition in Analytical Focus 1). As mentioned by one recipient (see example 4.1 above), the husband is depicted as a "caricature", namely in a satirical manner. In addition, the sounds signaling the beginning and the end of the husband's fantasy mark the humorous framing of that part of the advertisement (Language and Meta-Knowledge Resource).

On the other hand, those who perceived the advertisement as sexist rather than humorous appear to put forward a quite different, resistant (in Fairclough's 1992b: 136 terms; see Section 4.5) reading of it:

Analytical Focus 1: Sociocultural assumptions
Those who interpreted the advertisement as sexist seem to point out that women should not be perceived and/or represented as merchandize and as part of a transaction between their husbands and their parents. Even if a script opposition could be identified here (Script opposition: return the mobile phone to the store/ return the wife to her mother; women should not be treated/are treated as merchandize; Target: the wife and all married women), it cannot be considered to be a humorous one as it denigrates and insults women. According to such an interpretation, such topics should not become reasons for humor or laughter, because the script opposition is perceived as threatening rather than innocuous for contemporary Greek women. The following extract is indicative:

(4.2) Η αναπαραγωγή στερεοτύπων του παρελθόντος σε μια κοινωνία σαν την ελληνική, που *εξακολουθεί* όχι μόνο βάσει κοινής αίσθησης αλλά και βάσει στατιστικών στοιχείων *να είναι δέσμια αρνητικών συνεπειών αυτού του παρελθόντος*, δεν είναι χρήσιμη, είναι αντιθέτως εξαιρετικά άστοχη, θα πρόσθετα, και βαρετή. Όταν δε η ευρηματικότητα και η πλακίτσα έχουν μονομερώς και μονότονα το ίδιο περιεχόμενο τότε και η πλακίτσα χάνεται και το πράγμα αλλάζει.
The reproduction of stereotypes of the past in a society such as the Greek one, which –it is not only common belief but a statistically confirmed finding– *still suffers from the negative consequences of this past*, is not useful, but, on the contrary, it is totally pointless, I would add, and boring. Moreover, when creativity and kidding have the same one-sided and monotonous content, then kidding is not funny anymore and the thing changes [i.e. the message of the advertisement is interpreted literally, thus favoring sexism] (Apostolaki 2011, emphasis mine; see also example 2.34).

In humor theory terms, the *anesthesia of the heart* (Bergson [1901] 1911) and/or the *enjoyment of incongruity* (Morreall 1983: 47) as prerequisites for humor have no place here and seem to be out of the question.

It therefore seems that the non-humorous, sexist uptake of this advertisement presupposes male chauvinist views on the social position and roles of women especially in the context of marriage, which are still common among Greeks. In particular, male chauvinist phrases such as *Θα σε γυρίσω στη μάνα σου* 'I will return you to your mother' or *Αν δε σ' αρέσει, να γυρίσεις στη μάνα σου* 'If you don't like [it], go back to your mother' are reminiscent of the patriarchal structure of the Greek society and may still be used as threats by husbands who are not satisfied with their wives' behavior or who want to respond to their wives' complaints. Even today women (together with their dowries) are sometimes part of a financial transaction between the woman's parents and the future son-in-law; women cannot have a say in such transactions, and thus they are incapable of defending themselves (Context knowledge resource).

To understand the advertisement, one also has to be familiar with the fact that, stereotypically speaking, many Greek people are not particularly fond of okras. Although okras are part of the famous Mediterranean diet, they are not very popular among Greeks and many Greek children or adults have been forced to eat them by their mothers, on the grounds that they are nutritious and delicious (Context knowledge resource).

Analytical Focus 2: Genre
In terms of generic category, the humorous text is a TV advertisement (Narrative Strategy knowledge resource). Advertisements are often deliberately entertaining in order to attract audience attention (see among others Simpson 2001; Hatzithomas 2008; Politis and Kakavoulia 2010; Archakis, Lampropoulou, and Tsakona 2018; Dore 2018a), hence the presence of humor in the one examined here comes as no surprise to the members of audience watching the advertisement on TV and discussing it online. From a sociopragmatic perspective, humor here aims at rendering memorable the advertisement message concerning the possibility of returning a mobile phone to the store if the buyer is not satisfied. However, it is pointed out by some recipients that such "humor" denigrates women. In their view, advertisements are public discourse and their humor should not be considered without limits:

(4.3) Προσθέτει [η γενική γραμματέας Ισότητας των Φύλων κυρία Μαρία Στρατηγάκη] ότι εν προκειμένω οι διαφημιστές έχουν υπερβεί τα όρια του

χιούμορ, καθώς «το ιδιωτικώς εκφερόμενο χοντρό αστείο μπορεί απλώς να είναι κακόγουστο, το δημοσίως προβαλλόμενο όμως είναι απαράδεκτο, ειδικά όταν αναπαράγει ακραίες σεξιστικές συμπεριφορές».
[The General Secretary for Gender Equality Mrs. Maria Stratigaki] adds that, in the present case, the advertisers have exceeded the limits of humor, since "the tactless joke told in private settings may just be untasteful, but the one circulated in public is inadmissible, especially when it reproduces extreme sexist behaviors" (Ismailidou 2011; see also example 2.37).

According to such an interpretation, there are genre−related constraints on the use of sexist humor.

Analytical Focus 3: Text
Humor is produced during a lunch scene in the kitchen of a recently married couple and then at the doorstep of the wife's mother in front of the latter (Situation knowledge resource). The husband's words (see the utterances in example 2.29: *Wha::::t's that?, Okras! {with fake enthusiasm} Okras again, Get up! Get up you! {in an angry tone}, So dear mother-in-law do you see her? Well, I am bringing her back [exactly] as I took her [from you]. Untouched, unworn, and in her packaging, She has cost me 650 coffees, 152 meals, 1 birthday present and 2 nameday ones, Maria dear {he addresses his wife}, can you tell me, did we watch it together that great movie "Love in Swaziland"? Well, plus 39 movie tickets*) including the accompanying paralinguistic features (intonation, prosody, gestures, facial expressions, body movements), as well as the wife's and her mother's facial expressions (mostly of surprise and indignation), all contribute to portraying him as incongruous. His incongruity is not, however, perceived by some recipients as humorous but instead as aggressive and insulting. This time, the contextualization cues are not interpreted as a means of caricaturing the husband and ridiculing his views (see above), but as indicative of his aggressive, offensive, and eventually sexist behavior towards his wife (and his mother-in-law). In addition, in this particular reading of the advertisement, the sounds signaling the beginning and the end of the husband's fantasy do not entail that a non–*bona-fide* mode of communication allowing for a non–literal, inconsequential interpretation of humor (see Raskin 1985) is at work (Language and Meta-Knowledge Resource).

The proposed analysis using the Discourse Theory of Humor has tried to take into consideration both the advertisement text and the ensuing recipients' reactions in order to account for the contradictory readings that dominated the Greek public discourse on the advertisement. It has highlighted the ambiguity of several features of the text (intonation, prosody, paralinguistic features, jab lines), the different script oppositions and targets identified in the text, and the diverse sociocultural assumptions concerning the more or less powerful presence of sexist values in contemporary Greece.

Those who perceived the advertisement as "humorous" were based on the assumption that male chauvinist views and practices are outdated in contemporary Greece and as such they are incongruous, laughable, and hence can be ridiculed in public texts such as advertisements. Humor appears to "succeed" because the jab lines and related contextualization cues are interpreted as humorous. In other words, humor is recognized, comprehended, and appreciated. On the other hand, for those who opted for the "sexist" interpretation of the advertisement, this attempt at humor is of "low" quality or has "failed", because they do not align with the assumption that male chauvinist views and practices are outdated in contemporary Greece; on the contrary, they see them as alive and even prevailing. Hence, incongruous behaviors such as the husband's one are not to be taken light-heartedly, because they are threatening and disparaging for women. In addition, they would rather not be reproduced in the public sphere through advertisements, among other genres. Such an interpretation constitutes a non-humorous but rather discriminatory reading of the contextualization cues and utterances of the advertisement characters (especially the husband's ones). In this sense, whether humor was recognized on not, it was definitely not appreciated.

It therefore seems that the proposed analytical tools could help us account not only for what is perceived as funny/humorous (or not funny/humorous) in a specific text, but also why and how it is perceived as funny/humorous (or not funny/humorous; cf. Raskin 2012a in Section 4.2). The questions of "when" and "to whom", unfortunately, cannot be adequately addressed in the case study examined here. The "when it is funny" question would entail comparing different interpretations coming from different time periods or, if we had oral interactional data at our disposal (e.g. from informal peer interactions), from discussions among interlocutors who participate in different occasions or settings (e.g. same- or mixed-gender groups, private or public interactions). In addition, the partial anonymity or the pseudonyms used by the participants in this study and the lack of ethnographic or demographic information do not allow for elaborating on the "to whom it is funny" question by establishing whether participants' social characteristics (gender, class, education, profession, age, ethnicity, political orientation, religious beliefs, etc.) correlated with their "humorous" or "sexist" reading. This, however, confirms not so much the limitations of the analysis using the Discourse Theory of Humor, but rather the limitations that may be

4.6 An example of analysis using the Discourse Theory of Humor

imposed by the design and the methods of data collection. Working, for instance, with reception data coming from interviews, focus groups, or oral interactions would allow for answering more of Raskin's (2012a) questions through the analysis via the Discourse Theory of Humor.

The data analyzed here demonstrates that resistant readings of humor (in the present case, the "sexist" one) are not uncommon nowadays, especially in online environments where speakers often choose to express themselves and participate in various debates. Similar disagreements on the meaning(s) and sociopragmatic functions of humor are not rare, so it is expected that they become part of our knowledge about humor and of our experience(s) with humorous texts. In an effort to elaborate on such issues, the next Chapter is dedicated to educational applications exploring how humor works, how and why it may engender multiple interpretations, and what aligning or disaligning with one interpretation or another means and entails. This, as I intend to suggest, could be achieved by teaching about humor with a critical literacy educational framework.

Rounding up this discussion, I would like to underline, like many researchers have done before me, that the present proposal is a step towards an account of humor from a sociolinguistic perspective. It is in no way put forward as the most complete or the final approach to how humor should be analyzed and accounted for. The proposed Discourse Theory of Humor tries to overcome a few of the shortcomings of the previous linguistic theories of humor, namely the Semantic Script Theory of Humor and the General Theory of Verbal Humor: mostly their inability to take into consideration a number of contextual factors that have been pointed out as significant for the (linguistic or other) analysis of humor as developed within the past few decades. In this sense, emphasis has been placed on the dynamic character of humor: humor is perceived as jointly constructed and negotiated by interlocutors who take into account more than the semantic content of a humorous utterance/text to reach an interpretation, and who may eventually disagree on their interpretations. This could be considered to be an important step away from a competence theory of humor, but at the same time a necessary one, if we wish to explain why humor sometimes fails and sometimes succeeds. It could therefore be suggested that the three linguistic theories address different questions and may be perceived as each other's expansion:

- The Semantic Script Theory of Humor addresses the question: "How can we account for humor in semanticopragmatic terms?"
- The General Theory of Verbal Humor addresses the questions: "How can we account for joke similarity?" and "How can we analyze humorous texts different from canned jokes?"

– The Discourse Theory of Humor addresses such sociopragmatic questions as: "How can we account for different (humorous and non–humorous) perceptions and representations of social reality?" and eventually "How can we account for humor failure?"

4.7 Summary

This Chapter has built on the previous three to put forward a performance theory of humor, here called the Discourse Theory of Humor. After a relatively brief presentation and critical discussion of the most influential linguistic theories of humor nowadays, namely the Semantic Script Theory of Humor and the General Theory of Verbal Humor, the main attempts of expanding the latter have been presented. All these form the basis for the analytical model proposed here: the Discourse Theory of Humor borrows concepts and tools from the Semantic Script Theory of Humor and the General Theory of Verbal Humor (i.e. the script opposition, the knowledge resources, the jab lines and the punch lines). Concurrently, it presupposes a view of humorous discourse as a dynamic, jointly negotiated activity where participants draw from several aspects of context to create and interpret humor. Given the above, the Discourse Theory of Humor includes three Analytical Foci accounting for humor performance as well as for humor failure and assessments concerning the "high" or "low" quality of humor. These are the *Sociocultural assumptions*, *Genre*, and *Text* ones. To illustrate how the Discourse Theory of Humor works in practice, an advertisement intended as humorous was analyzed, which engendered both humorous and non–humorous readings.

Since humorous discourse is a significant part of our everyday communication (see Sections 3.1–3.3) and may yield multiple readings, our next step is to discuss all this within an educational context. As nowadays humor seems to become part of classroom communication and language learning, we could exploit humorous discourse to enhance students' communicative and critical skills. This is the focus of the next Chapter.

5 Teaching about humor within a critical literacy framework

5.1 Introductory remarks

The present study has so far placed particular emphasis on speakers' multiple ways of conceptualizing and interpreting humor (Chapter 2) as well as on the variety of contexts and genres where it may occur (Chapter 3). Such aspects of humor use are not only relevant to humor theory (as has been suggested in Chapters 1 and 4), but also to language learning, especially to teaching *about* humor. So, in the present Chapter, we will explore how we could teach about humor while taking into serious consideration that it may indeed yield multiple and often opposing interpretations as well as that it surfaces in most communicative settings and texts/genres.

Humor is often neglected or even deliberately excluded from educational settings and procedures *because* its multiple interpretations are difficult to handle in school classrooms, where peacefulness, consensus, and "seriousness" are expected to prevail. It is also neglected and excluded *despite* the fact that it is a significant part of our everyday communication and experiences with discourse. This means that we need to come up with an educational/teaching framework that will open the door to multiple perceptions of humorous discourse and simultaneously will create space for everyday texts with humor and will not limit students' textual experiences in class to the texts/genres proposed by the official curriculum. One such educational/teaching framework could be that of *critical literacy*.

So, in what follows, first, I discuss why humor has so far been resisted in educational settings and what recent research tells us about its advantages or disadvantages as a classroom management tool or as a facilitator of learning (Section 5.2). Focusing on language teaching, Section (5.3) considers the fact that the use of humor is more often than not recommended for teaching a second/foreign/additional language (henceforth L2) and not so much for first language/mother tongue teaching (henceforth L1). In this context, more studies are dedicated to teaching *with* humor rather than teaching *about* humor. In the same Section, I will refer to approaches advocating a critical approach to humor in classroom settings without usually making a distinction between L1 and L2 students. Section (5.4) elaborates on what critical literacy is and how it is usually practiced within educational settings. In Sections (5.5–5.6), I elaborate on the reasons why humor could be part of critical language courses, while also trying to diffuse common or potential reservations and objections. A brief overview of relevant applications reported in the literature is provided in Section (5.7).

Given that there seem to be significant advantages in teaching about humor within a critical literacy framework, and that some attempts have already been made in this direction, I present some main tenets for teaching about humor during critical literacy courses (Section 5.8). Then, in Section (5.9), I illustrate how this could be done using humorous texts referring to political issues (Section 5.9.1), gender roles and identities (Section 5.9.2), and racist views and practices (Section 5.9.3). In these tentative proposals, I exploit the Analytical Foci of the proposed Discourse Theory of Humor to design and organize potential questions that could be explored in class in relation to the humorous material at hand.

5.2 Humor in education

Even though it is a truism by now to say that humor is one of the most common resources in interaction, surfacing in many contexts or genres (see Chapter 3), education could be considered as one of the contexts where humor is faced with ambivalent feelings and resisted mostly by teachers rather than students. The reservations expressed by teachers and often discussed in the relevant literature come as no surprise if we consider the fact that humor has been perceived as morally suspect, hostile, and inappropriate behavior. Its "opposition" to "serious" behavior and meanings has rendered it undesirable, irrelevant, or inconsequential and has led to its rejection in/by institutions with "serious", "practical", "useful", and "moral" methods and goals such as education.[73] Commenting on the exclusion of playful and humorous discourse from education, Cook (2000: 160, 169, 170, 186) observes that

> many current approaches to language teaching assume, without either reflection or evidence, that it is the mundane transactional discourse of modern work, rather than the ancient playful discourse concerning intimacy and power, which should stimulate interest in language learning. (...) [I]t is the bizarre and unusual uses of language which, outside the classroom, seem to capture attention, take on importance, and remain in the mind. (...) We may pay far more attention to words of personal significance, such as a joke or an insult, a sarcastic or loving comment (...). Although contemporary Western society is not among the most repressive in its attitude to play, it does tend often to see it as childlike – even childish. Play is conceived as something immature, trivial, and superfluous, an appendage to be tagged on to the serious business of life.

---

[73] See among others Cook (2000), Bell and Pomerantz (2016: viii), Tsakona (2013b: 283–296), Trousdale (2018: 71–73). On the negative ethics and moral objections to humor, see Morreall (2008, 2009, 2010), Marciniak (2011), Saelid Gilhus (2011: 123–124), Taels (2011: 23), Larkin-Galiñanes (2017: 5–9); on how such objections and negative or positive language attitudes have influenced humor research and theory, see Tsakona (2013b: 77–118).

Nevertheless, there has recently been a "playful turn" in education (Bell and Pomerantz 2016: 5) and relevant research. This could be considered part of the cultural shift from negative to positive evaluations and perceptions of humor (Morreall 2010; see also Billig 2005b; Tsakona 2013b: 90–97). Scholars and teachers increasingly argue for the inclusion of humor in contemporary classrooms as well as for the benefits of such a change. The discussion of some potential drawbacks still accompanies the relevant proposals, and this shows the mixed findings, experiences, and eventually feelings concerning the exploitation of humor in educational settings.[74] More specifically, humor is more often than not perceived and proposed as a classroom management tool smoothing and regulating student–teacher interaction, and as a facilitator of learning improving its outcomes. Thus, humor seems to improve the conditions of the educational context, because:

- it motivates students and increases their collaboration, creativity, and self-confidence;
- it makes teaching content more appealing, thus it attracts and retains students' attention;
- it breaks classroom routine and contributes to the creation of a more informal and pleasant atmosphere in class;
- it allows students to project attractive and popular identities for themselves (e.g. as humorous individuals or even class clowns);
- students appreciate humor and evaluate its producers (whether teachers or students) in a positive manner;
- humor diffuses conflict and hostility and can strengthen the solidarity bonds among classroom participants;
- it allows teachers to restore order or their authority when necessary.

On the other hand, the use of humor in class is not always recommended or preferred, because:

- it distracts or even confuses students who may not grasp its meanings;
- it intimidates, demotivates, and eventually excludes students, especially if they feel targeted by it;
- it fosters or aggravates the power differential and conflicts in class;
- it could backfire, if classroom participants have diverse interpretations of it;

---

[74] See among others Holcomb (1997), Wallinger (1997), Cekaite and Aronsson (2004), Lytra (2007), Norrick and Klein (2008), Chaniotakis (2010), Archakis and Tsakona (2013a), Tsakona (2013b: 283–333), Bell and Pomerantz (2014, 2016: 69–99, 130–142), Hale (2016), Kontio (2017), Neff and Rucynski (2017), Van Praag, Stevens, and Van Houtte (2017), Gonulal (2018), Pozsonyi and Soulstein (2019).

- it weakens teachers' authority, disrupts the learning process, and results in loss of classroom control;
- it compromises teachers' professionalism, as it is often disapproved of by students' parents or teachers' superiors (e.g. school directors);
- it is usually not part of the curriculum, hence teachers feel that they are not properly trained to teach with/about humor in class.

The above-mentioned advantages and disadvantages of using humor as a classroom management tool or as a facilitator of learning are based on the assumption that humor is produced mostly by the teacher him/herself (and more or less appreciated by the students) or that it is jointly constructed by the whole group. Few, but not less significant, studies are dedicated to the humor produced by the students as a means of resistance to classroom discourse and procedures: "whether or not we as teachers opt to introduce humor, students are likely to find something about us amusing" (Bell and Pomerantz 2016: 144). Among others, Van Praag, Stevens, and Van Houtte (2017) argue that students may use humor to resist learning, especially if learning is perceived as the imposition of a curriculum on them. Thus, humor allows students to create an oppositional culture in class and brings to the surface the lack of social congruence between students and teachers.[75] Such critical analyses of humorous classroom discourse could help us understand how humor resists, or further contributes to, the reproduction of social inequalities in class. In general, the use of humor in class seems to be more complex than usually assumed, since the power dynamics and role asymmetries between classroom participants are often overlooked by relevant research (Nesi 2012; Hale 2016; Gonulal 2018).

The objections to using humor in class become even stronger when it is proposed that humor could become an *object* of study. As we will discuss in the following Sections, very few studies explore the process of teaching students what humor is and how it works in communication. This is directly related to the fact that teachers have not been trained in humor theory or analysis and are usually unfamiliar with what humor is, how it works, etc., so they feel inadequate in teaching about humor as a pragmatic phenomenon during language courses. The same, however, does not seem to hold for teaching other pragmatic phenomena such as speech acts or politeness conventions, which have for quite some time been considered to be more "mainstream" objects of study

---

[75] See also Jaspers (2005), Norrick and Klein (2008), Pomerantz and Bell (2007, 2011), Lefkowitz and Hedgcock (2017: 360–364), Jonsson (2018).

and are sometimes part of teachers' training and teaching. Actually, teachers (and parents) never seem to question the "usefulness" and "appropriateness" of using speech acts and politeness in class, as these phenomena are unanimously accepted as a significant part of communication. Then, *why not humor?* It seems that, in such cases, the prejudice against the "morally suspect", "irrelevant", "inconsequential", and "useless" humor prevails.

In sum, there appears to be a vicious circle here: negative evaluations and reservations against humor prevent it from being accepted as a useful resource for classroom management and/or for enhancing learning. The subsequent absence of humor from educational settings further fosters such negative evaluations and reservations as students and teachers seem to naturalize the "insignificance" of humor and its "non–serious" quality. Hence, humor is undervalued and not welcome as an object of study within education and its functions and affordances remain unexplored and implicit among its users. This, in turn, takes us back to where we started from: the "non seriousness", "inconsequentiality", and "immorality" of humor. Since humor is not part of language learning, there "must" be something "unacceptable" and "insignificant" about it. In this sense, teaching about humor appears to be one of the most powerful ways to break this vicious circle. If dispelling prejudice against humor is one of the goals of humor research in general, the analysis of humor in language courses should be promoted as a means to this end.

So, in what follows, we will concentrate on what happens with the use of humor in language teaching contexts. Given that humor is a common communicative resource, teaching about it is expected to be(come) part of language courses.

5.3 Humor in language teaching

One of the most striking facts that researchers are faced with when looking for studies in humor and language teaching is that the vast majority of these studies pertain to foreign/second/additional language (henceforth L2) teaching. It seems that humor is used and/or perceived as a particularly useful tool for familiarizing students with L2 communicative resources and sociocultural assumptions. First language/mother tongue (henceforth L1) teaching remains a "most serious" business and eventually much less fun. It appears to be implied that there is no need to attract students' attention and increase their motivation to a language they already have important reasons to use anyway. So let's see in more detail why humor is deemed important within L2 teaching contexts.

Many of the pros and cons of using humor in education in general (see Section 5.2) are identified in L2 teaching settings as well.[76] More specifically, humor appears to be useful for classroom management and better L2 learning outcomes as:
- it makes L2 forms more memorable and facilitates learning;
- it raises metalinguistic/metapragmatic awareness of L2 forms;
- it enhances L2 students' interest in the course;
- it helps L2 students to cope with linguistic inadequacies and alleviates communication problems, thus reducing their anxiety;
- it strengthens the solidarity bonds among classroom participants and mitigates potential face threats;
- it creates a pleasant atmosphere in class and a safe environment for experimentation with L2;
- it restores harmony in cases of conflict or tension;
- it offers momentary relief from institutional roles and constraints;
- students appreciate it and are eager to (learn how to) use it;
- it highlights potential differences between L1 and L2 cultures and helps teachers to familiarize students with L2 culture.

On the other hand, it is also observed that in L2 classrooms:
- humor reproduces inequalities (e.g. between students and teachers) and may be used for bullying;
- it tests the limits of acceptable behavior;
- it undermines the "serious" and "task-oriented" nature of classroom interaction;
- it renders communication a demanding task as L2 students may not understand it.

In general, there are no conclusive results concerning whether or not humor facilitates or impedes L2 learning; research findings suggest both (Bell and Pomerantz 2016: 101, 120–121; see also Attardo 2016: 1). As a result, humor is not accepted without reservations within L2 teaching contexts, or it is recommended only for classes with advanced students, whose linguistic proficiency may limit the possibility of humor failure or backfiring.

---

[76] See among others Schmitz (2002), Takouda (2002), Bushnell (2008: 50–51), Wagner and Urios–Aparisi (2008, 2011), Bell (2009), Forman (2011), Rucynski (2011), Archakis and Tsakona (2013a), Shively (2013), Tsakona (2013b: 283–333), Ahn (2016), Bell and Pomerantz (2016), Gasteratou (2016), Hann (2017), Huth (2017), Kim (2017), Van Dam and Bannick (2017), Alexander and Wood (2019).

Besides the affordances of teaching *with* humor discussed above, research in L2 teaching exploits the possibility of teaching *about* humor in L2 classrooms, albeit not frequently. The most powerful and popular argument in favor of teaching about humor in L2 is that humor is a significant part of students' communicative competence[77] in L2.[78] It seems beneficial to expose students to everyday, authentic L2 use so as to familiarize them with how, when, why, etc. humor is constructed and employed in L2. In particular, the use of humor in class could assist students in realizing how humor helps us to:
- build relationships and establish rapport with others;
- mitigate face threats, relieve tension, and release emotions;
- subvert, resist, or critique social norms and conventions (albeit often in a safe or deniable fashion); and
- highlight or redraw certain relations of power (Bell and Pomerantz 2016: viii).

Such an emphasis on the sociopragmatic functions of humor is expected to enhance students' *metalinguistic/metapragmatic awareness* of humor, namely their ability to recognize what is interactionally achieved through humor, in which contexts, and in relation to which topics (Bell and Pomerantz 2016: 148). Furthermore, Bell and Pomerantz (2016: 170–176) suggest that students should become capable of *identifying, comprehending, producing*, and *responding* to humor. More specifically, L2 students could become capable of:
- recognizing the contextualization cues[79] pointing to a humorous interpretation of an utterance (*identify*);
- evoking the relevant sociocultural knowledge to process the humorous message (*comprehend*);

---

77 *Communicative competence* refers to speakers' ability to use language appropriately so as to communicate effectively in diverse social situations, namely to their functional knowledge and control of the principles of language usage. As a reaction to Chomsky's (1965) *linguistic competence* (see Sections 1.2 and 4.2 in this book), Hymes (1972) proposes the concept of *communicative competence* and claims that a child

> acquires knowledge of sentences not only as grammatical, but also as appropriate. He or she acquires competence as to when to speak, when not, and as to what to talk about with whom, when, where, in what manner. In short, a child becomes able to accomplish a repertoire of speech acts, to take part in speech events, and to evaluate their accomplishment by others (Hymes 1972: 277).

78 See among others Cook (2000), Davies (2003), Archakis and Tsakona (2013a), Shively (2013), Tsakona (2013b: 283–333), Reddington and Waring (2015), Ahn (2016), Bell and Pomerantz (2016).
79 See Section (1.2).

- creating and performing humor in accordance with the contexts they participate in (*produce*); and
- selecting among a continuum of reactions to humor, ranging from clear rejection to full support and appreciation (*respond*).

The use of humor in class and, most importantly, students' and teachers' explicit discussion and experimentation on such skills are expected to cultivate students' communicative competence and metalinguistic/metapragmatic awareness (see also Kim 2017). An ethnographic investigation of L2 humor is significant here, as it will assist L2 students in acquiring "the necessary content knowledge about humor and the intercultural competence to recognize when, where, why, and with whom it might be OK to use particular expressions or joke about particular topics" (Bell and Pomerantz 2016: 173–174; see also Tsakona 2013b: 307–309).

Even though the ambiguity of humor is often perceived as one of the reasons humor may fail and backfire in class, hence its use is not recommended (see Section 5.2), it is exactly this quality of humor that could help students realize how language works in general. The multiple interpretations of humor and its context-dependent nature highlight the importance of context for interpreting all utterances, whether humorous or not: utterances have meaning potential and interactants jointly construct and negotiate their meaning(s). In this sense, communication (whether humorous or not) is not an exchange of words or expressions with inherent, fixed, pre-arranged meanings, but an act of interpretation (Linell 1998; Bell and Pomerantz 2016: 6, 12–13, 17–18, 197). Consequently, teaching about humor could enable students to understand their own contributions to interpreting discourse, and to reconsider their role in communication: as discourse producers and recipients, they do not merely repeat words or reach "intended" or "pre-determined" meanings, but they play an active role in interpreting and re-contextualizing meanings.

One of the very few proposals for teaching about humor in tertiary education, is put forward by Hempelmann (2016). Hempelmann (2016: 44) explicitly refrains from following the distinction between L1 and L2: "with the increasing student diversity in classrooms, scholars are currently advocating for a shift towards thinking beyond L1/L2 binaries and enacting pedagogies based on translanguaging and multiliteracies (Canagarajah, 2013), which draw on students' repertoires across languages".[80] His proposal aims to train humor scholars in particular and researchers in the humanities in general to do micro-ethnographic research and critical

---

[80] On conceptualizing and designing language teaching beyond L1/L2 binaries, see also Archakis (2019).

readings of scholarly literature. Among other things, students are expected to read and critically discuss literature on humor with particular emphasis on aggressive humorous discourse, keep a micro–ethnographic field diary including everyday humorous instances, focus on humorous practices of a group they have access to, study the humor produced by fictional characters (e.g. on television), and deliver an essay analyzing the humorous data collected.

Even though Hempelmann's proposal is not explicitly critical, it is in fact critically–oriented[81] as it encourages the students to follow an ethnographic approach to document, analyze, and discuss sociocultural differences in the use of aggressive humor across genres, so as "to make the familiar unfamiliar by close–up observation of what is normally taken for granted" (Hempelmann 2016: 46). He concludes that "[h]umor as an explicit topic in the classroom (...) has been argued to facilitate students' participation and their learning outcomes. (...) [H]umor can provide students with intrinsic motivation, insight into the working of language, and a window into human interaction in general" (Hempelmann 2016: 50). Thus, his approach highlights the critical potential of teaching about humor, which has also been underlined by Bell and Pomerantz (2016: 177, 178):

> our desired results or learning outcomes must extend to include opportunities for learners not only to expand their communicative repertoires but also to reflect on issues of identity and positionality. We cannot just encourage learners to engage in humor and language play without alerting them to the potential risks and rewards. For us, this means designing curricular units that don't merely proscribe what to say in particular specific situations, but engage learners in *critical reflection* about how we make meaning within and through interaction and what this means in terms of who we are and who we aspire to be. (...) [T]he decision to concentrate on humor in the language classroom should be motivated by *the desire to expand learners' communicative repertoires, metalinguistic awareness, and critical reflexivity* (emphasis mine).

To sum up, there indeed is a "playful turn" (Bell and Pomerantz 2016: 5) in language education, since a significant number of studies discuss the use of humor in L2 classrooms and its potential positive or negative effects on students, teachers, and their relationships. To teachers' question "Isn't being funny just too dangerous for L2 users?" (Bell and Pomerantz 2016: 176), the proposed answer is "Yes, of course, and this is why they need to learn more about it". Relevant research and proposals have already moved beyond teaching *with* humor; teaching *about* humor has also become an object of study and experimentation. Given that humor is an important aspect of our communicative competence in any language we may use, being able to produce and interpret it helps us to enhance our repertoires and

---

81 On critical approaches to language teaching, see Section (5.4).

eventually our metalinguistic/metapragmatic awareness about how humor in particular and language in general work.

In what follows, and building on Bell and Pomerantz's (2016) and Hempelmann's (2016) observations above, I intend to suggest that teaching about humor can be fruitfully done within a *critical literacy* framework. Such a framework allows for the exploitation of a wide variety of humorous texts and genres, contributes to students' familiarization with the workings of humor in accordance with their age or linguistic proficiency level, and draws on students' everyday experiences with discourse and the respective needs. Instead of debating whether to include or not humor in language teaching, why, and how, it would be preferable to come up with theoretical and methodological frameworks and applications which could facilitate such an inclusion and eventually cultivate students' communicative competence and metalinguistic/metapragmatic awareness or eventually their *critical language awareness*. Such frameworks and applications could also welcome and exploit humorous material from different sociocultural communities and languages, thus covering all students' interests and experiences with humor.

5.4 What is critical literacy?

As mentioned in Section (5.3), teaching with/about humor has recently been connected with students' metalinguistic/metapragmatic awareness and their critical processing of humorous interaction and other genres. So, here I will try to argue for teaching about humor within a critical literacy framework. In this Section, I offer a definition of critical literacy and describe some of its main principles, methodologies, and goals.[82] In this context, my next step will be to elaborate on the reasons why, in my view, critical literacy is suitable for teaching about humor (Section 5.5) as well as to discuss some restrictions or problems surfacing when attempting a critical approach to humorous texts in class (Section 5.6).

---

[82] The present accounts of critical literacy and critical language awareness draw on the following studies: Street (1984, 1995), Comber (1993), Fairclough (1992a, 1995), Baynham (1995), Shor (1999), Luke (2000), Cervetti, Pardales, and Damico (2001), Comber and Simpson (2001), Bean and Moni (2003), Wallace (2003), Evans (2004), Vasquez (2004, 2017), Behrman (2006), Lam (2006), Van Sluys, Lewison, and Flint (2006), Curdt-Christiansen (2010), Lau (2010), Luke and Dooley (2011), Archakis and Tsakona (2012), Janks et al. (2014), Tentolouris and Chatzisavvidis (2014), Tsakona (2014, 2016b), Felipe Fajardo (2015), Stamou, Archakis, and Politis (2016: 30–34), Koutsogiannis (2017: 232–291), Deliroka and Tsakona (2018).

5.4 What is critical literacy? — 149

Critical literacy is premised on the assumptions that neither discourse nor our interpretations of it are neutral, and that discourse shapes our understandings of the worlds, ourselves, and others. By representing aspects of social reality, texts offer value–laden, ideological interpretations of it, whether their producers or recipients are aware of it or not. All texts include and presuppose specific ideologies and evaluations of social reality and thus position not only their producers but also their potential addressees in specific ways in terms of background knowledge and ideological standpoints.[83] Texts have "designs on us" (Janks et al. 2014: 1). They shape and affect social relations and are shaped and affected by them. Hence, critical literacy aims to assist text producers or recipients in realizing the power relations and ideological standpoints implicitly or explicitly evoked and reproduced in the construction of various texts and genres: "[c]ritical literacy uses texts (...) in ways that enable students to examine the politics of daily life within contemporary society with a view to understanding what it means to locate and actively seek out contradictions within modes of life, theories, and substantive intellectual positions" (Bishop 2014: 52).

In this sense, critical literacy has often been associated with *critical language awareness*: "[c]ritical language awareness emphasizes the fact that texts are constructed. Anything that has been constructed can be de–constructed. This unmaking or unpacking of the text increases our awareness of the choices that the writer or speaker has made. Every choice foregrounds what was selected and hides, silences or backgrounds what was not selected" (Janks 2000: 176, cited in Rogers and Mosley Wetzel 2014: 9). More specifically, critical language awareness is based on the main assumption of critical discourse analysis that language as a social practice forms, and is formed by, values, convictions, and power relations. It therefore is a means and a product of social constitution (Fairclough 1989: 238; Clark and Ivanič 1999: 64; see also Freire 1972). From this perspective, the social world around us is not a static and neutral extension of the natural environment but a human construction, to a large degree a linguistic one, which is subject to negotiation and change. In the conventional educational environment of school, however, this view is usually suppressed (Fairclough 1989: 239).[84]

Critical literacy has also been perceived as a pedagogical application of critical discourse analysis to (language) education. Given that the main goal of critical discourse analysis is to unveil and scrutinize how discourse (re)produces social inequalities and social injustice (see among others Fairclough 1989; Wodak and

---

83 On the subtle yet significant differences between critical literacy and critical thinking, see Cervetti, Pardales, and Damico (2001), Wallace (2013: 35–39).
84 See also Wallace (2003), Farias (2005), Archakis and Tsakona (2012: 125–128).

Meyer 2001; Blommaert 2005; van Dijk 2008b), critical literacy explores how this can be achieved when analyzing texts in classroom settings. Its aim is to enable students to detect and expose how texts may be infused with manifestations of social inequality such as racism, sexism, classism, and linguistic discrimination, thus perpetuating discrimination against specific social groups. In this sense, critical discourse analysis and, by extension, critical literacy bring to the surface the hegemonic power of discourse and the struggle against the marginalization of certain opinions or points of view, mostly those coming from powerless and/or minority groups. It should also be noted here that, even though traditionally literacy refers to processing written forms of discourse, several approaches to critical literacy involve both written and oral skills, as they seem to be inseparable in everyday literacy practices (see among others Baynham 1995; Archakis and Tsakona 2012, 2013c; Tsakona 2014, 2016b; Cadiero–Kaplan 2002: 377, and references therein).

Behrman (2006: 490) maintains that "critical literacy is usually described as a theory with implications for practice rather than a distinctive instructional methodology". Indeed, critical literacy proponents such as Luke (2000) have argued *against* an explicit methodology for doing critical literacy in class, because this would result in applying pre–fabricated activities to diverse educational contexts and would limit students' and teachers' potential to design and implement critical discussions and analyses of texts according to their own interests and experiences. "Critical literacy needs to be continually redefined in practice" (Comber 1993: 82).[85]

However, there seem to be certain recurring broad categories of activities or tasks that are often discussed in critical literacy studies. In an effort to map and classify the main teaching practices proposed by such studies, Behrman (2006) identifies six broad categories of activities or tasks, all reflecting basic principles of critical literacy. Needless to say, critical literacy courses may include a combination of the activities described below:

1. *Reading supplementary texts*: School textbooks and the texts included therein more often than not offer specific dominant perceptions of social reality and simultaneously exclude or silence voices coming from powerless, marginalized, or minority groups. On the contrary, critical literacy places particular emphasis on students' and teachers' ability to design their own curricula by selecting texts and material to be introduced and discussed in class. It encourages students and teachers to move beyond

---

85 See also Vasquez, Tate, and Harste (2013), Bishop (2014: 57), Zacher Pandya & Ávila (2014), Vasquez (2017), Deliroka and Tsakona (2018).

canonical and literary texts to popular culture, to various everyday texts coming from students' sociopolitical realities, thus promoting an ethnographic approach to literacy.[86]

2. *Reading multiple texts*: The material selected (see above) could be read and juxtaposed with texts coming from school textbooks, thus allowing students to approach a specific topic from different and often opposing perspectives. One of the main goals of critical literacy is to move beyond text comprehension, namely the detection and reconstruction of the author's intended meanings of the text, to text's multiple interpretations offered by the readers/students themselves. In other words, to move from a text–oriented view of reading to a reader–oriented one: "text is given meaning as opposed to containing meaning" (Behrman 2006: 497; see also Wallace 2003). Within a critical literacy framework, students are expected to "unpack the multiplicity of meanings that resides in any text" (Rogers and Mosley Wetzel 2014: 10), to view the world from the perspectives of others, and to realize the inequality among different perspectives (e.g. dominant/majority vs. marginalized/minority ones). Contrary to what is often promoted within school settings, "authorship [is a] situated activity" and "text is not 'true' in any absolute sense but a rendering as portrayed by an author" (Behrman 2006: 493).

3. *Reading from a resistant perspective*: The texts included in traditional school textbooks or curricula represent a single, usually dominant view of a specific topic and give the impression that this view is the only "available" or "acceptable" one. Thus, students are usually encouraged or even forced to converge or acquiesce to it, and sometimes further develop it, through specific tasks. Such practices deliberately prevent students from (re)constructing deviant, resistant readings of a text, from considering opposing identities, and from questioning the values and ideologies presupposed in the text. Reading from a resistant perspective incites students to revisit and disagree with the standpoints, values, and knowledge they often take for granted and to gain some distance from their own ideological presuppositions.[87] Among the diverse, often conflictual meanings reconstructed from the text, none should be considered privileged or dominant in a critical literacy classroom. Resistant readings evolve around questions such as the following:[88]

---

[86] See also Wallace (2003), Vasquez, Tate, and Harste (2013), Bell and Pomerantz (2014: 36).
[87] See also Fairclough (1995), Bean and Moni (2003), Wallace (2003), Vasquez (2004: 1), Jones and Clarke (2007), Majors (2007), Deliroka and Tsakona (2018).
[88] See among others Coe (1994: 161), Freedman and Medway (1994: 10), Baynham (1995: 2), Fairclough (1995: 233–252), Behrman (2006: 496), Archakis and Tsakona (2012: 124), Janks et al. (2014: 1), Tsakona (2016b: 32).

- For what reason and for what purpose has a text been created?
- How and why does a specific text/genre gain acceptance and prominence?
- Whose interests and expectations does it serve and whose does it undermine?
- Could the text be created and function differently?
- How are the represented actions, persons, situations, etc. construed?
- Are there other possible ways of interpreting and representing these actions, persons, situations, etc.?
- What are the possible social consequences of this view of the world?
- Why is a specific linguistic variety, register, or text structure suitable for a genre – and not some other?
- Who decided on it?
- Who benefits from it and who is excluded from it?
- Does this variety, register, or genre empower some people and silence others?
- Why does communication in a specific context evolve (or should evolve) in a specific way and not in another?
- What kinds of communication does a variety, register, or genre encourage? What does it constrain against?
- Why are certain varieties, registers, or genres valorized?
- What kinds of social organization and institutions are put or kept in place by such valorizations?
- Which representations of social reality are favored (or even imposed) by such valorizations?
- When and with what consequences could someone decide to deviate from what is expected in a certain communicative setting?

Critical literacy incites students to make what Jones and Clarke (2007) call *disconnections*, namely to identify and critically discuss the sociocultural differences between, on the one hand, the social reality and characters as depicted in texts included in the curriculum and, on the other, their own social experiences and personal relationships.[89]

4. *Producing counter-texts*: While language teaching has traditionally placed more emphasis on text comprehension rather than production, critical literacy underlines the significance of creating opportunities for

---

[89] See also Archakis and Tsakona (2012: 109–163, 2013a, 2013c), Deliroka and Tsakona (2018).

text production in class (see among others The New London Group 1996; Cope and Kalantzis 2000; Silvers, Shorey, and Crafton 2007). Counter-texts, in particular, are considered to be most relevant to critical literacy goals as they allow students to represent non-dominant voices and to resist the values and ideologies put forward by school textbooks and curricula.

5. *Conducting student-choice research projects*: Students are encouraged to pick their topics of interest. More specifically, "the activity must go beyond simply selecting a topic and finding library books or websites on the topic. Students must become engaged participants in a problem affecting them and be able to reflect upon the social and cultural forces that exacerbate or mitigate the problem" (Behrman 2006: 485). Thus, students can exploit "experience as a curricular resource" (Shor 1999), develop a curriculum from engagement rather than memory (Vasquez, Tate, and Harste 2013: 19), and reflect on it.[90] This may not only enhance students' interest in language teaching, but will also allow teachers to share their power and authority with their students (Felipe Fajardo 2015: 34–35). Students' topics may result in open and perhaps heated or conflictual debates on controversial, even provocative issues in class. Such debates would rather *not* be avoided within a critical literacy course aiming at scrutinizing social inequalities and discriminatory phenomena (see Beck 2005: 343, 394; Parker 2012, 2016; Archakis and Tsakona 2018, and references therein).

6. *Taking social action*: As already mentioned, critical literacy is a social (not necessarily private) process, whereby critical readers are expected to share their opinions on texts publicly and not to be silenced as "deviating" from any "intended", "authentic", or "authoritative" meanings (see also Wallace 2003: 190–191). Critical literacy also involves taking social action moving students' real-life concerns beyond classroom walls and requiring students to become involved as members of a larger community (Behrman 2006: 485). In other words, critical literacy places particular emphasis on individuals' engagement and commitment as members of communities and on designing activities prompting social change and justice. "A critical literacy curriculum needs to be lived. It arises from the social and political conditions that unfold in communities in which we live" (Vasquez 2004: 1; see also Silvers, Shorey, and Crafton 2007).

---

90 See also Wallace (2003), Silvers, Shorey, and Crafton (2007).

Even though the above description and classification may lead us to think that critical literacy is meant predominantly or exclusively for students of secondary or tertiary education or for L2 students of advanced proficiency, critical literacy proponents and scholars underline the possibility of working with a critical literacy approach with young students, academically low–achieving ones, or early L2 learners. They also consider significant to familiarize all students with critical literacy practices and ways of processing discourse from an early age or from a low language proficiency level.[91] Comber (1993: 75), in particular, explicitly questions "any suggestion that critical literacy is a developmental attainment rather than social practice which may be excluded or deliberately included in early literacy curriculum".[92] Felipe Fajardo (2015: 41, 44) insists that teachers would rather not underestimate their students' skills and potential or using them as an excuse for refraining from critical literacy activities.

In sum, the goal of critical literacy is to enable text producers and recipients to detect, scrutinize, and critically discuss more or less latent ideologies and stereotypes pertaining to diverse forms of social inequality such as racism, sexism, classicism, and linguistic discrimination. Critically attending to discriminatory discourses and views may incite text producers and recipients to refrain from (re)producing such discourses and views, to understand and question the sociopolitical conditions they live in, and to realize that in texts certain voices are included and positively framed, while others are negatively framed, stigmatized, or even excluded and silenced. In Wallace's (2003: 42) terms, "critical reading does not privilege an author's communicative intent but is concerned with *effect*" (emphasis in the original). Furthermore, the multiplicity of texts and their meanings/interpretations are expected to highlight the fact that "texts are socially constructed artefacts and vehicles for different kinds of reality representations" (Comber 1993: 78). Such an approach is most compatible with our approach to humor so far, as I will discuss in detail in the following Section.

---

[91] On research and teaching proposals cultivating critical literacy in L2, see among others Wallace (2003), Zinkgraf (2003), Farias (2005), Correia (2006), Cots (2006), İçmez (2009), Zhang (2009), Koupaee Dar, Rahimi, and Shams (2010), Archakis and Tsakona (2013a, 2013b), Deliroka and Tsakona (2018).

[92] See also Comber and Simpson (2001), Cadiero-Kaplan (2002: 378–379), Evans (2004), Vasquez (2004), Harwood (2008), Curdt-Christiansen (2010: 186, 192), Stamou (2012), Tsakona (2016b), Maroniti (2017), Karagiannaki and Stamou (2018).

5.5 Why teach about humor within a critical literacy framework?

So far, research has shown that humor in class is more often than not employed as a classroom management tool or as a means of enhancing students' interest and learning. When it comes to language (mostly L2) teaching in particular, teaching with and about humor is expected to cultivate students' communicative competence and metalinguistic/metapragmatic awareness (Sections 5.2–5.3). Here, my aim is to underline the significance of teaching about humor as part of language courses as well as to argue for a critical literacy approach to humorous materials. Humor may be fun and incite us to become not only observers but also participants in interaction, but is never neutral or innocent, and students would rather be aware of that. Students are expected to be able to detect potential positive or negative effects of humor as well as to be aware that such effects may co-occur in a single interaction or context, as people may use and interpret humor in different ways.

First of all, critical literacy allows for the inclusion and processing in class of texts coming from students' social, political, and cultural realities, whether as supplementary readings or as the main ones (see Section 5.4). Diverse humorous texts may indeed be part of students' out-of-school activities and experiences, while many of them could be characterized as *social issue texts* as they "address the socio-political issues that students may face on a day-to-day basis" (Vasquez, Tate, and Harste 2013: 51–52). As Bell and Pomerantz (2016: 120) suggest, "humor often indexes social, historical, and political conflicts, thereby allowing learners to access and analyze attitudes about these issues".[93] By complementing or leaving aside official school textbooks often including outdated texts or texts reproducing exclusively dominant ideologies and cultures, humorous supplementary readings may spark students' interest and motivate them to explore how humor works. Teachers are expected to be attentive to students' preferences and proposals rather than introduce material which they themselves consider to be "funny" and/or "suitable", as their own humorous practices and preferences may not always be compatible or coincide with their students' ones. In some cases, teachers' chosen material may also be obsolete and hence incomprehensible to students or may not serve all classes' desires and needs. Besides, inciting students to provide their own humorous texts to class allows for flexibility and adjustment to students' age,

---

93 See also Trousdale (2018: 78–81, 84).

gender, previous (linguistic or other) knowledge, and contexts of humor use. Contrary to what educational research may sometimes suggest (see among others Schmitz 2002; Takouda 2002: 53, 56–57), there is no form or kind of humor that is universal, namely that could be understood and laughed with by everybody in class anyway (see also Bell 2009: 246–249; Tsakona 2013b: 295).

Within a critical literacy framework, teaching about humor could enable students to realize the diverse sociopragmatic functions of humor. Among other things, we use humor to build rapport, mitigate face threats, and criticize (see Chovanec and Tsakona 2018 in Section 1.2; also Bell and Pomerantz 2016: viii in Section 5.3). Sociopragmatic research on humor has brought to the surface a wide range of potential humorous effects, thus underlining the fact that humor is never "just for fun". Critical humor studies[94] have also concentrated on a wide range of sociopragmatic effects such as the following: how and why humor may reproduce and maintain social discrimination and inequality; how humor that seems at first sight to subvert stereotypes may eventually reinforce and naturalize them; how and why the generic conventions of humorous genres (e.g. jokes, film comedies, stand-up comedy) do not incite the audience to think critically of their content but instead enhance their tolerance for discriminatory standpoints; how discriminatory humor may force the targeted individuals to assimilate to prevalent social norms so as to avoid being ridiculed due to their differences, etc. Such sociopragmatic functions and effects may go unnoticed, as, whether consciously or subconsciously, recipients tend to acquiesce to humor's ideological presuppositions in their effort to establish coherence and comprehend the meanings of humorous texts (see Tsakona 2018a, 2018b and references therein). After all, as superiority/aggression theories of humor remind us,[95] humor (re)constructs relations of power: humorists portray themselves as superior to their targets and attack them for their "foibles". In this context, a critical approach to humorous texts calls us to rethink things that seem "normal" so as to defuse systems of meanings and values operating within humorous texts. If humor may render discriminatory and/or aggressive contents easy to escape our attention, critical literacy "requires active engagement and inquiring minds" (Vasquez, Tate, and Harste 2013: 64), thus revealing what may be swept under the humorous carpet.

---

[94] See among others Billig (2001, 2005a, 2005b), Howitt and Owusu-Bempah (2005), Park, Gabbadon, and Chernin (2006), Hill (2008), Lockyer and Pickering (2008), Santa Ana (2009), Chun and Walters (2011), Weaver (2011, 2013, 2016), Sue and Golash-Boza (2013), Malmquist (2015), Archakis and Tsakona (2019).
[95] On superiority/aggression theories of humor, see among others Gruner (1978, 1997), Raskin (1985: 36–38), Attardo (1994: 49–50), Morreall (2009: 4–9).

Critical literacy has been strongly influenced by poststructuralism (see among others Cervetti, Pardales, and Damico 2001), thus placing particular emphasis on multiple meanings and interpretations. This makes critical literacy suitable for analyzing and teaching about linguistic phenomena such as humor, which are inherently ambiguous and engender diverse, often contradictory interpretations by different people. Drawing on Kramsch (2008), Bell and Pomerantz (2016) discuss the fluidity of meanings and the importance of individual and cultural assumptions for making sense of (humorous) texts (see also Chapters 2 and 4 in this book). More specifically, they argue for "creating contexts in which learners can consider the social, political, cultural, and historical significance of different texts for different people" (Bell and Pomerantz 2016: 119). Such practices may bring to the surface a wide range of interpretations of, and positionings towards, humorous texts, which are most welcome in critical literacy courses and actually the cornerstone of such courses (see also Bell and Pomerantz 2014: 38–41, 2016: 170–176). An open, critical discussion of various perceptions and effects of humorous texts may sensitize students to discourse's potential to reinforce power asymmetries and perpetuate social inequalities, especially if dominant readings (e.g. perceiving humorous texts as "inconsequential" and mere "fun" while eventually promoting social discrimination) prevail while resistant readings (e.g. denying the "light–hearted" and "innocuous" nature of texts intended as humorous) are marginalized or silenced.

Such open critical discussions on what humor is and how it works in communication could be fostered by questions such as the following:
- Why does humor occur in certain genres or contexts and not in others?
- Who decides on such "proper" use of humor and who benefits from it?
- What are the consequences for someone who violates the "norms" of humor use?
- What is projected as "incongruous" and what is projected as "normal" or at least "acceptable" through a specific humorous utterance/text?
- Who benefits from the distinction between "incongruous" and "normal"/"acceptable" acts?
- Is such a distinction understood and accepted by all speakers? Why may some speakers disagree with it?
- Who is targeted through humor and why?
- Who benefits from such targeting? (see also Tsakona 2013b: 302).

Such questions could assist students and teachers in digging below the entertaining surface of humorous texts and in looking for readings different from their own initial ones. In addition, they will incite them to contextualize humor, thus reducing its authority and taken–for–granted–ness: decontextualized texts (whether humorous or not) "deny readers the space to question the grounds or sources of statements, effectively precluding challenge" (Wallace 2003: 9; see also Olson 1990: 21; Wallace 2013: 37). It should also be noted that such questions are not too different from the ones asked by those scholars who explore the social repercussions or sociopragmatic functions of humorous texts.

Furthermore, the fluidity and multiplicity of meanings derived from humorous texts as well as the significance of context (including background knowledge and ideological presuppositions; see Chapters 1 and 4) are expected to help students to realize not only the different and often competing value systems surrounding them (Bell and Pomerantz 2014: 42), but also how language works in general. Language is not a set of recyclable words and phrases with pre-determined, stable meanings but rather an endless act of interpretation, of jointly producing and negotiating meanings taking into consideration interactants' identities, needs, and desires (see also Bell and Pomerantz 2014: 36–41, 2016: 197; Hempelmann 2016: 50).

Finally, it should be underlined here that it is *definitely not* among the goals of a critical approach to humor to ban, censor, or restrict humor in any way. It is of primary importance, however, to familiarize students with what happens in interaction when humor is used, what various reactions to humor mean and entail for human communication and social relationships, how humorous texts, like all texts, shape the social world and the power differentials therein (see also Lockyer and Pickering 2008). Being a form of aggressive behavior, and through pointing out violations of expectations (i.e. incongruities/script oppositions), humor conveys specific views and is premised on specific values that may not be shared or accepted by everybody, or that may denigrate or victimize certain people or social groups. Critical literacy could help us make such sociopragmatic effects explicit in class through scrutinizing humorous texts and allowing for the expression of diverse reactions to them, including, but not limited to, laughter. As Pozsonyi and Soulstein (2019: 154, 152) remark, "[i]t is all too often said that explaining a joke ruins the fun of it. Granted, it changes how we hear the joke next time, but that is precisely the point of much of our work as educators"; after all, "it's pedagogically valuable to get students to reflect on their laughter".

5.6 Addressing some reservations concerning critical literacy and humor

Earlier in this Chapter, we discussed how and why humor has been considered incompatible with educational settings and irrelevant to educational goals for a

5.6 Addressing some reservations concerning critical literacy and humor

long time. It is only recently that it has been re-evaluated as an educational tool and as a teaching subject, albeit still not unanimously. Among other things, the emphasis placed on students' (prospective and often speculated) professional needs as well as on "serious" forms of discourse has kept humor away from classrooms, including language-oriented ones (see among others Cook 2000; Bell and Pomerantz 2016 in Section 5.2).

Reservations and objections to teaching about humor in a critical manner could multiply if one considers that teachers and students tend to resist critical literacy practices and goals, in general.[96] First, teachers are often not properly trained to design and implement critical literacy activities in class. Feeling unprepared, they are reluctant to try and they often question the validity and effectiveness of such an endeavor. In addition, many of them are exclusively trained to follow the official pre-determined curricula for language teaching and are not willing to consider an approach lacking a sequence of pre-planned, well-defined steps, such as critical literacy (see Section 5.4; also Beck 2005: 395–396; Bishop 2014: 57). On the other hand, "instructors may lack awareness about the use of laughter and humor" (Neff and Rucynski 2017: 283), which is indeed a prerequisite for a critical course involving humorous texts. This, however, should not, in my view, be perceived as a reason for avoiding the critical analysis of humor in class; it could instead become an important *motivation* for such an analysis. Given the pervasiveness of humor in everyday (con)texts, both teachers' and students' critical language awareness of humor could be enhanced through scrutinizing humorous texts in class.

Since critical literacy is usually not part of the official curricula and material for language teaching, teachers may consider it unnecessary and time-consuming, especially in courses that prepare students for language proficiency texts (mostly in L2 courses). Open critical discussions are expected to last long (or at least longer than other tasks which do not incite students to scrutinize texts), as they encourage students' reflection on the deeper (perhaps latent and discriminatory) meanings of discourse, and the expression of their stances towards them. In addition, humorous texts are not usually part of language learning curricula and material or of the tasks included in language proficiency tests. In this sense, teaching about humor within a critical literacy framework may sound not only unnecessary but

---

[96] The discussion concerning the reservations and difficulties for designing and implementing critical literacy projects in class in general draws on Brown (1999), Beck (2005), Norton (2008), Curdt-Christiansen (2010), Lau (2010: 277–279, 287, 293), Archakis and Tsakona (2012, 2013a, 2013c, 2018), Parker (2012, 2016), Kontovourki and Ioannidou (2013), Felipe Fajardo (2015: 40–44), Stamou, Archakis, and Politis (2016: 37–40), Tsakona (2016b), Koutsogiannis (2017: 278–279, 283–291).

even harmful to students (Wallace 2003: 45), as it distracts them from their "serious" goals.

During language courses, teachers often select topics and texts that are assessed as "safe", namely they are not expected to cause negative reactions or confrontations among students (see among others Wallace 2003: 53). Humorous texts may turn out to be controversial texts (see Sections 2.5.2–2.5.2.3), especially within a critical literacy context encouraging students to trace and critically discuss the more or less latent ideologies and values of texts and their own diverse interpretations of these texts. As the sociopragmatic analysis of humor suggests, humorous texts often make fun of certain people or groups, convey criticism against them, and may even stigmatize them. Therefore, the aggressive and denigrating content of humorous texts may discourage teachers from using them in class as potentially "dangerous" and hence "ineffective" material. This, however, perpetuates the impression that humorous texts are "just for fun", they cannot hurt or disparage anyone, they are "inconsequential" (see the vicious circle described in Section 5.2).

On the other hand, within a critical literacy framework, humorous texts selected by the students themselves could become the most suitable means not only for attracting their attention, but, most importantly, for sensitizing them to how humor may reproduce social inequalities and discredit certain people of groups, even in a mitigated, latent, or misleading manner ("just for fun"; see Pozsonyi and Soulstein 2019). If teachers are looking for a text which will unanimously be perceived as humorous/funny and not offensive by all the students, humor will never be introduced in class. Humor may be a universal phenomenon, but it is also a culturally-specific one: different linguocultural communities and different people within the same linguocultural community may more or less disagree on what they perceive as humorous or funny, and on how humor works or should work (see Chapter 2 and references therein). The "universally humorous" text thus becomes a pretext for not teaching about humor in class.

Voicing conflicting interpretations of humor and allowing for diverse reactions to it during a critical literacy course may also be considered undesirable by teachers. Teachers are sometimes reluctant to engage in conflictual discussions with students, fearing that they may lose control of the class and appear inadequate in their professional roles (see among others Parker 2012, 2016; Bell and Pomerantz 2014: 42; Felipe Fajardo 2015; Archakis and Tsakona 2018). After all, the exams students have to deal with more often than not require and accept one and only "correct" answer, namely one and only interpretation of the texts included in them (Curdt-Christiansen 2010: 190). Still, different interpretations of texts (whether humorous or not) and, by extension, different perceptions of social reality would rather not be discouraged in class. The diversity and juxtaposition of ideas and values are the *sine qua non* within a critical literacy course. As already mentioned, students are not expected to trace, accept, and take for granted the text producer's intended meaning(s), but instead to extract their own meaning(s) from the texts and critically process them with other students, as well as to familiarize themselves with value systems other than their own ones (see Section 5.5). The ambiguity of humorous texts render them ideal for such endeavors and goals: humor may help students and teachers "purposefully generate conflict dialogue" (Parker 2012: 624) based on their own lived experiences of humorous texts or incidents. In this sense, the exchange of diverse ideas and eventually confrontation should not be perceived as an indication of the failure of language teaching, but as one of its desired effects.

Critical literacy involves a shift from teacher authority to teacher–student sharing of authority or even student–authority, since students are expected to bring their own texts to class, design the curriculum, conduct their own research projects, and take social action (see Sections 5.4–5.5; also Beck 2005: 395–396). Such a shift may disorient students or make them feel uncomfortable, especially if they are socialized into a teacher–centered form of instruction, where the teacher is the main source of knowledge and the evaluator of students' contributions. Moreover, students may be socialized into text–analytical practices that are not compatible with critical literacy, such as accepting the author's (and/or the teacher's) opinions and representations without questioning them, and treating reading as a means for information gathering and entertainment and not for social critique; hence, they may think that critical skills have nothing to do with language learning (Felipe Fajardo 2015: 40). As a result, students may resist a critical approach, perceive the teacher as incompetent or inadequate in his/her role, and eventually distrust him/her (Brown 1999: 22–23). Humor may aggravate this, as students may be used to a "serious" mode in class and/or to processing exclusively "serious" texts as part of language teaching. The absence of humorous texts from language courses will, however, make it harder for students to develop their communicative competence and their critical skills towards humorous discourse. It will also reinforce the widespread view of humorous texts as merely entertaining, "un–serious", "unimportant", and "inconsequential" texts (see Section 5.2).

Questions concerning the appropriate age and level of language proficiency for either critical literacy or teaching with/about humor are frequently posed. Critical literacy scholars seem to agree that critical tasks and activities can be designed and implemented for students of any age or level of language proficiency (see Section 5.5). At the same time, recent research suggests that children use and recognize humor from a very young age.[97] Young children are also capable of explaining what humor is and what humor means or entails (Dowling 2014). Critical literacy offers an important advantage in this respect: by allowing students to select their own texts and thus contribute to designing their projects, language courses can be adjusted to students' age, language proficiency, interests, desires, and experiences (see also Bell 2009: 243–246). Besides, students' level of proficiency (including their metalinguistic/metapragmatic awareness and critical skills) is doomed to remain low if students do not become familiar with how a common and multifunctional linguistic resource such as humor works. And a low level of language proficiency in general and limited skills in processing humor in particular may result in the negative evaluation and marginalization of the speaker (Bell 2007: 28).

Last but not least, critical literacy could render the distinction between L1 and L2 teaching rather irrelevant: by collecting material from students' sociocultural realities, it welcomes texts from different languages and linguistic varieties to enter class and become part of language courses. Thus, students come into contact with different forms and expressions of humor, enrich their repertoires across languages, and could compare different sociopragmatic functions and effects achieved in each case (see Stein 2001; Hempelmann 2016: 44).

Finally, within critical literacy courses focusing on humorous texts and genres, students may be given the opportunity to analyze appealing material from their own sociocultural realities. At the same time, they may have to confront issues that are sensitive to them, they may be asked to consider different perspectives, and eventually to make changes in the ways they think about or use humor. This does not mean that they will stop enjoying humor or laughing with it, but they would be more conscious and critical of the uses of humorous discourse. Such goals could convince both teachers and students to attempt a critical approach to humorous texts. Critical literacy teaching and the respective analytical practices may be different from the ones students and teachers are usually socialized into, but this should not discourage them from trying a different approach to learning and thinking about language in general and humor in particular.

---

97 See among others Cekaite and Aronsson (2004), Lytra (2007), Hoicka (2016), Loizou and Kyriakou (2016), Timofeeva–Timofeev (2016).

5.7 Using humorous texts in critical literacy courses

Albeit not very often, humorous texts have been included in critical literacy proposals or projects. This shows that scholars and teachers sometimes recognize the importance of such texts for students; in other words, they perceive humorous texts as an important part of students' social, political, and cultural realities and everyday experiences with discourse. In what follows, I will briefly present some critical approaches to humorous texts within language courses, so as to demonstrate the main tendencies identified so far.

Janks et al. (2014: 91–97) exploit political cartoons to design a critical literacy course, thus providing a sequence of specific steps and goals that could be followed in class. The data examined involves cartoons reproducing racist and colonial stereotypes and representing politicians either in a positive or in a negative manner. Their approach seems to be a bottom–up one as they first focus on both the visual and verbal elements of cartoons asking questions such as the following:
- Who is/are represented? How are they physically portrayed?
- What is/are the represented person/s doing? Where are they placed in relation to one another? What are their relative sizes?
- Where and when is the described event taking place?
- What are the words represented in the form of speech bubbles, captions, headings, banners, or other bits of texts?
- Is the style, shape, or placement of the writing significant?
- How do the words provided shape our interpretation of the represented events? (Janks et al. 2014: 91).

Janks et al. (2014) also take into consideration the cartoons' context of publication (e.g. in newspapers alongside the editorial column or other articles reflecting a newspaper's political stance or agenda) as well as the wider sociopolitical context (e.g. the real–life events at the moment of the cartoon's publication). Their analysis in class is shaped by the presupposition that

> political cartoons are positioned and positioning. (...) [Their] *choices* shape the way we interpret the cartoon, working to position us as *ideal readers* who share the cartoonist's attitude. But as critical readers we should be able to use or own beliefs and values to challenge the text. If we find the cartoon's assumptions problematic and we choose not to go along with them, we become *resistant readers* (Janks et al. 2014: 91, emphasis in the original).[98]

---

[98] On resistant readers and readings, see also Sections (4.5–4.6 and 5.4) in this book.

Janks et al. (2014) also discuss the significant role intertextuality plays in the creation and interpretation of political cartoons: intertextuality may engage the readers in making connections between the cartoons and previous texts, thus underlining the cartoonists' evaluation of political figures and events and (more or less directly) forcing the readers to make the same associations with him/her and acquiesce to his/her ideological standpoints. The significance of tracing intertextual connections between political cartoons and other texts within a critical literacy framework is also highlighted by Werner (2004) who suggests that political cartoons often carry unquestioned hegemonic assumptions concerning politics and cultural memory, thus naturalizing certain stereotypes of political figures and events within the public sphere (see also Tsakona 2018a, 2018b).

Gasteratou (2016) also discusses the exploitation of political comics and cartoons in critical literacy courses for teaching Greek as L2, so as to familiarize students with the sociopolitical particularities of the Greek cultural context. She specifically uses the *multiliteracies model*[99] which is expected to allow students and teachers to explore political values, views, and stereotypes which are widespread among Greeks and concern politicians' hypocrisy, corruption, and unreliability. Such material also touches upon recent developments in Greece after the eruption of the current debt crisis which aggravated political mistrust and caused significant changes in the social and financial status of people living in Greece.[100] In Gasteratou's (2016) proposal, emphasis is placed on the incongruities and targets of the data examined, so as to reveal and scrutinize in class the ideological presuppositions and the positions expressed by the producers of such texts and identified by the students analyzing them.

An interesting research project within critical literacy, also based on political cartoons, is reported in Paximadaki (2016). The author designed and implemented critical literacy courses for Greek students of the first two grades of High school (12–14 year–olds). She used cartoons about a variety of sociopolitical topics, such as unhealthy eating habits and consumerism, fan violence, standardization in education, sexism and sexual harassment at the workplace. Although her purpose was not explicitly to teach about humor, humor and the concepts of *incongruity* and *subversion* emerged as part of the critical discussions that took place in the classroom. Both students and teachers seemed to realize that the messages conveyed by the examined cartoons involved

---

99 See The New London Group (1996), Cope and Kalantzis (2000), Silvers, Shorey, and Crafton (2007); also Archakis and Tsakona (2012: 134–163, 2013c), Tsakona (2013b: 310–332, 2014, 2016b), Fterniati et al. (2015), Tsami (2018).
100 See also Tsakona (2015, 2017c, 2017f, 2018a, 2018b) and Sections (2.5.1–2.5.1.2.3 and 5.9.1) in this book.

cartoonists' reflections on aspects of social reality, which were framed as containing a humorous incongruity/subversion. Thus, it appears that part of the outcomes of these courses was students' familiarization with the use of humor to convey criticism, to depict cartoonists' ideological standpoints, and to sensitize the public on social or political problems. At the same time, it is observed that the exploitation and analysis of humorous material in class significantly increased students' interest and involvement in the course, even for those who spoke Greek as L2 and those with low academic records. Finally, Paximadaki (2016) underlines the positive evaluation and feedback offered by the teachers who participated in the project, concerning the learning outcomes, students' engagement, and their own reconsiderations about how to teach (about) language at school.

The humorous representation of language variation has also attracted the interest of critical literacy proponents. Stamou (2012) argues for the exploitation of humorous fairy tales to sensitize young students to the differences between standard and non-standard linguistic varieties (including the unequal status assigned to them) and to register/stylistic humor (i.e. the co-existence of more than one linguistic variety in a single context or the replacement of the expected variety with an unexpected, "incongruous" one).[101] Stamou (2012) maintains that using children's books including various stylistic resources and stylistic humor could bring young students into contact with non-standard varieties which are more often than not excluded from school textbooks and curricula, thus enhancing their awareness of language variation. Furthermore, drawing students' attention to the mixing and juxtaposition of various "incompatible" stylistic resources could help students to reflect on these resources and realize the dynamic character of stylistic conventions; eventually, it "could prevent against the danger of seeing registers as fixed categories to be simply deciphered and internalized, and could help children to adopt a more critical stance towards language use in general" (Stamou 2012: 325).

Elaborating on such a critical approach to language variation addressed to young students of 5–7 years old, Maroniti (2017) uses humorous sitcoms, TV advertisements, and cartoon films to familiarize students with language variation and to cultivate their critical skills concerning the representation of linguistic varieties in such texts. Maroniti's (2017) teaching proposal includes texts that have been collected after investigating young students' experiences with media

---

101 On register/stylistic humor, see Attardo (1994: 230–253, 262–268, 2001: 104–110, 2009: 315); also Woolard (1987), Canakis (1994), Georgakopoulou (2000), Bainschab (2009), Berglin (2009), Gardner (2010), Hiramoto (2011), Stamou (2011), Tsiplakou and Ioannidou (2012), Adetunji (2013: 4–6), Archakis et al. (2014, 2015), Tsami et al. (2014), Piata (to appear).

genres, and involves tasks inciting students to detect the differences and inequality between standard and non-standard linguistic varieties (i.e. dialects and sociolects). Her findings indicate that humorous texts can be creatively and fruitfully exploited within critical literacy courses, significantly increasing young students' involvement in, and enjoyment of, language teaching activities. Such texts appear to be particularly suitable for addressing in class widespread stereotypes concerning standard and non-standard linguistic varieties and their users.

Humorous media texts become the teaching material in Tsami's (2018) critical project as well. Her research is based on a corpus of humorous advertisements and sitcoms which were selected by 11–12 year-old elementary school students. Her analysis shows that the stylistic humor attested therein more often than not promotes standard varieties and denigrates non-standard ones (and their speakers). It also denigrates style-mixing phenomena by framing them as incongruous and "inappropriate". The teaching activities designed are meant to sensitize elementary school students to the reasons and effects of using stylistic humor in media texts and eventually to enhance their critical awareness concerning the use of both stylistic humor and language varieties in specific contexts. The implementation of the teaching material reveals that, besides increasing students' interest in language courses, such critical activities and humorous media texts do assist students in detecting non-standard varieties and the respective language ideologies and in critically reflecting on them (see also Fterniati et al. 2015).

The validation of marginalized discourses and languages is the basic aim of Stein (2001) who concentrates on her students' oral storytelling performances. Her goal is to enhance students' learning through inciting them to perform, analyze, and critically reflect upon oral stories coming from their own linguocultural communities and belonging to their out-of-school literacy practices. Working in a multicultural and multilingual environment (South Africa), Stein (2001) encouraged students to perform their fictional or real-life stories in class, thus constructing their diverse identities as part of the linguistic course. In their performances, students feel free to use their own languages or linguistic varieties, to present their sociocultural backgrounds, and to resort to a variety of genres, such as jokes, comic radio routines, rap songs, dialogues, and dramatized storytelling. In her study, Stein (2001) reports on a humorous traditional story/folktale with political content performed by one of her students in Zulu (i.e. the student's native language) and translated by another student into English so that the whole group could understand. Such an approach to language teaching is meant to challenge the hegemony of the dominant/official language at school (i.e. English) and of pre-determined material and literacy practices. It constitutes a critical literacy approach to language teaching as it also allows students to select (and even perform) the texts to be analyzed in class, to discuss their meanings and sociocultural significance, and to scrutinize the more or less hidden ideological standpoints lurking therein. Furthermore, allowing students to perform their own texts in class brought to the limelight their different sociocultural identities and languages which may be marginalized or banned at school. Once again, even though humor is not the main focus of the project, its presence in students' sociocultural experiences and students' preference for it are important.

Humorous narratives from everyday interaction are also explored by Archakis and Tsakona (2012: 134–163, 2013a, 2013c) in the framework of critical literacy. Using the multiliteracies model (see above) in particular, they come up with a series of questions and steps which are expected to enable students to scrutinize their own identities and those ascribed to other narrative characters, the sociocultural presuppositions of their stories, and, most importantly in the present context, the role humor plays in all this. The following questions are illustrative:
- Through which linguistic mechanisms is humor produced?
- Who is/are humorously targeted because they violated what is perceived as expected?
- Which social values are implicit in these narratives and are brought to the surface through the analysis of humor?
- What kind of identities do narrators construct for themselves and for others via the use of humor?

In a similar vein, other genres originating in students' everyday experiences with texts (e.g. jokes, comic strips, Harry Potter novels, student essays) are exploited within the same framework (in Tsakona 2013b: 310–332) to familiarize students with what humor is, what its main sociopragmatic functions are, and how it contributes to the construction of various identities.

Finally, a recent effort aiming at cultivating students' critical literacy and specifically concentrating on humorous texts can be found at the online platform Χιούμορ και κριτικός γραμματισμός [Humor and critical literacy] (2018). The platform includes a data–base of Greek humorous texts (mostly canned jokes, comics, cartoons, memes, oral interactions, online articles) which have been classified by genre, topic (e.g. marriage, gender relations, language, ethnic origin, profession, age, religious beliefs, political orientation), and mode (monomodal or multimodal texts). The project is addressed to language teachers and includes useful information on humorous phenomena and humor research as well as tentative analyses of humorous texts to be used in class. The analyses offered focus on the structural and linguistic characteristics of humorous texts, their cultural and intertextual allusions, and the ideologies underlying them. Relevant tasks and lesson plans are also provided, while the users of the platform are allowed to upload their own material and to interact with other users on relevant issues (see also Tsami et al. 2019).

Critical literacy approaches to language teaching may, as we have seen so far, involve humorous texts to explore various topics, such as racism, stereotypes, linguistic inequality, and sociocultural identities. Although the studies presented here do not always have an explicit focus on humor, some of its sociopragmatic functions are discussed, mostly humor as criticism of political affairs in political cartoons (Janks et al. 2014; Gasteratou 2016), as a means of undermining non–standard varieties or style–mixing practices (Stamou 2012; Fterniati et al. 2015; Maroniti 2017; Tsami 2018), or as a resource for identity construction (Stein 2001; Archakis and Tsakona 2012, 2013a, 2013c; Tsakona 2013b). Teaching *with* humor seems to yield positive results: most of the studies presented here suggest that teaching with humorous texts significantly increases students' interest and participation in language courses (Stein 2001; Stamou 2012; Maroniti 2017; Tsami 2018). Some reservations are, on the other hand, expressed concerning the background knowledge and ideological presuppositions necessary for processing humor, for example, in political cartoons (Werner 2004; Janks et al. 2014; Gasteratou 2016).

To sum up, humorous texts have sometimes been employed to design and implement critical literacy courses involving various forms of social inequality and discrimination. Such efforts usually combine teaching *with* humor with teaching *about* humor, as humorous texts are often included in the material to attract students' attention and maintain their interest in the critical discussions of "serious" issues – with the exception of Archakis and Tsakona's (2012, 2013a, 2013c), Tsakona's (2013b), Gasteratou's (2016) and Tsami's (2018) works and the online platform *Χιούμορ και κριτικός γραμματισμός* [Humor and critical literacy] (2018), which have an explicit focus on teaching about how humor works. In what follows, I will try to make some suggestions for teaching *about* humor through humorous texts, thus reinforcing the claim that humor is serious and important enough to become the main focus of critical literacy projects.

5.8 Designing critical literacy courses on humor

Taking into consideration the above discussion about critical literacy and its suitability for teaching about humor, let's summarize here some main tenets on which the following tentative proposals will be based:
1. The humorous material intended to be used as main or supplementary readings in class is expected to be collected by the students in collaboration with

the teachers: the former could bring to class humorous texts that attract(ed) their attention and collaborate with the latter in determining the goals of reading and analyzing such texts in class.
2. The material under scrutiny is not expected to be humorous to everybody in class: some may have grasped the humor and laughed, while others may have not; some may align with the humorous meanings, while others may not. It is crucial within a critical literacy framework to consider different perceptions of discourse and to allow them to become part of the analysis and discussion in class (see also below).
3. Teachers are expected to be familiar (or to be interested in becoming familiar) with some main theoretical concepts and analytical tools from humor research (e.g. the incongruity, aggression/superiority, and relief theories of humor, its sociopragmatic functions, the genres with humor). Thus, they will be able to assist students in exploring in depth how humor works in each case and why different readers may have different reactions to, and interpretations of, humor (see also Bell 2009: 255).
4. Humorous texts may be examined in parallel or in juxtaposition with non–humorous ones dealing with the same topic from a more or less different perspective. Thus, students could realize that humor stems from our evaluation of certain aspects of social reality as incongruous and simultaneously laughable, but such an evaluation is not the only way to perceive and frame aspects of social reality.
5. Students are expected to go through the humorous texts and identify whether or not they consider them humorous, why, which specific utterances are funny and what makes them think so, whether they agree or disagree with the humorous messages, what are the potential effects of such messages for the readers or the targeted entities, etc. (see also Bell and Pomerantz 2014: 39). Questions such as those in Section (5.4) could be used to foster the discussion in class, after adjusting them to the specific material at hand:
    - For what reason and for what purpose has the humorous text been created?
    - How and why does/did a specific humorous text/genre gain acceptance and prominence?
    - Whose interests and expectations does it serve and whose does it undermine?
    - Could the humorous text be created and function differently?
    - How are the represented actions, persons, situations, etc. framed so as to be perceived as humorous?

- Are there other possible non-humorous ways of interpreting and representing these actions, persons, situations, etc.?
- What are the possible social consequences of this humorous view of the world?
- Why is humor considered to be suitable for a specific genre?
- Who decided on it?
- Who benefits from it and who is excluded from it?
- Does the use of humor empower some people and silence others?
- Which representations of social reality are favored (or even imposed) within the humorous text under scrutiny?

Such questions will assist students and teachers in contextualizing humor, questioning its more or less hidden assumptions, and bringing to the surface its underlying values and norms. The latter are directly related to humor's potential to target and denigrate individuals and social groups and, by extension, to its potential to sustain certain social asymmetries and relations of power. Contextualizing humorous texts in class could therefore undermine their authority and taken-for-granted-ness (see Section 5.5).

6. Both teachers and students are expected to bear in mind that, just like it happens with non-humorous discourse, humorous discourse is not unambiguous: several and often opposing interpretations may be heard in class, which may even lead to conflict occasionally. This is a crucial point and goal for critical literacy courses: participants are expected to become familiar with different perceptions of humor as well as to consider different views than their own, thus shifting (even for a moment) their perspective. The aim of the critical analysis and discussion in class is not to reach and impose a single "correct" and "unambiguous" humorous meaning or interpretation, but to allow students and teachers to share their own views and critically reflect on them.
7. Students could finally recontextualize their knowledge and experiences with humor through various text-producing and performing activities and through further disseminating the conclusions of their analyses and discussions outside the classroom, so as to sensitize the wider audience or community to the uses and meanings of humorous discourse.

In what follows, and based on these tenets, I will try to offer a few examples so as to demonstrate how critical literacy courses about humor could work. It should be underlined here that these proposals are not considered to be suitable (in their current form) for all classes, independently of students' age, linguistic proficiency, sociocultural characteristics, and interests. After all, I align myself with those researchers within critical literacy studies who question and eventually resist the transference and imposition of pre–determined critical activities from one sociocultural context to the other, from one class to the other. Critical courses about humor would rather be designed, negotiated, and implemented *in situ* by students and teachers together (see Section 5.4). Even though the absence of a rigid pre–determined methodology and specific steps for critical literacy is often perceived as a disadvantage, it would rather be considered as an advantage: it gives students and teachers the opportunity to follow their own teaching and analytical trajectories and to choose among various practices and tasks which could be relevant to their own teaching and learning goals. So, the following examples could serve as potential inspiration for constructing and working on critical courses about humor.

5.9 Tentative proposals for teaching about humor within critical literacy

Given that the following tentative proposals have not been implemented in class, the data that will be used here comes from the examples discussed so far in this book and from similar sources (Archakis and Tsakona 2012, 2019; Tsakona 2013a, 2015, 2017c, 2017e, 2017f) and have not been selected by students, as would be expected (see Sections 5.4 and 5.8). In this sense, this kind of humorous material is by no means the only "suitable" for critical analysis in class. Furthermore, I would like to demonstrate that the model for the analysis of humor proposed in Chapter (4) could also serve as means for framing and enhancing teaching about humor. In other words, the Analytical Foci of the Discourse Theory of Humor could (hopefully) help students and teachers to organize their analysis in class and gather information on the data examined by posing and answering critical questions concerning the sociocultural assumptions, the genres of humor, and the humorous texts themselves (see Section 4.4.3).

5.9.1 Critically reflecting on political jokes and political reality

One of the most common kinds of humor nowadays is humor concerning political affairs. This may take the form of cartoons, memes, satirical TV shows, and, of course, jokes. Here we will concentrate on political jokes referring to the current financial crisis in Greece, assuming that (Greek) students would be interested in exploring such material in class.

As already mentioned (see Section 2.5.1.1 and examples therein), Greek crisis jokes are created and disseminated by Greek people complaining about their deteriorated living conditions and unemployment, and feeling deprived of goods and services available to them before the crisis. Greek people also humorously blame themselves for a luxurious lifestyle beyond their means and for not reacting dynamically against the austerity measures imposed. On the other hand, crisis jokes target politicians, thus depicting Greek people's mistrust and disapproval: politicians are blamed for not being able to handle the problems of the country effectively and for defending their own interests instead of the country's ones. Concurrently, Greek people seem to feel responsible for electing such politicians, and occasionally to become aggressive towards them, even in a humorous frame. So, in relation to such jokes, questions such as the following ones could be discussed in class:

Sociocultural assumptions
- In what sociopolitical circumstances did these jokes emerge and are circulated?
- What does one need to know about the sociopolitical context in Greece to understand what these jokes talk about?
- Would it be possible for someone who is not familiar with what happens/ed in Greek politics and economy to understand the content and aims of these jokes?
- Even though such jokes are usually anonymous creations, do students have any ideas concerning who could create them? What could the social characteristics of those who come up with such humorous texts be?
- What political and financial changes do these jokes refer to?
- Who is/are held responsible for all these changes and become/s the target of humor?
- How are Greek people and Greek politicians represented in these jokes? Are these representations humorous or not – and why?
- Eventually, why did students come up with the idea that such humor could or should be discussed in class?

By first discussing the sociopolitical context in Greece and the background knowledge necessary to grasp such jokes, students could confirm and enhance what they know about the current financial crisis. They could also ponder on why Greek people decide to laugh with such serious changes in their own lives, as well as on how difficult it could be for non–Greeks to understand and appreciate such texts. Moreover, they could discuss whether there could be Greek people who would not understand and/or appreciate such humor, and try to identify their social characteristics (e.g. upper class people not significantly affected by the crisis, lower class people devastated by the consequences of the crisis, politicians held responsible for the crisis).

Students could also elaborate on the changes in people's lives referred to in the jokes and realize that it is the unexpectedness or the incongruity of such changes (in relation to Greek people's living conditions before the eruption of the crisis) that triggers crisis humor. Another trigger for such humor is politicians' behaviors and roles in such circumstances: even though politicians are expected to be honest, trustworthy individuals fighting for the well–being of citizens, these jokes represent (and target) them as failing in their roles and letting down Greek people. On the other hand, Greek people also become the targets of humor for being "partly responsible" for their current situation (e.g. because they lived beyond their means or they elected "incompetent" politicians) and for not resisting the austerity measures imposed on them.

Genre
– What are the sources of these jokes? Where did students collected them from?
– Do all these jokes have the same form? What are the differences between the different forms attested?
– Why, in students' views, do speakers create and circulate such jokes? What could their intentions be?
– Why may such jokes become popular?

Focusing on generic features, students could elaborate on the different forms political jokes may take (e.g. narrative jokes, riddle–jokes, one–liners, intertextual jokes, monological fictionalizations, memes) and on what these texts have in common: among other things, they presuppose familiarity among interlocutors sharing them as well as shared perspectives and feelings about the crisis and related political issues. This discussion could lead to one of the most significant questions – the one concerning the sociopragmatic functions of such humor: *why* do Greek people joke about the financial crisis and its repercussions on their lives? Potential answers to these questions could bring students closer to the main theories of humor:[102] people create and disseminate crisis jokes because they find the sociopolitical changes unexpected and abnormal (incongruity theory); because they express their disappointment, disapproval, anger, etc. towards

---
102 See also Trousdale (2018: 73–76).

politicians and themselves (aggression/superiority theory); or because they attempt to release the pressure they feel from their current living conditions and to cope with their frustration (relief theory).

Text
- Are there any linguistic or other cues (e.g. puns, fictional elements, emoticons, titles/labels) indicating that these texts are intended as humorous?
- What could recipients think or feel when they read or listen to such jokes?
- What did the students themselves think or feel? How did they react to such humor? Did they laugh? Did they not laugh? And why?

The textual analysis of crisis jokes will allow students, first, to concentrate on the linguistic/discursive resources employed to create humor or to indicate humorous effect (e.g. puns, metaphors, similes, style–mixing, unconventional punctuation, emoticons), thus exploring the pragmatic functions of such resources. Then, students will offer their own thoughts, understandings, and assessments of such humor. Such reactions are not expected to be the same for all students and sharing them in class could enable students to realize the polysemy of humor and individuals' divergent perceptions of what humor is (and is not), whether a particular text is humorous or not, how humor works in communication, etc. Thus, students could understand that not all of us laugh with the same texts, and this happens because we perceive social reality differently and consider different reactions as "appropriate" to the same potentially humorous instances.

As already mentioned, such discussions should not be concluded with forcing students to converge to a specific "correct" and "appropriate" interpretation of crisis humor. Instead, it could incite them to document (and perhaps present in a wider audience) the different aspects of humor they explored in class, the particularities of the data examined (targets, situations, sociopolitical changes, etc.), and, most importantly, to document and classify their own different interpretations of such humor. They could also compare all these with representations of the Greek crisis and its repercussions in non–humorous texts, such as newspaper articles, TV stories and documentaries, whether coming from Greek sources or not. Comparing and contrasting humorous and non–humorous texts and/or Greek and non–Greek representations of the crisis could enable them not only to explore various perspectives, but also to understand how and why humor may or may not be used depending on how text producers wish to evaluate and frame aspects of sociopolitical reality. Finally, students could create their own humorous texts about the crisis. This will give them the opportunity to select the experiences or events they consider incongruous and frame them accordingly. Such creations could be compared with the data initially used for critical analysis in class.

5.9.2 Scrutinizing humorous representations of gender roles and identities

Another task within critical literacy could involve the critical analysis of the humor used for the representation of specific versions of gender roles and identities. Here, we could compare humorous texts belonging to different genres and offering diverse accounts of gender. For this teaching proposal in particular, I will use the TV advertisement analyzed earlier (in Sections 2.5.2.1–2.5.2.3 and 4.6) and an oral humorous narrative by a female school student (Archakis and Tsakona 2012: 152–155). The main aim of this proposal is once again to assist students in tracing the role of humor in depicting and evaluating specific representations of gender identities, as well as to help them realize the ambiguity and multifunctionality of such representations.

As already discussed, the advertisement involving the undesirable okra dish pictures a young, recently married couple: the man is not satisfied with the food his wife cooked for them and dreams of returning her to her mother, while also asking back the money he spent for/with her. The advertisement has been perceived as both humorous (i.e. ridiculing the husband's exaggerated and hence incongruous reaction) and non-humorous/sexist (i.e. demeaning women and reproducing patriarchy). In other words, the recipients of the advertisement derived opposing interpretations from it (as shown in the analysis in Sections 2.5.2.1–2.5.2.3 and 4.6).

The oral narrative examined in parallel with the advertisement comes from a conversation among Lyceum students (17–18 years old), in particular a tight-knit group of girlfriends who hang out in and outside school.[103]

---

[103] It should be mentioned here that as part of critical literacy courses, students could be asked to document (e.g. using the cameras of their computers or mobile phones) and to bring to class their own humorous stories. Their experiences and increased familiarity with the digital media could be exploited here for the collection of data for critical analysis. Their narratives could be transcribed (see also examples 3.3, 3.32, and 5.1) or reproduced in class using a computer. Students could also be asked to provide information concerning the time, place, and goals of interaction, the social characteristics of the participants (gender, age, level of intimacy, etc.) and the specific purposes of the telling of each of the collected narratives. Alternatively, they could produce their own narratives *in situ*, namely in class, while students and teachers either record them or take notes for the discussion to follow (see also Archakis and Tsakona 2012, 2013a, 2013c; Tsakona 2013b).

Hara, an undergraduate university student, is the researcher who collected the material. She became Danae's and Vasiliki's friend after hanging out with them for months (see also Archakis and Tsakona 2012: 152–155). Narrative (5.1) refers to the cooking skills of Danae's father:

(5.1) Δανάη: Εμένα όταν του λέει {του πατέρα μου} ζέστανε, του λέει η μητέρα μου απ' το τηλέφωνο, γιατί δεν προλαβαίνει τώρα καθόλου, είναι λογίστρια. Μιλάμε με τις δηλώσεις έχει φρίξει, ξέρεις, δεν αναλαμβάνει καθόλου σπίτι//
Χαρά: //Ωου
Δανάη: Και λέει στον πατέρα μου ζέστανε, ξέρω 'γω, τα φασολάκια ή τη φασολάδα ας πούμε. Ε και μέσα σε τρία λεπτά ας πούμε έχει βρομίσει όλο το σπίτι, έχει καεί το από κάτω το τέτοιο καταλαβαίνετε τι. Έχει ζεσταθεί το μισό σπίτι {γέλια}. Τα φασόλια έχουνε γίνει μαύρα. Το βάζει στο τρία στο μεγαλύτερο τέτοιο που μπορεί να πάρει το μάτι. Βάλτο στο ένα ρε άνθρωπε να γίνει σιγά–σιγά. Υπομονή ρε παιδί μου, περίμενε. Τακ το βάζει στο τρία και μυρίζει όλο το σπίτι. Μα δεν τα κάψα, μα φάτε {γέλια}. Τρώει μόνο αυτός εν τω μεταξύ.
Χαρά: Έχει την εντύπωση ότι δεν τα 'χει κάψει κιόλας.
Βασιλική: Ναι ναι ναι έτσι {γέλια}
Δανάη: Ε πήρανε, λίγο λέει και το κάνατε θέμα.
Danae: Mine {i.e. my father} when she tells him warm it up, my mother tells him on the phone, because she has no time anymore, she's an accountant. We're talking tax forms, she's freaked out, you know, she doesn't do any housework at all//
Hara: //Oh
Danae: And she tells my father warm it up, or something, the green beans or the bean soup, say. Well, in three minutes, say, the whole house stinks, the underneath, the thing, you know what {i.e. the hotplate} is burnt. Half the house is warmed up {laughs}. The beans have become black. He sets it at {mark} 3, the maximum the hotplate can take. Set it at {mark} 1, my good man, so that it warms up slowly. Be patient man, wait. Zoom he sets it to {mark} 3 and the whole house stinks. But I didn't burn it, but do eat {laughs}. Mind you, he is the only one eating.
Hara: He is under the impression he hasn't burned it on top of everything.
Vasiliki: Yes yes yes that's right. {laughs}
Danae: Well, they've just stuck a bit he says and you've made a big deal out of it.

The main narrator here is Danae, while Vasiliki and Hara also intervene and agree with Danae's evaluations. From the beginning of the narrative, Danae positions herself positively towards her hard-working mother, and she fully understands why her mother does not do the household chores (*γιατί δεν προλαβαίνει τώρα καθόλου ... δεν αναλαμβάνει καθόλου σπίτι* 'she has no time anymore ... she doesn't do any housework at all'). Therefore, Danae justifies her mother giving orders to her husband over the phone (*ζέστανε, ξέρω γω, τα φασολάκια ή τη φασολάδα* 'warm it up, or something, the green beans or the bean soup'). At the climax of narrative, the father is represented as incapable even of warming up the food properly (*Το βάζει στο τρία στο μεγαλύτερο τέτοιο που μπορεί να πάρει το μάτι* 'He sets it at 3, the maximum the hotplate can take'). His daughter gives him directives in a rather derogatory manner (*Βάλτο στο ένα ρε άνθρωπε να γίνει σιγά–σιγά. Υπομονή ρε παιδί μου, περίμενε* 'Set it at 1, my good man, so that it warms up slowly. Be patient man, wait'). The father is represented as clumsily justifying himself in response to her derogatory comments (*Μα δεν τα κάψα, μα φάτε ... Ε πήρανε, λίγο ... και το κάνατε θέμα* 'But I didn't burn them, but do eat ... Well, they've just stuck a bit ... and you've made a big deal out of it'), causing the girls to laugh.

The laughter particles dispersed at various points of the narrative indicate that father's behavior is framed and evaluated as incongruous and funny. The results of father's inability (*Έχει ζεσταθεί το μισό σπίτι* 'Half the house is warmed up') and his incongruous effort to undermine the damage (*Μα δεν τα κάψα, μα φάτε* 'But I didn't burn it, but do eat') appear to be the main reasons for his humorous targeting. Thus, interlocutors position themselves negatively towards his inability to adjust himself to the modern way of life and the ensuing daily domestic chores, whereas they fully approve of the mother's new active role. For them, father's inability to do basic household tasks is unexpected and hence humorous.

For a critical comparison of these two texts, students and teachers could explore questions such as the following ones:

Sociocultural assumptions
- How are the characters of the texts represented? Do they conform to gender roles according, for example, to the patriarchal, traditional norms and values – or do they distance themselves from such roles?
- Through promoting specific versions of gender roles, do text-producers marginalize and devalue other versions? Why? How does/could this affect recipients' perception of gender identities?
- How does humor contribute to such representations?

- Which characters are targeted and why?
- What are the assumptions underlying our assessment of the characters' behaviors as humorous/funny?
- What would be the "expected" (non-humorous) behavior for each character?
- What gender identities are dominant in students' sociocultural context?

In the advertisement, the husband is portrayed as sitting at the kitchen table ready to eat the lunch his wife prepared for them. He also seems to be expecting a dish that would please him (obviously not okras "like his mother-in-law cooks them"). So, in the next scene, he fantasizes getting rid of his wife by returning her to her mother, because he is not satisfied with the meal she cooked. The wife, on the other hand, seems initially happy to have cooked a dish that, she thinks, her husband would appreciate. We do not see her actual reaction to her husband disapproval, but we watch her surprise and confusion in his fantasy. Still, she does not react dynamically and does not resist her husband's decision to return her to her mother.

On the one hand, it could be suggested that, according to traditional gender roles, the husband is "correct" in his protest: the wife "must" have prepared a meal that would satisfy him (instead of okras). Her silent reaction conforms to, and confirms, such traditional gender roles. On the other hand, it could be maintained that both characters' behaviors are incongruous and hence humorous: the husband's one because he conforms to traditional gender roles in an exaggerated manner; the wife's one because she does not fully comply with traditional gender expectations by frowning upon her husband's behavior and by not cooking his favorite meal to satisfy him (even though she seems to be the one who cooks in the house). Humor here appears to be ambiguous as it helps to reproduce traditional gender norms and simultaneously frames them as incongruous and hence humorous. The different interpretations of humor seem to correlate with the gender norms and identities recipients may have in mind and endorse. The Greek context, where this advertisement comes from and refers to, plays a significant role in the interpretation of humor, as traditional gender roles are often perceived as dominant therein.

In the oral humorous narrative also referring to the Greek context, the father is portrayed as incapable of warming up a meal, when his wife has to work long hours. His daughter appears to give him directions and to negatively comment on his failure. The target of humor here is quite clearly the father who conforms to traditional gender norms and is not effectively helping around the house. His "inability" is judged as incongruous from a more "modern" perspective promoting a more balanced division of household chores and non-traditional gender identities involving, among other things, mothers working long hours outside the house and fathers taking care of the family. In other words, his daughter's humor implies that the father should have been able to do basic chores around the house without causing further problems – and her girlfriends agree with her humorous evaluation of father's "inadequacy".

Moving on to the discussion of genres, questions such as the following ones could be explored in class:

Genre
- What are the sources of these humorous texts? Where did students collected them from?
- Do all these texts have the same form? What are the differences between the different forms attested?
- How do such humorous texts function in terms of reproducing or questioning gender stereotypes?

In this activity we have two different forms of gender-related humor: a TV advertisement addressing a wider audience and aiming at promoting a service which only incidentally and metaphorically relates to gender issues; and an oral narrative performed among peers to share their experiences and enhance their solidarity bonds. Such differences are significant for the interpretation of humor by its recipients and for the sociopragmatic functions served in each case.

More specifically, in the first case, representing gender stereotypes in a humorous manner appears to be the aim of the advertisement, but eventually led to its banning from TV: it is the issue of gender and not the advertised service that a part of the audience considered insulting (see Sections 2.5.2–2.5.2.3). Even though advertisers tried to render their commercial message memorable and to attract potential customers via humor, the advertisement (at least partly) failed to do so, according to the negative reactions to it.

On the contrary, gender-related humor seems to have succeeded in bringing closer the three female friends in the case of the oral humorous narrative. They seem to agree on the evaluation of father's behavior as incongruous, thus aligning themselves with specific norms and standpoints concerning gender roles.

Text
- Are there any linguistic or other cues (e.g. intonation/prosody, visual elements, laughter) indicating that these texts are intended as humorous?

- What aspects of the characters' behavior are framed as humorous and via what cues?
- What could recipients think or feel when they read or listen to such humorous texts?
- What did the students themselves think or feel? How did they react to such humor? Did they laugh? Did they not laugh? And why?

A close analysis of the advertisement text is expected to identify the husband's jab lines and paralinguistic features (intonation, prosody, gestures, facial expressions, body movements), as well as the wife's and her mother's facial expressions (mostly of surprise and indignation), all contributing to portraying him as exaggerating and hence incongruous (see the analysis in Section 4.6). Furthermore, students could discuss their own thoughts and understandings of what happens in the advertisement, so as to come into contact with various – and perhaps conflicting– reactions to the humorous representations of gender roles therein.

In the oral humorous narrative, students could explore the role of laughter in signaling humorous utterances (i.e. jab lines) and of other evaluative elements such as repetition, exaggeration, constructed direct speech, which frame father's behavior as unexpected and abnormal. Students' own views and feelings on the narrated events are also expected to be shared and analyzed in class.

To sum up, the Discourse Theory of Humor and the questions related to the different Analytical Foci could help students and teachers analyze in detail *and compare* humorous texts evolving around similar topics. As already mentioned, different sociocultural assumptions on gender roles, generic conventions, and discursive/semiotic resources could enable students understand how humor is materialized in each case and how it fulfills diverse sociopragmatic functions. It should also be underlined once again that the plurality and diversity of students' perceptions and reactions to humorous texts are not to be downplayed or ignored in class, but, on the contrary, they are expected to become the focus of analytical attention and the main goal of class discussions. All such discussions can be continued through, for example, imagining or even performing in class what happened in these texts after their prescribed/conventional endings. Students could come up with different scenarios and fictional dialogues enacting various versions of gender roles and identities, whether humorously or not.

5.9.3 Unveiling racism in contemporary migrant jokes

Migrant jokes have become quite common nowadays in many countries (at least) of the Western world.[104] Such humor has been associated with the maintenance of national boundaries, monoculturalism, and monolingualism in contemporary nation–states: migrants are perceived as a threat to monoculturalist values and norms, hence they become targets of humor. In this sense, humor allows speakers to downplay or even disguise racial aggression. In other words, humor in such cases allows speakers to strike a balance between two conflicting experiences: their reluctance to distance themselves from the "one state–one nation" norm (Irvine and Gal 2000: 63); and their effort to align themselves with discourses of tolerance and acceptance of the "Other" that become widespread nowadays.

More specifically, feeling threatened by the arrival of migrants, nation–states of the Western world put forward racist discourses and attitudes which seem to be one of the most efficient means for the achievement and maintenance of linguocultural homogeneity. Lentin (2004: 38, 44) argues that racism is "a structuring ideology of the nation–state": "where groups could not be assimilated so as to be classified in nationally acceptable terms, racism intervened to oppress them". As a consequence, migrants are forced to marginalization unless they assimilate themselves to the host community (Archakis 2018: 4). Simultaneously, racism maintains the social inequality between majority and minority people and is rooted in negative stereotypes and prejudice for minority people resulting in their marginalization and exclusion (van Dijk 2005: 2, 3, 7). As a result, power abuse against minority groups takes the form of racist views perceiving the cultural difference between majority and minority groups as a weakness on the part of the latter.

Despite the fact that manifestations of racism in the Western world are not uncommon, we should not overlook the humanitarian and anti–racist values of acceptance of difference that are in wide social circulation nowadays (van Dijk 1992: 95–97). As a matter of fact, in the Western world, extreme racist behaviors are usually hindered or banned, hence verbal racist attacks have acquired a mitigated form. Such mitigation is often achieved through the creation and circulation of racist jokes which may more or less disguise their denigrating

---

104 The discussion and analysis of migrant jokes draws on Archakis and Tsakona (2019). On contemporary migrant humor, see also Laineste and Voolaid (2016), Özdemir and Özdemir (2017), Dilmaç and Kocadal (2018), Constantinou (2019).

or aggressive effect and meanings through laughter and the creation of a light-hearted context.[105] Thus, a new, "liquid" kind of racism is attested, which allows for ambivalent and often opposing interpretations (Weaver 2016; see also Archakis 2018: 4–5, 9).

The data exploited here comes from a collection of Greek jokes[106] concerning the recent migrant crisis (from 2014 onwards; see Archakis and Tsakona 2019). Due to recent geopolitical changes (e.g. the collapse of the Eastern Bloc, the deregulation of the Balkan states, the wars at Syria and North Africa), millions of migrants have moved towards Greece the last thirty years: the first twenty years, Greece received migrants mainly from the Balkans and Eastern Europe; the last few years, Greece has received mostly Muslim migrants. All these migrant populations were faced with an intense national–racist discourse. Due to their cultural and linguistic differences, migrants have been perceived and represented as an "abnormal" and "suspect community", as a "security risk" and "an existential threat" to the Greek nation–state (Charalambous et al. 2016; see also Archakis 2018: 7). Suspicion and xenophobia have been the most common reactions of Greek people towards migrants forcing the latter to assimilate, if they wish to be accepted by the former.

In this context, migrant jokes can be perceived as "derivative of racist discourse" (Weaver 2011: 431), as they reproduce the above-mentioned discriminatory ideologies and practices. As such, critically analyzing them in class could sensitize students and teachers to their discriminatory meanings. Let's consider some examples that could be discussed during a critical literacy course about humor.

In the joke included in Figure 5.1, a Pakistani migrant is supposed to have won a huge amount of money at a lottery game and is considering buying one of the biggest and most notorious (for its bad living conditions) refugee camps near Athens. The humorous incongruity mainly evolves around the fact that migrants are not supposed to become estate owners in Greece (thus menacing its sovereignty and cultural homogeneity), but also around the fact that instead of buying a beautiful or luxurious house somewhere in Greece, he prefers one of the most notorious refugee camps as his "home". In this sense, the joke represents migrants not only as unwanted "invaders" but also as stupid (i.e. inferior).

---

105 See among others Park, Gabbadon, and Chernin (2006), Santa Ana (2009), Chun and Walters (2011), Sue and Golash-Boza (2013), Malmquist (2015), Weaver (2016).
106 The term *joke* is here used as a hypernym for canned jokes, one-liners, and memes.

5.9 Tentative proposals for teaching about humor within critical literacy —— **183**

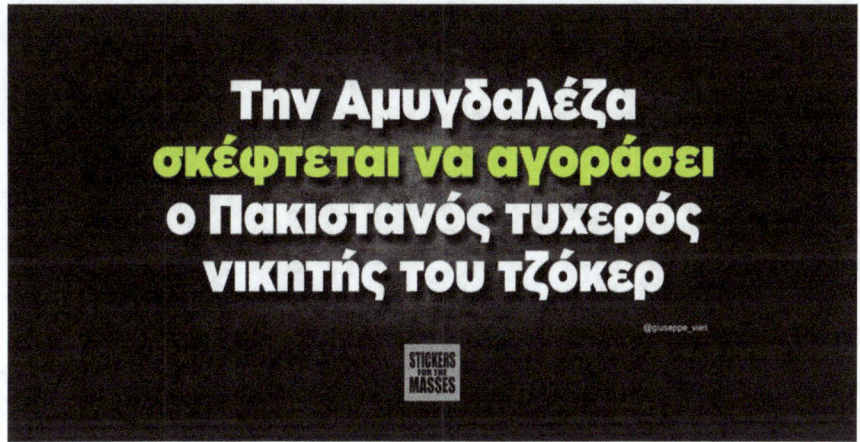

Figure 5.1: 'The Pakistani lucky winner of Joker [i.e. a popular lottery game] is thinking of buying Amygdaleza [i.e. a refugee camp near Athens]'.

Cultural "invasion" is emphasized in the meme of Figure 5.2:

Figure 5.2: 'The parade on March 25th, 2020'.

March 25th is the Greek Independence Day: Greeks celebrate their revolution against the Ottoman Turks, which began in 1821 and resulted in Greece becoming an independent state in 1830. Every year on that day, a military parade still takes place in the center of Athens as part of the celebrations. In this joke, it is implied that in a few years' time, Muslims/Arabs on camels will incongruously replace Greek soldiers after the former's (military and cultural) "invasion" in Greece.

The "terrorist" script is also ascribed to migrants in such jokes (Figure 5.3):

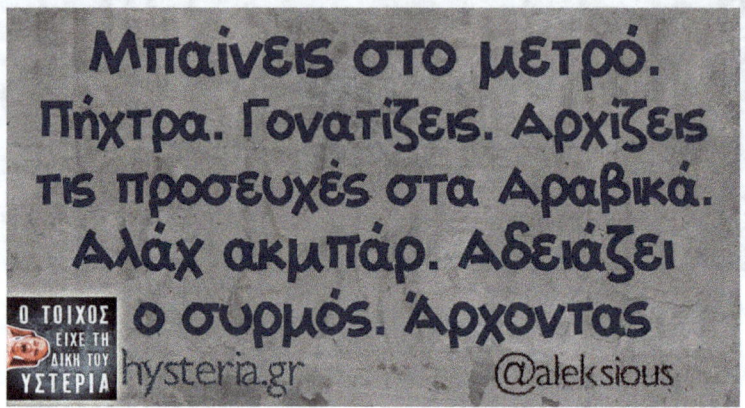

Figure 5.3: 'You get on the metro. It is packed with people. You get on your knees. You start praying in Arabic. Allahu Akbar. The metro wagon is evacuated. You rule'.

The joke provides incongruous instructions on how to find an empty seat at the metro. More specifically, it suggests that, instead of asking for a seat or wait for one to become available, one could pretend that s/he is a Muslim suicide bomber and start praying in the metro wagon before sacrificing oneself as part of a suicide attack. This will force all passengers to evacuate the metro wagon to save their lives. The joke is based on a rather common stereotype portraying Muslims as dangerous, inhumane terrorists and thus denigrating them.[107]

An explicit rejection of Muslim religion and culture appears in joke (5.2):

(5.2) Ένας αφοσιωμένος Μουσουλμάνος Άραβας μπήκε σε ένα ταξί κάπου στην Αθήνα. Ζήτησε κοφτά από τον ταξιτζή να απενεργοποιήσει το ραδιόφωνο, επειδή, όπως συνάγεται από τη θρησκευτική διδασκαλία του, δεν πρέπει να ακούει μουσική, επειδή την εποχή του προφήτη δεν υπήρχε μουσική και κυρίως Δυτική μουσική που είναι η μουσική των άπιστων.
Ο ταξιτζής σβήνει το ραδιόφωνο, σταματάει το ταξί και ανοίγει την πόρτα. Οπότε ο Μουσουλμάνος Άραβας τον ρώτησε, «Γιατί σταμάτησες, τι κάνεις;» Και ο οδηγός του απαντάει:

---

107 See also Weaver (2013: 491–494), Laineste and Voolaid (2016).

5.9 Tentative proposals for teaching about humor within critical literacy — 185

«Αγαπητέ μου φίλε στην εποχή του προφήτη όπως γνωρίζεις δεν υπήρχαν ταξί, γι'αυτό κατέβα και περίμενε για καμήλα!»

A dedicated Muslim Arab [sic] got on a taxi somewhere in Athens. He briskly asked the taxi driver to turn off the radio because, according to his religious education, he should not listen to music, because in the Prophet's era there was no music, and specifically no Western music which is the music of the infidels.

The taxi driver turns off the radio, stops the taxi, and opens the door. Then, the Muslim Arab asked: "Why did you stop? What are you doing?" And the driver replies:

"My dear friend, in the Prophet's era, as you know, there were no taxis, so get off and wait for a camel!"

The Muslim passenger is represented as too demanding, irrational, uncultivated, and impolite and as trying to impose his own religious beliefs and cultural practices on the Greek taxi driver. The latter's reaction indicates that, in his view, his passenger's culture and religion are inferior to the Greek ones: Muslims are supposed to be culturally underdeveloped and backward, as they still use camels instead of cars/taxis and they do not appreciate Western music. Consequently, they do not "deserve" to use the services provided by the Greeks.

To sum up, Greek jokes against migrants portray them as foreigners who invade the Greek territory and threaten local people (Figures 5.1–5.2), while at the same time their culture and practices are "inferior" to the Greek ones and hence would rather be rejected (Figures 5.1–5.3 and example 5.2). Therefore, the jokes appear to align with widespread racist discourses dominating not only the Greek public sphere but also those of other Western nation-states, which perceive migrants as dangerous for their security and cultural homogeneity. The two overarching script oppositions identified in the examples discussed here are the following:

1. Greece should not accept migrants so as to maintain its sovereignty and cultural homogeneity/Migrants invade the Greek territory threatening the Greek sovereignty and cultural homogeneity (Figures 5.1–5.2);
2. Greek culture is superior and should be dominant/Migrants' cultures are inferior and should not become dominant (Figures 5.1–5.3 and example 5.2).

Aiming at a critical approach of such material in class, students and teachers could consider questions such as the following ones:

Sociocultural assumptions
- How are migrants represented in such humorous texts?
- Why do they become the targets of humor?
- What aspects of their behaviors are framed as incongruous?
- What are the sociopolitical ideologies and attitudes underlying the representations of migrants as "alien", "undesirable", "threatening", "inferior", and "invaders"?
- Would there be such jokes in a state where multiculturalism would prevail?
- Who/Which social groups benefit from, or are gratified by, such humor?
- Which social behaviors and norms are promoted and reinforced by this kind of humor?

As already mentioned, migrant jokes portray such groups as "inferior" and "dangerous" "invaders" who are not welcome by the majority population due to cultural differences which are perceived as significant and threatening for the host culture. Therefore, migrants are targeted for their actions and characteristics and it is implied that they should not be allowed to enter the Greek territory, or they would rather be expelled from it. In this sense, humor reproduces racist views and practices (even in a mitigated manner), thus leading to further marginalization and exclusion of such groups and to the justification and endorsement of racist practices. This reminds us of the aggression/superiority theories of humor suggesting that through humor humorists portray themselves as "superior" to those targeted by humor and attack the latter for being "inferior" and not meeting their expectations (in the present case, for being culturally different).[108] In addition, if monoculturalist and monolingualist norms and values did not prevail in Greece (or other nation–states), newcomers would not be perceived as threatening to the host community and would not be forced to assimilate to local values and norms in order to become accepted some day.

Genre
- What forms does anti-migrant humor takes?
- Who, in students' views, creates and disseminates such humor and for which purposes?
- Where can one find this kind of humor?

---

[108] On such theories, see among others Gruner (1978, 1997), Raskin (1985: 36–38), Attardo (1994: 49–50), Morreall (2009: 4–9).

Such jokes appear to be created and circulated by Greek people mostly online and more rarely orally (see Archakis and Tsakona 2019). They take the form of canned jokes (e.g. narrative jokes, riddle–jokes, one–liners) and memes. The producers of such humor may be familiar with, or even endorse, racist values and views. Some of them may also try to hide or mitigate such views by taking advantage of the ambiguity and "non–seriousness" of humorous discourse. Such jokes make fun of migrants by representing them as "inferior" to Greek people, since the former do not conform to the "Greek" way of thinking and living. It therefore seems that humor can be used to convey and bolster social discrimination in a covert, not always obvious manner.

Text
- What are the linguistic/semiotic resources employed to frame migrants and their actions as incongruous/humorous?
- What could recipients think or feel when they read or listen to such humorous texts?
- What did the students themselves think or feel? How did they react to such humor? Did they laugh? Did they not laugh? And why?

As the textual analysis in class is expected to show, migrants are often represented using their ethnic names so as to underline their cultural differences with the majority. Their languages, traditional attires, religious beliefs, and other traits are also evoked in such jokes as part of widespread stereotypes. All such traits are explicitly or implicitly compared to Greek ones so as to denigrate migrants. Moreover, students are expected to share their own reactions and feelings when faced with such jokes and humorously reproduced stereotypes. They could also be asked to imagine how it would feel to be targeted, even in a humorous manner, by people living in the same geographical area with them but being different in sociocultural terms. Creating jokes targeting the host population as viewed by migrants would be another task that could incite students to shift perspective and enhance their empathy. Such conflictual and shifting perspectives are a significant goal within critical literacy courses, and the critical analysis of racist humor appears to be a suitable means for attaining them.

Finally, such humorous texts could be analyzed in parallel with other texts representing migrants in a non–humorous manner, such as news articles, TV shows, advertisements,[109] literary texts, online posts in the social media. Students

---

[109] On migrant representations in anti–racist advertisements, see Archakis, Lampropoulou, and Tsakona (2018) and Tsakona, Karachaliou, and Archakis (to appear).

could be asked to identify similarities and differences between humorous and non–humorous representations and trace their underlying assumptions and ideologies.

5.10 Summary

This Chapter is based on the premise that, since humor is a significant part of everyday interaction and communication in general, contemporary language education should familiarize students with what humor is and how it works, as well as with the fact that humor is not unambiguous, thus resulting in disagreements and conflicts among speakers. So, first, I provided a brief overview of recent developments and proposals of how humor is (to be) used in education, placing particular emphasis on language teaching. There, researchers and practitioners mostly concentrate on humor as a pedagogical tool employed to create a more pleasant and effective learning environment. Instead, my focus here was on teaching not with humor but about humor, so as to enhance students' communicative and critical skills. I argued that critical literacy could provide a suitable educational context for cultivating students' critical awareness about humor and I presented its main principles and practices. In an effort to defuse potential criticism and reservations, I discussed the advantages critical literacy offers for teaching about humor, and referred to previous attempts to design and implement critical literacy courses using humorous texts. Finally, based on some main tenets for designing such courses, I presented some tentative teaching proposals exploiting humorous texts from various topics and genres. In these proposals, I also demonstrated that the proposed Discourse Theory of Humor can be used to help teachers and students to come up with relevant and critical questions concerning the material at hand.

6 Conclusions

The main aim of this book, as indicated already in its title, has been to incite us to revisit the importance of contextual factors for the analysis of humor and its reception. Especially within linguistics, and under the heavy shade of generative theories about language, context has been more or less neglected and has not been included as a basic parameter for the identification, interpretation, and perception of humorous phenomena. This effect was encouraged or even aggravated by the fact that for many years humor research has mainly concentrated on decontextualized canned jokes which were/are thought to convey the "same" meaning independently of where they are (re)told.

However, as discussed in Chapter (1), context has been considered important by humor scholars coming mostly from outside generative linguistics. Studies in the pragmatics, discourse analysis, sociolinguistics, folklore, anthropology, etc. of humor underline the central role context plays in analyzing and accounting for the reasons why some utterances/texts may be intended as humorous, but are not always understood as such – and vice versa. The aspects of context usually taken into consideration are the sociocultural assumptions of humor use, the humorous genres, the specific communicative settings where humor occurs, the humorous text and co-text, the contextualization cues for humor, the characters of a humorous text and their speech, the reactions to and comments on humor, and speakers' differences and preferences in humor use. Here two of these aspects have been chosen for a more detailed discussion: the reactions to humor and its genres.

Reactions to humor have been explored within the wider context of metapragmatic research in Chapter (2). Following recent trends in pragmatic and sociolinguistic studies (mostly on the metapragmatics of politeness and register), I have tried to account for reactions to humor as indicators of speakers' metapragmatics stereotypes of humor, namely as visible or audible manifestations of speakers' internalized models of what humor is, how it functions (or should function), and where its limits (should) lie. Speakers' knowledge on such issues is based on their previous experiences with humor as part of their socialization processes. It therefore seems that the metapragmatic comments speakers offer on utterances/texts intended and/or perceived as humorous not only provide us with useful information about what they think about humor, but also demonstrate how they align with or disalign from other speakers on the basis of shared or deviating metapragmatic stereotypes of humor respectively. In other words, one of the main sociopragmatic functions of humor (if not the most significant one), namely its potential to bring speakers together or drive them apart, can be investigated not exclusively through the analysis of humorous content and its *potential* or *assumed* (by humor scholars) interpretations, but, perhaps most importantly, through *attested* and *documented* framings of humor or reactions to it. Such a turn in humor research could motivate more researchers to look for actual clues indicating how meaning is constructed and derived in context rather than try to conjecture how meaning would be constructed by studying decontextualized texts whose humorous quality is presupposed and taken for granted.

The other contextual parameter examined here is genre. One does not have to be a humor scholar to understand that humor is not perceived as appropriate behavior in every occasion: language users calibrate their use of humor according to the communicative settings they find themselves in, and the respective oral, digital, or written texts produced therein. So, in Chapter (3), I have tried to classify genres according to whether humor is attested in them and to whether its presence or absence is compulsory or not. Four categories have been identified: (a) genres produced predominantly for the amusement of the audience, where humor is indispensable; (b) genres that may often but not necessarily include humor and constitute humorous realizations of non–humorous genres; (c) genres where humor may occasionally occur but it is not normally or always expected therein; and (d) genres where humor hardly ever (or never) occurs. Such categories reflect speakers' metapragmatic stereotypes on the occasions where humor may/should or may not/should not be attested. Furthermore, humorous genres are not resistant to change but, on the contrary, adapt to speakers' communicative goals and needs and to the new affordances offered by contemporary technology and media. Thus, new humorous genres may emerge, while old ones may be transformed, lose their popularity, or even fade away as time goes by. The production of humor and the emerging genres are therefore perceived as dynamic processes and often presuppose speakers' creative negotiation of generic conventions and humorous meanings.

The emphasis placed on context so far cannot, in my view, but be reflected in linguistic humor theories and leads us to reconsider already existing analytical concepts and tools. The main linguistic theories accounting for humor, namely the Semantic Script Theory of Humor (Raskin 1985) and the General Theory of Verbal Humor (Attardo 1994, 2001), have programmatically refrained from taking context into consideration, as they focus on humor competence, that is, on how humor could ideally be perceived by an ideal (in Chomsky's 1965 sense) speaker. Chapter (4) has first attempted to demonstrate that both theories have not completely excluded context from their accounts and analytical tools; among other things, the very concept of *script opposition* is premised on speakers' contextual knowledge about the world, which is indispensable for processing any text, whether humorous or not. Then, I have tried to come up with an analytical model that explicitly incorporates and highlights the significance of context for the analysis of humor. The Discourse Theory of Humor proposed here includes three Analytical Foci:

1. *Sociocultural assumptions* involving the background knowledge necessary for processing humor and determining what is perceived as incongruous in a certain sociocultural community (i.e. the script opposition) and who is held responsible for it (i.e. the target of humor). Such knowledge coincides to a significant extent with what we earlier defined as the metapragmatic stereotypes of humor.
2. *Genre*, namely the types of texts including humor, which is directly related to the communicative settings where humor is obligatory, more or less expected, or forbidden. Genre also involves speakers' sociopragmatic goals when using humor.
3. *Text* pertaining to the specific discursive resources employed for framing discourse as humorous or even for rejecting a humorous framing of discourse. Semantic content, stylistic choices, contextualization cues, verbal or visual reactions, attested interpretations, etc. are all examined here.

A "contextualized" analytical model for humor cannot but account for humor failure as well, so it has been demonstrated that (and how) the same Analytical Foci can be used to explain why an utterance/text intended as humorous may not eventually be perceived as such, or why speakers sometimes distinguish between "good"/"high quality" humor and "bad"/"low quality" humor.

Last but not least, the present study has tried to connect a contextualized perspective on humor and its analysis with teaching about humor. In recent years, educational interest for teaching with and about humor has significantly increased, with particular emphasis being placed on the former rather than the latter. Among other things, the "non-serious" meanings of humor and its diverse interpretations have in the past discouraged teachers from inserting it in teaching materials. In Chapter (5), I have argued that a critical literacy educational/teaching framework allowing for everyday humorous texts, multiple interpretations of humor, and open discussions in class about the positive and/or negative functions and effects of humor could be suitable for teaching about humor. More specifically, I have suggested that teaching about humor should not be confined to L2 language courses: L1 students equally need to be critically aware of what humor is and how it works in communication. Moreover, a critical perspective on humor will enable students to understand that discourse, whether humorous or not, is jointly constructed and negotiated in context and that the emergence of multiple meanings from a single utterance/text is not necessarily due to some "failure" or "miscommunication" among speakers. To illustrate how a critical literacy approach to humor could work in class, I have provided some tentative proposals exploiting humorous texts on controversial topics (political, gender, and migrant humor). Furthermore, the Discourse Theory of Humor has been employed to show how the critical analysis and discussion of such material could be organized in class. Besides, a discourse analytic approach to discourse, such as the one proposed by the Discourse Theory of Humor, is a prerequisite for its critical investigation (see among others Rogers and Mosley Wetzel 2014).

Needless to say, further research could validate (or not) what this study puts forward. Among other things, we definitely need to test the Discourse Theory of Humor to diverse kinds of data to see whether its analytical tools (i.e. the Analytical Foci) are helpful and revealing for the phenomena investigated each time. The present initial proposal may improve through such feedback. We also need to test whether and how a critical processing of humorous texts in class would be accepted by, and become beneficial for, students and teachers. And whether the Discourse Theory of Humor would indeed contribute to productive and successful results in teaching about humor.

In addition, even though the present study has examined the metapragmatics of humor and its failure in separate Chapters (2 and 4 respectively), their interconnection needs to be highlighted and further explored in future studies. More research also needs to be oriented towards humorous genres, in particular towards how speakers modify and/or recontextualize the generic conventions of humorous texts, or in other cases draw on non–humorous genres to produce humor. It is equally important to investigate how such changes affect humor reception (e.g. making it easier or more difficult) and how humor recipients respond to them.

As a final thought, I would like to underscore the need for more metapragmatic research on humor, that is, for a stronger emphasis on the recipient end. As humor scholars, we may find it useful and beneficial to reflect more on our own tastes and/or prejudices on humor, and on how these influence what we choose to analyze as well as the methods and results of our analyses. As discussed in Sections (2.5.1.3 and 2.5.2.3), before becoming humor scholars, most of us are humor enthusiasts or at least humor producers and recipients and this cannot but affect the ways we see humor, the data we select for analysis, and the methods we opt for. We do not operate in a context devoid of our own experiences and preferences concerning humor. Nevertheless, utterances/texts that may make us laugh may (and, most probably, will) not cause the same reaction to everybody. This is something that tends to be forgotten by studies looking for humorous "universals" or for texts "unanimously" accepted as humorous. The actual, spontaneous, and documented reactions to humor are not insignificant or of secondary importance, especially if we view discourse as co-constructed and negotiated among speakers and if we wish to be attentive to what our informants are really telling us. Especially within the discourse analytic and sociolinguistic approaches to humor, humorous intent or generic conventions are often not by themselves adequate in accounting for what happens in interaction. This entails that, even if we cannot always have access to or consider in detail "the recipient end" of humor, we would rather at least acknowledge this as a limitation to our claims.

This is not at all irrelevant to the critical perspective on humor. Critical readings are not exclusively meant for educational/teaching environments, but are expected to be part of our everyday practices and experiences with discourse (see among others Fairclough 1992b: 136; Cadiero-Kaplan 2002: 378; Wallace 2003; Bishop 2014: 57–61). In other words, a critical literacy approach to humorous discourse should not be restricted to educational settings, but pertains to all of us and to our everyday encounters with, or uses of, humor, as critical humor studies have recently underlined (see among others Lockyer and Pickering 2008; Weaver 2011, 2013, 2016; Archakis and Tsakona 2019). Becoming critical readers of humor will enhance our understanding of it, whether we are humor scholars or not. And this cannot happen unless we (re)contextualize humor and consider its multiple and often opposing meanings and sociopragmatic effects for different speakers in different occasions.

References

Adetunji, Akin. 2013. The interactional context of humor in Nigerian stand-up comedy. *Pragmatics* 23(1). 1–22.
Agha, Asif. 1998. Stereotypes and registers of honorific language. *Language in Society* 27(2). 151–193.
Agha, Asif. 2000. Register. *Journal of Linguistic Anthropology* 9(1/2). 216–219.
Agha, Asif. 2004. Registers of language. In Alessandro Duranti (ed.), *A companion to linguistic anthropology* (Blackwell Companions to Anthropology 1), 23–45. Malden: Blackwell.
Agha, Asif. 2007. *Language and social relations* (Studies in the Social and Cultural Foundations of Language). Cambridge: Cambridge University Press.
Ahn, So-Yeon. 2016. Bridging notions of language play and language awareness. *Humor: International Journal of Humor Research* 29(4). 539–544.
Akinola, Ayodele James. 2018. Pragmatics of crisis-motivated humor in computer mediated platforms in Nigeria. *Journal of Language and Education* 4(3). 6–17.
Alba-Juez, Laura. 2016. The variables of the evaluative functional relationship: The case of humorous discourse. In Leonor Ruiz-Gurillo (ed.), *Metapragmatics of humor: Current research trends* (IVITRA: Research in Linguistics and Literature 14), 11–34. Amsterdam: John Benjamins.
Alexander, Richard J. 1997. *Aspects of verbal humor in English* (Language in Performance 13). Tübingen: Gunter Narr.
Alexander, Stephanie & Lana Mariko Wood. 2019. No news is good news? Satirical news videos in the information literacy classroom. *Libraries and the Academy* 9(2). 253–278.
Anderson, Benedict. 1991. *Imagined communities: Reflections on the origins and spread of nationalism*, revised edn. London: Verso.
Andriotakis, Manolis. 2011. Ειδήσεις από το δικό μου δωμάτιο [News from my own room]. http://andriotakis.wordpress.com/2011/02/27/germanos_sexist (accessed 28 June 2011). [in Greek]
Antonopoulou, Eleni. 2003. Parody and perverted logic in humorous film and sitcom scripts: A GTVH based account for humorous devices. *Antares* 6. 21–25.
Antonopoulou, Eleni & Kiki Nikiforidou. 2011. Construction grammar and conventional discourse: A construction-based approach to discoursal incongruity. *Journal of Pragmatics* 43(10). 2594–2609.
Antonopoulou, Eleni, Kiki Nikiforidou & Villy Tsakona. 2015. Construction grammar and discoursal incongruity. In Geert Brône, Kurt Feyaerts & Tony Veale (eds.), *Cognitive linguistics and humor research* (Applications of Cognitive Linguistics 26), 13–47. Berlin: Mouton de Gruyter.
Antonopoulou, Eleni & Maria Sifianou. 2003. Conversational dynamics of humor: The telephone game in Greek. *Journal of Pragmatics* 35(5). 741–769.
Antonopoulou, Eleni & Villy Tsakona. 2006. The importance of being Wilde: Τα γλωσσικά χαρακτηριστικά και η διαγλωσσική μεταφορά των χιουμοριστικών αφορισμών του Oscar Wilde [The importance of being Wilde: Linguistic characteristics and interlingual transference of Oscar Wilde's humorous aphorisms]. In Ioannis K. Probonas & Panos Valavanis (eds.), *EVERGESII. Festschrift for Panagiotis Kontos, Volume 1* (Parousia 17–18 2004–2005), 11–17. Athens: National and Kapodistrian University of Athens. [in Greek]

Apostolaki, Milena. 2011. Πόλεμος στα στερεότυπα. Διάλογος γύρω από ένα αθώο σποτάκι [War against stereotypes. Dialogue on an innocent advertising spot]. *Τα Νέα* [The News], 17 March. http://www.tanea.gr/news/greece/article/4622921/?iid=2 (accessed 28 June 2011). [in Greek]

Archakis, Argiris. 2018. The representations of racism in immigrant students' essays in Greece: The "hybrid balance" between legitimizing and resistance identities. *Pragmatics* 28(1). 1–28.

Archakis, Argiris. 2019. Από τον εθνικό στον μετα-εθνικό λόγο: Ανάλυση δεδομένων από μαθητικά γραπτά μεταναστών και προτάσεις γλωσσικής πολιτικής στο πλαίσιο της κριτικής γλωσσικής εκπαίδευσης [From national to post-national discourse: Critical language policy proposals based on the analysis of immigrant students' essay texts]. In Maria Chondrogianni, Simon Courtenage, Geoffrey Horrocks, Amalia Arvaniti & Ianthi Tsimpli (eds.), *Proceedings of the 13th Conference on Greek Linguistics*. London, 2–16. http://icgl13.westminster.ac.uk/wp-content/uploads/sites/55/2019/09/ICGL2013_Proceedings.pdf (accessed 11 December 2019). [in Greek]

Archakis, Argiris, Maria Giakoumelou, Dimitris Papazachariou & Villy Tsakona. 2010. The prosodic framing of humor in conversational narratives: Evidence from Greek data. *Journal of Greek Linguistics* 10(2). 187–212.

Archakis, Argiris, Sofia Lampropoulou & Villy Tsakona. 2018. "I'm not racist but I expect linguistic assimilation": The concealing power of humor in an anti-racist campaign. *Discourse, Context and Media* 23. 53–61.

Archakis, Argiris, Sofia Lampropoulou, Villy Tsakona & Vasia Tsami. 2014. Linguistic varieties in style: Humorous representations in Greek mass culture texts. *Discourse, Context and Media* 3(1). 46–55.

Archakis, Argiris, Sofia Lampropoulou, Villy Tsakona & Vasia Tsami. 2015. Style and humor in Greek mass culture texts. In Dorota Brzozowska & Władysław Chłopicki (eds.), *Culture's software: Communication styles*, 16–38. Newcastle upon Tyne: Cambridge Scholars Publishing.

Archakis, Argiris & Villy Tsakona. 2005. Analyzing conversational data in GTVH terms: A new approach to the issue of identity construction via humor. *Humor: International Journal of Humor Research* 18(1). 41–68.

Archakis, Argiris & Villy Tsakona. 2006. Script oppositions and humorous targets: Promoting values and constructing identities via humor in Greek conversational data. *Stylistyka* XV. 119–134.

Archakis, Argiris & Villy Tsakona. 2011. Informal talk in formal settings: Humorous narratives in Greek parliamentary debates. In Villy Tsakona & Diana Elena Popa (eds.), *Studies in political humor: In between political critique and public entertainment* (Discourse Approaches to Politics, Society and Culture 46), 61–81. Amsterdam: John Benjamins.

Archakis, Argiris & Villy Tsakona. 2012. *The narrative construction of identities in critical education*. Basingstoke: Palgrave Macmillan.

Archakis, Argiris & Villy Tsakona. 2013a. Χιούμορ, κριτικός γραμματισμός και Γ2 [Humor, critical literacy and L2]. In *Routes in teaching Modern Greek*. Supportive material for teaching Modern Greek as a second/foreign language, Articles for teaching Modern Greek as a second/foreign language, 4. Sociolinguistics. Center for the Greek Language. http://elearning.greek-language.gr/mod/resource/view.php?id=308 (accessed 15 November 2018). [in Greek]

Archakis, Argiris & Villy Tsakona. 2013b. Διαβάζοντας ειδησεογραφικά άρθρα στη Γ2 [Reading news articles in L2]. In *Routes in teaching Modern Greek*. Supportive material for teaching

Modern Greek as a second/foreign language, Articles for teaching Modern Greek as a second/foreign language, 4. Sociolinguistics. Center for the Greek Language. http://elearning.greek-language.gr/mod/resource/view.php?id=307 (accessed 15 November 2018). [in Greek]

Archakis, Argiris & Villy Tsakona. 2013c. Sociocultural diversity, identities, and critical education: Comparing conversational narratives at school. *Critical Literacy: Theories and Practices* 7(1). 48–62.

Archakis, Argiris & Villy Tsakona. 2018. A critical literacy proposal for exploring conflict and immigrant identities in the classroom – or how *not* to sweep conflict under the multicultural classroom carpet. *Journal of Language Aggression and Conflict* 6(1). 1–25.

Archakis, Argiris & Villy Tsakona. 2019. Racism in recent Greek migrant jokes. *Humor: International Journal of Humor Research* 32(2). 267–287.

Attardo, Salvatore. 1994. *Linguistic theories of humor* (Humor Research 1). Berlin: Mouton de Gruyter.

Attardo, Salvatore. 1997. The semantic foundations of cognitive theories of humor. *Humor: International Journal of Humor Research* 14(1). 395–420.

Attardo, Salvatore. 2001. *Humorous texts: A semantic and pragmatic analysis* (Humor Research 6). Berlin: Mouton de Gruyter.

Attardo, Salvatore. 2002. Beyond humor competence and toward a theory of humor performance. Paper presented at the 14th Conference of the International Society for Humor Studies (ISHS), Bertinoro, Italy, 3–7 July.

Attardo, Salvatore. 2008. A primer for the linguistics of humor. In Victor Raskin (ed.), *The primer of humor research* (Humor Research 8), 101–155. Berlin: Mouton de Gruyter.

Attardo, Salvatore. 2009. A commentary on Antonopoulou and Nikiforidou. In Geert Brône & Jeroen Vandaele (eds.), *Cognitive poetics: Goals, gains and gaps* (Applications in Cognitive Linguistics 10), 315–317. Berlin: Mouton De Gruyter.

Attardo, Salvatore. 2011. Humor. In Jan Zienkowski, Jan-Ola Östman & Jef Verschueren (eds.), *Discursive pragmatics* (Handbook of Pragmatics Highlights 8), 135–155. Amsterdam: John Benjamins.

Attardo, Salvatore. 2016. Humor, language, and pedagogy: An introduction to this special issue. *EuroAmerican Journal of Applied Linguistics and Languages* 3(2). 1–2.

Attardo, Salvatore. 2017a. The General Theory of Verbal Humor. In Salvatore Attardo (ed.), *The Routledge handbook of language and humor* (Routledge Handbooks in Linguistics), 126–142. New York: Routledge.

Attardo, Salvatore. 2017b. The GTVH and humorous discourse. In Władysław Chłopicki & Dorota Brzozowska (eds.), *Humorous discourse* (Humor Research 11), 93–105. Berlin: Mouton De Gruyter.

Attardo, Salvatore & Jean-Charles Chabanne. 1992. Jokes as a text type. *Humor: International Journal of Humor Research* 5 (1/2). 165–176.

Attardo, Salvatore, Christian F. Hempelmann & Sara Di Maio. 2002. Script oppositions and logical mechanisms: Modeling incongruities and their resolutions. *Humor: International Journal of Humor Research* 15(1). 3–46.

Attardo, Salvatore & Lucy Pickering. 2011. Timing in the performance of jokes. *Humor: International Journal of Humor Research* 24(2). 233–250.

Attardo, Salvatore & Victor Raskin. 1991. Script theory revis(it)ed: Joke similarity and joke representation model. *Humor: International Journal of Humor Research* 4(3). 293–347.

Attardo, Salvatore & Victor Raskin. 2017. Linguistics and humor theory. In Salvatore Attardo (ed.), *The Routledge handbook of language and humor* (Routledge Handbooks in Linguistics), 49–63. New York: Routledge.

Attardo, Salvatore, Manuela Wagner & Eduardo Urios-Aparisi (eds.). 2013. *Prosody and humor* (Benjamins Current Topics 55). Amsterdam: John Benjamins.

Badarneh, Muhammad A. 2011. Carnivalesque politics: A Bakhtinian case study of contemporary Arab political humor. *Humor: International Journal of Humor Research* 24(3). 305–327.

Bainschab, Alexandra Corinna Damaris. 2009. The humor of Christopher Moore. Vienna: Universität Wien MA thesis. http://othes.univie.ac.at/3440/1/2009-01-18_0201010.pdf (accessed 13 November 2018).

Bakhtin, Mikhail. 1981. *The dialogic imagination: Four essays* [Voprosy literatury i éstetiki] (Slavic Series 1). Austin: University of Texas Press.

Bakhtin, Mikhail. 1984a. *Problems of Dostoevsky's poetics* [Problemy poetiki Dostoevskogo] (Theory and History of Literature 8). Minneapolis: University of Minnesota Press.

Bakhtin, Mikhail. 1984b. *Rabelais and his world* [Tvorčestvo fransua Rable]. Bloomington: Indiana University Press.

Bakhtin, Mikhail. 1986. *Speech genres and other late essays* [Éstetika slovesnogo tvorchestva] (Slavic Series 8). Austin: University of Texas Press.

Balirano, Giuseppe & Marcella Corduas. 2008. Detecting semiotically-expressed humor in diasporic TV productions. *Humor: International Journal of Humor Research* 21(3). 227–251.

Bateson, Gregory. 1972 [1955]. A theory of play and fantasy. In *Steps to an ecology of mind*, 177–193. New York: Ballantine.

Bauman, Richard. 2004. Introduction: Genre, performance, and the production of intertextuality. In Richard Bauman (ed.), *A world of others' words: Cross-cultural perspectives on intertextuality*, 1–14. Malden: Blackwell.

Bawarshi, Anis S. & Mary Jo Reiff. 2010. *Genre: An introduction to history, theory, research, and pedagogy* (Reference Guides to Rhetoric and Composition). West Lafayette: Parlor Press and The WAC Clearinghouse.

Baym, Nancy K. 1993. Interpreting soap operas and creating community: Inside a computer-mediated fan culture. *Journal of Folklore Research* 30(2/3). 143–176.

Baym, Nancy K. 1995. The performance of humor in computer-mediated communication. *Journal of Computer-Mediated Communication* 1(2). http://onlinelibrary.wiley.com/enhanced/doi/10.1111/j.1083-6101.1995.tb00327.x (accessed 23 October 2018).

Baynham, Mike. 1995. *Literacy practices: Investigating literacy in social contexts* (Language in Social Life Series). London: Longman.

Bean, Thomas W. & Karen Moni. 2003. Developing students' critical literacy: Exploring identity construction in young adult fiction. *Journal of Adolescent and Adult Literacy* 46(8). 638–348.

Beck, Ann S. 2005. A place for critical literacy. *Journal of Adolescent and Adult Literacy* 48(5). 392–400.

Behrman, Edward H. 2006. Teaching about language, power, and text: A review of classroom practices that support critical literacy. *Journal of Adolescent and Adult Literacy* 49(6). 490–498.

Bell, Nancy D. 2007. How native and non-native English speakers adapt to humor in intercultural interaction. *Humor: International Journal of Humor Research* 20(1). 27–48.

Bell, Nancy D. 2009. Learning about and through humor in the second language classroom. *Language Teaching Research* 13(3). 241–258.

Bell, Nancy D. 2015. *We are not amused: Failed humor in interaction* (Humor Research 10). Berlin: Mouton De Gruyter.
Bell, Nancy D. 2017. Failed humor. In Salvatore Attardo (ed.), *The Routledge handbook of language and humor* (Routledge Handbooks in Linguistics), 356–370. New York: Routledge.
Bell, Nancy D. 2018. Pragmatics, humor studies and the study of interaction. In Cornelia Ilie & Neal R. Norrick (eds.), *Pragmatics and its interfaces* (Pragmatics and Beyond New Series 294), 291–309. Amsterdam: John Benjamins.
Bell, Nancy D., Scott Crossley & Christian F. Hempelmann. 2011. Wordplay in church marquees. *Humor: International Journal of Humor Research* 24(2). 187–202.
Bell, Nancy D. & Anne Pomerantz. 2014. Reconsidering language teaching through a focus on humor. *EuroAmerican Journal of Applied Linguistics and Languages* 1(1). 31–47.
Bell, Nancy D. & Anne Pomerantz. 2016. *Humor in the classroom: A guide for language teachers and educational researchers*. New York: Routledge.
Berglin, Ieva Tūna. 2009. "Really? You're gonna say 'tunes'?": The functions of register clashes in the television drama series *Gilmore Girls*. Västerås & Eskilstuna: Mälardalen University unpublished essay. http://mdh.diva-portal.org/smash/get/diva2:345243/FULLTEXT01.pdf (accessed 13 November 2018).
Bergson, Henri. 1911 [1901]. *Laughter: An essay on the meaning of the comic* [Le rire: Essai sur la signification du comique]. Temple of Earth Publishing. http://www.templeofearth.com/books/laughter.pdf (accessed 27 February 2018).
Bhatia, Vijay K. (1997). The power and politics of genre. *World Englishes* 16(3). 359–371.
Billig, Michael. 2001. Humor and hatred: The racist jokes of the Ku Klux Klan. *Discourse and Society* 12(3). 267–289.
Billig, Michael. 2005a. Comic racism and violence. In Sharon Lockyer & Michael Pickering (eds.), *Beyond a joke: The limits of humor*, 25–44. Basingstoke: Palgrave Macmillan.
Billig, Michael. 2005b. *Laughter and ridicule: Towards a social critique of humor* (Theory, Culture and Society). London: Sage.
Bishop, Elizabeth. 2014. Critical literacy: Bringing theory to praxis. *Journal of Curriculum Theorizing* 30(1). 51–63.
Blommaert, Jan. 2005. *Discourse: A critical introduction* (Key Topics in Sociolinguistics). Cambridge: Cambridge University Press.
Boespflug, François. 2011. Laughing at God: The pictorial history of boundaries not to be crossed. In Hans Geybels & Walter Van Herck (eds.), *Humor and religion: Challenges and ambiguities* (Continuum Religious Studies), 204–217. London: Continuum.
Boxman-Shabtai, Lillian & Limor Shifman. 2015. When ethnic humor goes digital. *New Media and Society* 17(4). 520–539.
Brandes, Stanley H. 1977. Peaceful protest: Spanish political humor in a time of crisis. *Western Folklore* 36(4). 331–346.
Briggs, Charles L. & Richard Bauman. 1992. Genre, intertextuality, and social power. *Journal of Linguistic Anthropology* 2(2). 131–172.
Brown, Gillian & George Yule. 1983. *Discourse analysis* (Cambridge Textbooks in Linguistics). Cambridge: Cambridge University Press.
Brown, Kristine. 1999. Developing critical literacy. Sydney: National Center for English Language Teaching and Research, Macquarie University. http://www.ameprc.mq.edu.au/docs/research_reports/professional_development_collection/Developing_Critical_Literacy.pdf (accessed 13 November 2018).

Bublitz, Wolfram & Axel Hübler (eds.). 2007. *Metapragmatics in use* (Pragmatics and Beyond New Series 165). Amsterdam: John Benjamins.

Bushnell, Cade. 2008. "Lego my keego!": An analysis of language play in a beginning Japanese as a foreign language classroom. *Applied Linguistics* 30(1). 49–69.

Cadiero-Kaplan, Karen. 2002. Literacy ideologies: Critically engaging the language arts curriculum. *Language Arts* 79(5). 372–381.

Caffi, Claudia. 1994. Metapragmatics. In Robert E. Asher & James Simpson (eds.), *The encyclopedia of language and linguistics*, 2461–2466. Oxford: Pergamon Press.

Cameron, Deborah. 2004. Out of the bottle: The social life of metalanguage. In Adam Jaworski, Nikolas Coupland & Dariusz Galasiński (eds.), *Metalanguage: Social and ideological perspectives* (Language, Power and Social Process 11), 311–321. Berlin: Mouton de Gruyter.

Canagarajah, A. Suresh. 2013. *Literacy as translingual practice: Between communities and classrooms*. New York: Routledge.

Canakis, Kostas. 1994. Diglossia as an agent of humor in the writings of Elena Akrita. *Journal of Modern Greek Studies* 12(2). 221–237.

Canestrari, Carla. 2010. Meta-communicative signals and humorous verbal interchanges: A case study. *Humor: International Journal of Humor Research* 23(3). 327–349.

Capelotti, João Paolo. 2016. Defending laughter: An account of Brazilian court cases involving humor, 1997–2014. *Humor: International Journal of Humor Research* 29(1). 25–47.

Carr, Jimmy & Lucy Greeves. 2006. *The naked jape: Uncovering the hidden world of jokes*. Harmondsworth: Penguin.

Cekaite, Asta & Karin Aronsson. 2004. Repetition and joking in children's second language conversations: Playful recyclings in an immersion classroom. *Discourse Studies* 6(3). 373–392.

Cervetti, Gina, Michael J. Pardales & James S. Damico. 2001. A tale of differences: Comparing the traditions, perspectives, and educational goals of critical reading and critical literacy. *Reading Online* 4 (9). https://eric.ed.gov/?id=EJ662487 (accessed 13 November 2018).

Chaniotakis, Nikos I. 2010. *Το χιούμορ στη διδασκαλία* [Humor in teaching]. Athens: Ellinika Grammata. [in Greek]

Charalambous, Constadina, Panayiota Charalambous, Kamran Khan & Ben Rampton. 2016. Security and language policy. *Working Papers in Urban Language and Literacies* 194. 1–19.

Chen, Khin Wee. 2013. The Singapore Mass Rapid Transport: A case study of the efficacy of a democratized political humor landscape in a critical engagement in the public sphere. *European Journal of Humor Research* 1(2). 43–68.

Chiaro, Delia. 1992. *The language of jokes: Analyzing verbal play* (The Interface Series). London: Routledge.

Chłopicki, Władysław. 1987. *An application of the script theory of semantics to the analysis of selected Polish humorous short stories*. West Lafayette: Purdue University dissertation.

Chłopicki, Władysław. 2002. How rich is rich? Or character frames in joke worlds. Paper presented at the 14th Conference of the International Society for Humor Studies (ISHS), Bertinoro, Italy, 3–7 July.

Chomsky, Noam. 1965. *Aspects of the theory of syntax*. Cambridge: MIT Press.

Chovanec, Jan. 2012. Conversational humor and joint fantasizing in online journalism. In Jan Chovanec & Isabel Ermida (eds.), *Language and humor in the media*, 139–161. Newcastle upon Tyne: Cambridge Scholars Publishing.

Chovanec, Jan & Marta Dynel. 2015. Researching interactional forms and participant structures in public and social media. In Marta Dynel & Jan Chovanec (eds.), *Participation in public and social media interactions* (Pragmatics and Beyond New Series 256), 1–23. Amsterdam: John Benjamins.

Chovanec, Jan & Villy Tsakona. 2018. Investigating the dynamics of humor: Towards a theory of interactional humor. In Villy Tsakona & Jan Chovanec (eds.), *The dynamics of interactional humor: Creating and negotiating humor in everyday encounters* (Topics in Humor Research 7), 1–26. Amsterdam: John Benjamins.

Chun, Elaine W. 2017. How to drop a name: Hybridity, purity, and the K-pop fan. *Language in Society* 46(1). 57–76.

Chun, Elaine & Keith Walters. 2011. Orienting to Arab orientalisms: Language, race, and humor in a *YouTube* video. In Crispin Thurlow & Kristine Mroczek (eds.), *Digital discourse: Language in the new media* (Oxford Studies in Sociolinguistics), 251–273. Oxford: Oxford University Press.

Clark, Romy & Roz Ivanič. 1999. Editorial. Raising critical awareness of language: A curriculum aim for the new millennium. *Language Awareness* 8(2). 63–70.

Coe, Richard M. 1994. Teaching genre as process. In Aviva Freedman & Peter Medway (eds.), *Learning and teaching genre* (Critical Perspectives on Literacy and Education), 157–172. Portsmouth: Heinemann/Boynton-Cook.

Comber, Barbara. 1993. Classroom explorations in critical literacy. *The Australian Journal of Language and Literacy* 16(1). 73–83.

Comber, Barbara & Anne Simpson (eds.). 2001. *Negotiating critical literacies in classrooms*. Mahwah: Lawrence Erlbaum Associates.

Constantinou, Maria. 2019. Charlie Hebdo's controversial cartoons in question: Stances, translational narratives and identity construction from a cross-linguistic perspective. *Social Semiotics* 29(5). 698–727.

Coogan, Peter. 2012. Genre: Reconstructing the superhero in *All-Star Superman*. In Matthew J. Smith & Randy Duncan (eds.), *Critical approaches to comics: Theories and methods*, 203–220. New York: Routledge.

Cook, Guy. 2000. *Language play, language learning* (Oxford Applied Linguistics). Oxford: Oxford University Press.

Cope, Bill & Mary Kalantzis (eds.). 2000. *Multiliteracies: Literacy learning and the design of social futures* (Literacies). London: Routledge.

Corduas, Marcella, Salvatore Attardo & Alyson Eggleston. 2008. The distribution of humor in literary texts is not random: A statistical analysis. *Language and Literature* 17(3). 253–270.

Correia, Rosane. 2006. Encouraging critical reading in the EFL classroom. *English Teaching Forum* 44. 16–19. https://files.eric.ed.gov/fulltext/EJ1107883.pdf (accessed 13 November 2018).

Cots, Josep M. 2006. Teaching "with an attitude": Critical discourse analysis in EFL teaching. *ELT Journal* 60(4). 336–345.

Coupland, Nikolas & Adam Jaworski. 2004. Sociolinguistic perspectives on metalanguage: Reflexivity, evaluation and ideology. In Adam Jaworski, Nikolas Coupland & Dariusz Galasiński (eds.), *Metalanguage: Social and ideological perspectives* (Language, Power and Social Process 11), 15–51. Berlin: Mouton de Gruyter.

Coutinho, Maria Antónia & Florencia Miranda. 2009. To describe genres: Problems and strategies. In Charles Bazerman, Adair Bonini & Débora Figueiredo (eds.), *Genre in a changing world* (Perspectives on Writing), 35–55. Fort Collins: The WAC Clearinghouse and Parlor Press.

Culpeper, Jonathan. 2011. *Impoliteness: Using language to cause offense* (Studies in Interactional Sociolinguistics 28). Cambridge: Cambridge University Press.

Culpeper, Jonathan & Michael Haugh. 2014. *Pragmatics and the English language.* (Perspectives on the English Language). Basingstoke: Palgrave Macmillan.

Curdt-Christiansen, Xiao Lan. 2010. Competing priorities: Singaporean teachers' perspectives on critical literacy. *International Journal of Educational Research* 49(6). 184–194.

Davies, Catherine Evans. 2003. How English-learners joke with native speakers: An interactional sociolinguistic perspective on humor as a collaborative discourse across cultures. *Journal of Pragmatics* 35(9). 1361–1385.

Davies, Catherine Evans. 2017. Sociolinguistic approaches to humor. In Salvatore Attardo (ed.), *The Routledge handbook of language and humor* (Routledge Handbooks in Linguistics), 472–488. New York: Routledge.

Davies, Christie. 1998. *Jokes and their relation to society* (Humour Research 4). Berlin: Mouton de Gruyter.

Davies, Christie. 2004. The right to joke (Research report 37). Great Britain: The Social Affairs Unit, St. Edmundsbury Press. http://socialaffairsunit.org.uk/digipub/index2.php?option=content&do_pdf=1&id=11 (accessed 17 November 2018).

Davies, Christie. 2007. Humor and protest: Jokes under Communism. *International Review of Social History* 52(15). 291–305.

Davies, Christie. 2008. The Danish cartoons, the Muslims and the new battle of Jutland. In Paul Lewis (ed.), *The Muhammad cartoons and humor research: A collection of essays. Humor: International Journal of Humor Research* 21(1). 2–7.

Davies, Christie. 2011. *Jokes and targets*. Bloomington: Indiana University Press.

Davies, Christie. 2018. Jokes and insults: Language and aggression. In Arie Sover (ed.), *The languages of humor: Verbal, visual, and physical humor* (Bloomsbury Advances in Semiotics), 15–35. London: Bloomsbury Academic.

de Jongste, Henri. 2013. Negotiating humor intent. In Marta Dynel (ed.), *Developments in linguistic humor theory* (Topics in Humor Research 1), 179–210. Amsterdam: John Benjamins.

Deliroka, Sideri & Villy Tsakona. 2018. Exploring identities in the ELF class: A critical proposal. *Brno Studies in English* 44(1). 5–26.

Dilmaç, Julie Alev & Özker Kocadal. 2018. Syrian refugees in Turkish cartoons: A social semiotic analysis. *Studii de Lingvuistică* 8. 211–229.

Dore, Margherita. 2018a. Controversial humor in advertising: Social and cultural implications. In Francois Maon, Adam Lindgreen, Joelle Vanhamme, Robert J. Angell & Juliet Memery (eds.), *Not All Claps and Cheers: Humor in Business and Society Relationships*, 132–145. London: Routledge.

Dore, Margherita. 2018b. Laughing *at* you or laughing *with* you? Humor negotiation in intercultural stand-up comedy. In Villy Tsakona & Jan Chovanec (eds.), *The dynamics of interactional humor: Creating and negotiating humor in everyday encounters* (Topics in Humor Research 7), 105–126. Amsterdam: John Benjamins.

Dowling, Jacqueline S. 2014. School-age children talking about humor: Data from a focus group. *Humor: International Journal of Humor Research* 27(1). 121–139.

Duranti, Alessandro & Charles Goodwin (eds.). 1992. *Rethinking context: Language as an interactive phenomenon* (Studies in the Social and Cultural Foundations of Language 11). Cambridge: Cambridge University Press.

Dynel, Marta. 2009. Beyond a joke: Types of conversational humor. *Language and Linguistics Compass* 3(5). 1284–1299.
Dynel, Marta. 2011. Joker in the pack. Towards determining the status of humorous framing in conversations. In Marta Dynel (ed.), *The pragmatics of humor across discourse domains* (Pragmatics and Beyond New Series 210), 217–241. Amsterdam: John Benjamins.
Dynel, Marta. 2017. Academics vs. American scriptwriters vs academics: A battle over the etic and emic "sarcasm" and "irony" labels. *Language and Communication* 55. 69–87.
Dynel, Marta. 2018. No child's play: A philosophical pragmatic view of overt pretense. In Villy Tsakona & Jan Chovanec (eds.), *The dynamics of interactional humor: Creating and negotiating humor in everyday encounters* (Topics in Humor Research 7), 205–228. Amsterdam: John Benjamins.
Dynel, Marta & Fabio I. M. Poppi. 2019. Risum teneatis, amici? The socio-pragmatics of RoastMe humor. *Journal of Pragmatics* 139. 1–21.
Ekdale, Brian & Melissa Tully. 2014. Makmende Amerudi: Kenya's collective reimagining as a meme of aspiration. *Critical Studies in Media Communication* 31(4). 283–298.
Ekdosi.com. 2011. Διαφήμιση Γερμανού "Μπάμιες όπως τις κάνει η μανούλα μου" [Germanos' advertisement "Okras like my mummy cooks them"]. http://christossainis.blogspot.com/2011/04/antispot.html (accessed 28 June 2011).
El Refaie, Elisabeth. 2011. The pragmatics of humor reception: Young people's responses to a newspaper cartoon. *Humor: International Journal of Humor Research* 24(1). 87–108.
Ermida, Isabel. 2008. *The language of comic narratives: Humor construction in short stories* (Humor Research 9). Berlin: Mouton de Gruyter.
Evans, Janet (ed.). 2004. *Literacy moves on: Using popular culture, new technologies and critical literacy in the primary classroom* (Informing Teaching Series). London: David Fulton.
Fairclough, Norman. 1989. *Language and power* (Language in Social Life Series 1). London: Longman.
Fairclough, Norman (ed.). 1992a. *Critical language awareness* (Real Language Series). London: Longman.
Fairclough, Norman. 1992b. *Discourse and social change*. Cambridge: Polity Press.
Fairclough, Norman. 1995. *Critical discourse analysis: The critical study of language* (Language in Social Life). London: Longman.
Farias, Miguel. 2005. Critical language awareness in foreign language learning. *Literatura y Lingüística* 16. 211–222. http://www.scielo.cl/scielo.php?pid=s0716-58112005000100012&script=sci_arttext (accessed 13 November 2018).
Felipe Fajardo, Margarita. 2015. A review of critical literacy beliefs and practices of English language learners and teachers. *University of Sydney Papers in TESOL* 10. 29–56.
Fetzer, Anita. 2004. *Recontextualizing context: Grammaticality meets appropriateness* (Pragmatics and Beyond New Series 121). Amsterdam: John Benjamins.
Fetzer, Anita & Etsuko Oishi (eds.). 2011. *Context and contexts: Parts meet whole?* (Pragmatics and Beyond New Series 209). Amsterdam: John Benjamins.
Filani, Ibukun. 2017. On joking contexts: An example of stand-up comedy. *Humor: International Journal of Humor Research* 30(4). 439–461.
Finkbeiner, Rita, Jörg Meibauer & Petra B. Schumacher (eds.). 2012. *What is context?* (Linguistik Aktuell/Linguistics Today 196). Amsterdam: John Benjamins.
Forman, Ross. 2011. Humorous language play in a Thai EFL classroom. *Applied Linguistics* 32(5). 541–565.

Freedman, Aviva & Peter Medway. 1994. Locating genre studies: Antecedents and prospects. In Aviva Freedman & Peter Medway (eds.), *Genre and the New Rhetoric* (Critical Perspectives on Literacy and Education), 2–18. London: Taylor and Francis.

Freire, Paulo. 1972. *Pedagogy of the oppressed* (Penguin Education). London: Penguin.

Freud, Sigmund. 1991 [1905]. *Jokes and their relation to the unconscious* [Der Witz und seine Beziehung zum Unbewussten] (The Penguin Freud Library 6). London: Penguin.

Fterniati, Anna, Argiris Archakis, Villy Tsakona & Vasia Tsami. 2015. Scrutinizing humorous mass culture texts in class: A critical language teaching proposal. *Israeli Journal of Humor Research* 4(1). 28–52.

Gardner, Scott. 2010. Discourse shifting for humorous effect: The Python method. *Bulletin of Graduate School of Education Okayama University* 145. 39–46.

Gasteratou, Spyridoula. 2016. *Διδάσκοντας το χιούμορ στη δεύτερη γλώσσα: Μία εναλλακτική προσέγγιση στα πλαίσια του κριτικού γραμματισμού* [Teaching about humor in L2: An alternative approach in the framework of critical literacy]. Athens: National and Kapodistrian University of Athens MA thesis. [in Greek]

General Secretariat for Gender Equality. 2011. Δελτίο τύπου. Καταγγελία στο Εθνικό Συμβούλιο Ραδιοτηλεόρασης [Press release. Complaint to the National Council of Radio and Television]. http://www.isotita.gr/var/uploads/PRESS%20%28APO%20SEP%202010%29/germanos%20advert%203_3_11.pdf (accessed 28 June 2011).

Georgakopoulou, Alexandra. 2000. On the sociolinguistics of popular films: Funny characters, funny voices. *Journal of Modern Greek Studies* 18(1). 119–133.

Georgakopoulou, Alexandra. 2007. *Small stories, interaction and identities* (Studies in Narrative 8). Amsterdam: John Benjamins.

Georgakopoulou, Alexandra & Dionysis Goutsos. 2004. *Discourse analysis: An introduction*, 2nd edn. Edinburgh: Edinburgh University Press.

Gérin, Annie. 2013. A second look at laughter: Humor in the visual arts. *Humor: International Journal of Humor Research* 26(1). 155–176.

Germanos advertisement–mpamies [money back]. 2011. http://www.youtube.com/watch?v=6kQhzPziRFs (accessed 28 June 2011). [in Greek]

Geybels, Hans & Walter Van Herck (eds.). 2011. *Humor and religion: Challenges and ambiguities* (Continuum Religious Studies). London: Continuum.

Goatly, Andrew. 2012. *Meaning and humor* (Key Topics in Semantics and Pragmatics). Cambridge: Cambridge University Press.

Gonulal, Talip. 2018. Investigating the potential of humor in EFL classrooms: An attitudinal study. *European Journal of Humor Research* 6(1). 141–161.

Grice, H. Paul. 1975. Logic and conversation. In Peter Cole & Jerry L. Morgan (eds.), *Syntax and semantics, Volume 3: Speech acts*, 41–58. London: Academic Press.

Gruner, Charles R. 1978. *Understanding laughter: The workings of wit and humor*. Chicago: Nelson-Hall.

Gruner, Charles R. 1997. *The game of humor: A comprehensive theory of why we laugh*. New Brunswick: Transaction.

Gumperz, John J. 1982. *Discourse strategies* (Studies in Interactional Sociolinguistics 1). Cambridge: Cambridge University Press.

Hale, Adrian. 2016. The risks and rewards of teaching with humor in Western Sydney: Adapting pedagogy to complex demographics. *EuroAmerican Journal of Applied Linguistics and Languages* 3(2). 22–41.

Hale, Adrian. 2018a. "I get it but it's just not funny": Why humor fails, after all is said and done. *European Journal of Humor Research* 6(1). 36–61.

Hale, Adrian. 2018b. There *is* an after–life (for jokes, anyway): The potential for, and appeal of, "immortality" in humor. *Humor: International Journal of Humor Research* 31(3). 507–538.

Hann, David. 2017. Building rapport and a sense of communal identity through play in a second language classroom. In Nancy D. Bell (ed.), *Multiple perspectives on language play* (Language Play and Creativity 1), 219–244. Boston: Mouton de Gruyter.

Harwood, Debbie. 2008. Deconstructing and reconstructing Cinderella: Theoretical defense of critical literacy for young children. *Language and Literacy* 10(2). http://ejournals.library.ualberta.ca/index.php/langandlit/article/view/9777 (accessed 15 November 2018).

Hatzithomas, Leonidas D. 2008. *Το χιούμορ στην τηλεοπτική διαφήμιση* [Humor in television advertisements] (Topics in Communication and Marketing 6). Thessaloniki: University Studio Press. [in Greek]

Hay, Jennifer. 2001. The pragmatics of humor support. *Humor: International Journal of Humor Research* 14(1). 55–82.

Hempelmann, Christian F. 2016. Humor in the teaching of writing: A microethnographic approach. *EuroAmerican Journal of Applied Linguistics and Languages* 3(2). 42–55.

Hempelmann, Christian F. 2017. Key terms in the field of humor. In Salvatore Attardo (ed.), *The Routledge handbook of language and humor* (Routledge Handbooks in Linguistics), 34–48. New York: Routledge.

Hill, Jane H. 2008. *The everyday language of White racism* (Blackwell Studies in Discourse and Culture 3). Malden: Wiley–Blackwell.

Hiramoto, Mie. 2011. Is dat dog you're eating?: Mock Philipino, Hawai'i Creole, and local elitism. *Pragmatics* 21(3). 341–371.

Hlynka, Anthony & Nancy Nelson Knupfer. 1997. A thinking person's comedy: A study of intertextuality in "Cheers". In Robert E. Griffin, J. Mark Hunter, Carole B. Schiffman & William J. Gibbs (eds.), *VisionQuest: Journeys toward visual literacy. Selected readings from the Annual Conference of the International Visual Literacy Association (28th, Cheyenne, Wyoming, October, 1996)*, 401–410. https://eric.ed.gov/?id=ED408995 (accessed 31 October 2018).

Hobbs, Pamela. 2007. Judges' use of humor as a social corrective. *Journal of Pragmatics* 39(1). 50–68.

Hoicka, Elena. 2016. Understanding of humorous intentions: A developmental approach. In Leonor Ruiz–Gurillo (ed.), *Metapragmatics of humor: Current research trends* (IVITRA: Research in Linguistics and Literature 14), 257–272. Amsterdam: John Benjamins.

Holcomb, Christopher. 1997. A class of clowns: Spontaneous joking in computer–assisted discussions. *Computers and Composition* 14(1). 3–18.

Hong, Nathaniel. 2010. Mow 'em all down grandma: The "weapon" of humor in two Danish World War II occupation scrapbooks. *Humor: International Journal of Humor Research* 23(1). 27–64.

Howitt, Dennis & Kwame Owusu–Bempah. 2005. Race and ethnicity in popular humor. In Sharon Lockyer & Michael Pickering (eds.), *Beyond a joke: The limits of humor*, 44–62. Basingstoke: Palgrave Macmillan.

Ήρθε ο ερπετολόγος Ολιβιέ Μπεχρά για τον Σήφη τον κροκόδειλο [Herpetologist Olivier Behra is here for Sifis the crocodile]. 2014. *Newsbomb.gr*, 26 August. http://www.newsbomb.

gr/ellada/news/story/487859/irthe-o-erpetologos-olivie-mpehra-gia-ton-sifi-ton-krokodeilo (accessed 23 October 2018). [in Greek]

Hübler, Axel. 2011. Metapragmatics. In Wolfram Bublitz & Neal R. Norrick (eds.), *Foundations of pragmatics* (Handbooks of Pragmatics 1), 107–136. Berlin: Mouton de Gruyter.

Hübler, Axel & Wolfram Bublitz. 2007. Introducing metapragmatics in use. In Wolfram Bublitz & Axel Hübler (eds.), *Metapragmatics in use* (Pragmatics and Beyond New Series 165), 1–26. Amsterdam: John Benjamins.

Hunston, Susan & Geoff Thompson (eds.). 1999. *Evaluation in text: Authorial stance and the construction of discourse*. Oxford: Oxford University Press.

Huth, Thorsten. 2017. Playing with turns, playing with action? A social-interactionist perspective. In Nancy D. Bell (ed.), *Multiple perspectives on language play* (Language Play and Creativity 1), 47–72. Boston: Mouton de Gruyter.

Hymes, Dell H. 1972. On communicative competence. In John B. Pride & Janet Holmes (eds.), *Sociolinguistics: Selected readings*, 269–293. Harmondsworth: Penguin.

İçmez, Simla. 2009. Motivation and critical reading in EFL classrooms: A case of ELT preparatory students. *Journal of Theory and Practice in Education* 5. 123–147. http://dergipark.gov.tr/download/article-file/63223 (accessed 13 November 2018).

Irvine, Judith T. & Susan Gal. 2000. Language ideology and linguistic differentiation. In Paul V. Kroskrity (eds.), *Regimes of language: Ideologies, polities, and identities* (School of American Research Advanced Seminar Series), 35–84. Santa Fe: School of American Research Press.

Ismailidou, Elli. 2011. Η διαφήμιση, οι μπάμιες και ο φεμινισμός [The advertisement, okras and feminism]. *Το Βήμα* [The Podium], 13 March. https://www.tovima.gr/2011/03/13/society/i-diafimisi-oi-mpamies-kai-o-feminismos (accessed 17 November 2018). [in Greek]

Jakobson, Roman. 1971 [1957]. Shifters, verbal categories, and the Russian verb. In *Selected writings II: Word and language*, 130–147. The Hague: Mouton.

Janks, Hilary. 2000. Dominance, access, diversity, and design: A synthesis for critical literacy education. *Educational Review* 52(1). 15–30.

Janks, Hilary, Kerryn Dixon, Ana Ferreira, Stella Granville & Denise Newfield. 2014. *Doing critical literacy: Texts and activities for students and teachers* (Language, Culture, and Teaching). New York: Routledge.

Jaspers, Jürgen. 2005. Doing ridiculous: Linguistic sabotage in an institutional context of monolingualism and standardization. *Working papers in Urban Language and Literacies* 28. https://www.kcl.ac.uk/sspp/departments/education/research/Research-Centres/ldc/publications/workingpapers/abstracts/WP028-Doing-ridiculous-Linguistic-sabotage-in-an-institutional-context-of-monolingualism-and-standardisation.aspx (accessed 13 November 2018).

Jaworski, Adam, Nikolas Coupland & Dariusz Galasiński (eds.). 2004a. *Metalanguage: Social and ideological perspectives* (Language, Power and Social Process 11). Berlin: Mouton De Gruyter.

Jaworski, Adam, Nikolas Coupland & Dariusz Galasiński. 2004b. Metalanguage: Why now? In Adam Jaworski, Nikolas Coupland & Dariusz Galasiński (eds.), *Metalanguage: Social and ideological perspectives* (Language, Power and Social Process 11), 3–8. Berlin: Mouton de Gruyter.

Johns, Ann M. (ed.). 2002. *Genre in the classroom: Multiple perspectives*. Mahwah: Laurence Erlbaum Associates.

Jones, Rodney. 2012. Introduction: Discourse and creativity. In Rodney Jones (ed.), *Discourse and creativity* (Longman Applied Linguistics), 1–13. Harlow: Pearson.

Jones, Stephanie & Lane W. Clarke. 2007. Disconnections: Pushing readers beyond connections and toward the critical. *Pedagogies: An International Journal* 2(2). 95–115.

Jonsson, Rickard. 2018. Swedes can't swear: Making fun at a multiethnic secondary school. *Journal of Language, Identity and Education* 17(5). 320–335.

Kádár, Dániel Z. & Michael Haugh. 2013. *Understanding politeness*. Cambridge: Cambridge University Press.

Kanaana, Sharif. 1995. Palestinian humor during the Gulf War. *Journal of Folklore Research* 32(1). 65–75.

Karachaliou, Rania & Argiris Archakis. 2018. Reactions to jab lines in conversational storytelling. In Villy Tsakona & Jan Chovanec (eds.), *The dynamics of interactional humor: Creating and negotiating humor in everyday encounters* (Topics in Humor Research 7), 29–56. Amsterdam: John Benjamins.

Karagiannaki, Evanthia & Anastasia G. Stamou. 2018. Bringing critical discourse analysis into the classroom: A critical language awareness project on fairy tales for young school children. *Language Awareness* 27(3). 222–242.

Kerkkänen, Paavo. 2006. Results of scientific humor studies in media interviews: How important is scientific significance? Paper presented at the 18th Conference of the International Society for Humor Studies, Danish University of Education, 3–7 July.

Kersten, Holger. 2019. America's faith in the laugh resistance – popular beliefs about political humor in the 2016 presidential election. *Humor: International Journal of Humor Research* 32(2). 299–316.

Kim, Jiyun. 2017. Teaching language learners how to understand sarcasm in L2 English. In Nancy D. Bell (ed.), *Multiple perspectives on language play* (Language Play and Creativity 1), 317–346. Boston: Mouton de Gruyter.

Klumbytė, Neringa. 2011. Political intimacy: Power, laughter, and coexistence in late Soviet Lithuania. *East European Politics and Societies* 25(4). 659–677.

Kolek, Leszek S. 1985. Toward a poetics of comic narratives: Notes on the semiotic structure of jokes. *Semiotica* 53(1–3). 145–163.

Kontio, Janne. 2017. Making fun of language use: Teasing practices and hybrid language forms in auto mechanic student peer interaction. *Linguistics and Education* 37. 22–31.

Kontovourki, Stavroula & Elena Ioannidou. 2013. Κριτικός γραμματισμός στο κυπριακό σχολείο: Αντιλήψεις, πρακτικές και στάσεις εκπαιδευτικών [Critical literacy in the Cypriot school: Teachers' views, practices and attitudes]. *Preschool and School Education* 1(1). 82–107. [in Greek]

Kotthoff, Helga. 1999. Coherent keying in conversational humor: Contextualizing joint fictionalization. In Wolfram Bublitz, Uta Lenk & Eija Ventola (eds.), *Coherence in spoken and written discourse. How to create it and how to describe it. Selected papers from the International Workshop on Coherence, Augsburg, 24–27 April 1997* (Pragmatics and Beyond New Series 63), 125–150. Amsterdam: John Benjamins.

Kotthoff, Helga. 2006. Pragmatics of performance and the analysis of conversational humor. *Humor: International Journal of Humor Research* 19(3). 271–304.

Kotthoff, Helga. 2007. Oral genres of humor: On the dialectic of genre knowledge and creative authoring. *Pragmatics* 17(2). 263–296.

Koupaee Dar, Zeinab, Ali Rahimi & Mohammad Reza Shams. 2010. Teaching reading with a critical attitude: Using Critical Discourse Analysis (CDA) to raise EFL university students' Critical Language Awareness (CLA). *International Journal of Criminology and Sociological*

Theory 3. 457–476. https://ijcst.journals.yorku.ca/index.php/ijcst/article/view/30585/28534 (accessed 13 November 2018).

Koutsogiannis, Dimitris. 2017. *Η γλωσσική διδασκαλία χθες, σήμερα, αύριο: Μια πολιτική προσέγγιση* [Language teaching yesterday, today, tomorrow: A political approach]. Thessaloniki: Institute of Modern Greek Studies (Manolis Triandaphyllidis Foundation). [in Greek]

Kramer, Elise. 2011. The playful is political: The metapragmatics of internet rape–joke arguments. *Language in Society* 40(2). 137–168.

Kramsch, Claire. 2008. Ecological perspectives on foreign language education. *Language Teaching* 41(3). 389–408.

Kristiansen, Tore. 2004. Social meaning and norm–ideals for speech in a Danish community. In Adam Jaworski, Nikolas Coupland & Dariusz Galasiński (eds.), *Metalanguage: Social and ideological perspectives* (Language, Power and Social Process 11), 167–192. Berlin: Mouton de Gruyter.

Κρήτη: Ο «Σήφης» κατάγεται από το Νείλο και είναι… καλοταϊσμένος [Crete: "Sifis" originates in the Nile and he is… well–fed]. 2014. *Skai.gr*, 29 August. http://www.skai.gr/news/environment/article/264545/kriti-o-sifis-katagetai-apo-to-neilo-kai-einai-kalotaismenos (accessed 23 October 2018). [in Greek]

Κροκόδειλος περίπου δύο μέτρων σε φράγμα στην Κρήτη [Crocodile almost two meters long in a dam in Crete]. 2014. *Το Βήμα* [The Podium], 4 July. http://www.tovima.gr/society/article/?aid=612462 (accessed 23 October 2018). [in Greek]

Kuipers, Giselinde. 2006. *Good humor, bad taste: A sociology of the joke* (Humour Research 7). Berlin: Mouton de Gruyter.

Kuipers, Giselinde. 2008a. The Muhammad cartoon controversy and the globalization of humor. In Paul Lewis (ed.), *The Muhammad cartoons and humor research: A collection of essays. Humor: International Journal of Humor Research* 21(1). 7–16.

Kuipers, Giselinde. 2008b. The sociology of humor. In Victor Raskin (ed.), *The primer of humor research* (Humor Research 8), 361–398. Berlin: Mouton de Gruyter.

Kuipers, Giselinde. 2009. Humor styles and symbolic boundaries. *Journal of Literary Theory* 3(2). 219–240.

Labov, William. 1972. *Language in the inner city: Studies in Black English Vernacular.* Philadelphia: University of Pennsylvania Press.

Laineste, Liisi. 2008. *Post–socialist jokes in Estonia: Continuity and change.* Tartu: University of Tartu dissertation. https://www.etis.ee/portaal/publicationInfo.aspx?PubVID=53&LanguageVID=1&FullTranslate=false (accessed 12 January 2014).

Laineste, Liisi. 2009. Conclusion. In Arvo Krikmann & Liisi Laineste (eds.), *Permitted laughter: Socialist, post–socialist and never–socialist humor*, 371–406. Tartu: ELM Scholarly Press.

Laineste, Liisi. 2011. Politics of taste in a post–Socialist state: A case study. In Villy Tsakona & Diana Elena Popa (eds.), *Studies in political humor: In between political critique and public entertainment* (Discourse Approaches to Politics, Society and Culture 46), 217–241. Amsterdam: John Benjamins.

Laineste, Liisi & Piret Voolaid. 2016. Laughing across borders: Intertextuality of internet memes. *European Journal of Humor Research* 4(4). 26–49.

Lam, Wan Shun Eva. 2006. Re–envisioning language, literacy and the immigrant subject in new mediascapes. *Pedagogies: An International Journal* 1(3). 171–195.

Larkin-Galiñanes, Cristina. 2017. An overview of humor theory. In Salvatore Attardo (ed.), *The Routledge handbook of language and humor* (Routledge Handbooks in Linguistics), 4–16. New York: Routledge.

Lau, Man Chu. 2010. *Practicing critical literacy work with English language learners: An integrative approach*. Toronto: University of Toronto dissertation. https://tspace.li brary.utoronto.ca/bitstream/1807/24804/1/Lau_Man_Chu_201006_PhD_thesis.pdf (accessed 13 November 2018).

Lefkowitz, Natalie & John S. Hedgcock. 2017. Anti-language: Linguistic innovation, identity construction, and group affiliation among emerging speech communities. In Nancy D. Bell (ed.), *Multiple perspectives on language play* (Language Play and Creativity 1), 347–376. Boston: Mouton de Gruyter.

Lentin, Alana. 2004. *Racism and anti-racism in Europe*. London: Pluto Press.

Lewis, Paul (ed.). 2008. The Muhammad cartoons and humor research: A collection of essays. *Humor: International Journal of Humor Research* 21(1). 1–46.

Linell, Per. 1998. *Approaching dialogue: Talk, interaction and contexts in dialogical perspectives* (Impact: Studies in Language and Society 3). Amsterdam: John Benjamins.

Lockyer, Sharon. 2006. Heard the one about... applying mixed methods in humor research? *International Journal of Social Research Methodology* 9(1). 41–59.

Lockyer, Sharon & Michael Pickering. 2001. Dear shit-shovellers: Humor, censure and the discourse of complaint. *Discourse and Society* 12(5). 633–651.

Lockyer, Sharon & Michael Pickering (eds.). 2005. *Beyond a joke: The limits of humor*. Basingstoke: Palgrave Macmillan.

Lockyer, Sharon & Michael Pickering. 2008. You must be joking: The sociological critique of humor and comic media. *Sociology Compass* 2(3). 808–820.

Loizou, Eleni & Maria Kyriakou. 2016. Young children's appreciation and production of verbal and visual humor. *Humor: International Journal of Humor Research* 29(1). 99–124.

Lucy, John A. (ed.). 1993. *Reflexive language: Reported speech and metapragmatics*. Cambridge: Cambridge University Press.

Luke, Allan. 2000. Critical literacy in Australia: A matter of context and standpoint. *Journal of Adolescent and Adult Literacy* 43(5). 448–461.

Luke, Allan & Karen T. Dooley. 2011. Critical literacy and second language learning. In Eli Hinkel (ed.), *Handbook of research on second language teaching and learning, Volume 2* (ESL and Applied Linguistics Professional Series), 856–868. New York: Routledge.

Lytra, Vally. 2007. *Play frames and social identities: Contact encounters in a Greek primary school* (Pragmatics and Beyond New Series 163). Amsterdam: John Benjamins.

Majors, Yolanda J. 2007. Narrations of cross-cultural encounters as interpretive frames for reading *word* and *world*. *Discourse and Society* 18(4). 479–505.

Malinowski, Bronislaw. 1989 [1923]. The problem of meaning in primitive languages. In Charles Kay Ogden & Ivor Armstrong Richards, *The meaning of meaning: A study of the influence of language upon thought and the science of symbolism*, 296–336. San Diego: Harvest/Harcourt Brace Jovanovich.

Malmquist, Karl. 2015. Satire, racist humor and the power of (un)laughter: On the restrained nature of Swedish online racist discourse targeting EU-migrants begging for money. *Discourse and Society* 26(6). 733–753.

Manteli, Vicky. 2011. Humor and... Stalin in a National Theatre of Greece postmodern production: *Stalin: A discussion about Modern Greek theatre*. In Villy Tsakona & Diana

Elena Popa (eds.), *Studies in political humor: In between political critique and public entertainment* (Discourse Approaches to Politics, Society and Culture 46), 243–270. Amsterdam: John Benjamins.

Marciniak, Przemysław. 2011. Laughing against all the odds. Some observations on humor, laughter and religion in Byzantium. In Hans Geybels & Walter Van Herck (eds.), *Humor and religion: Challenges and ambiguities* (Continuum Religious Studies), 141–155. London: Continuum.

Marone, Vittorio. 2015. Online humor as a community–building cushioning glue. *European Journal of Humor Research* 3(1). 61–83.

Maroniti, Katerina. 2017. *Η γλωσσική ποικιλότητα στον λόγο της μαζικής κουλτούρας: Αναπαραστάσεις της και ανάπτυξη ενός εκπαιδευτικού προγράμματος για παιδιά προσχολικής και πρωτοσχολικής ηλικίας* [Sociolinguistic diversity in popular culture discourse: Representations and development of a project for preschool children and pupils in the first school years]. Florina: University of Western Macedonia dissertation. https://www.didaktorika.gr/eadd/handle/10442/42063 (accessed 17 November 2018). [in Greek]

Mauranen, Anna. 2010. Discourse reflexivity – A discourse universal? The case of ELF. *Nordic Journal of English Studies* 9(2). 13–40.

McBride, Keally D. 2005. *Collective dreams: Political imagination and community.* Pennsylvania: The Pennsylvania State University Press.

McKinney, Julia & Elaine W. Chun. 2017. Celebrations of a satirical song: Ideologies of anti–racism in the media. In Nancy D. Bell (ed.), *Multiple perspectives on language play* (Language Play and Creativity 1), 377–401. Boston: Mouton de Gruyter.

Μένει Κρήτη ο «Σήφης» ο κροκόδειλος (;), που μπορεί να μην είναι μόνος [In Crete stays "Sifis" the crocodile (?), who may not be alone] 2014. *Skai.gr*, 10 July. http://www.skai.gr/news/environment/article/261798/menei-kriti-o-sifis-o-krokodeilos-pou-borei-na-min-einai-monos/?utm_source=feedburner&utm_campaign=Feed%3A+skai%2FUulu+%28%CE%A3%CE%9A%CE%91%CE%AA+-+%CE%9A%CF%85%CF%81%CE%B9%CF%8C%CF%84%CE%B5%CF%81%CE%B5%CF%82+%CE%95%CE%B9%CE%B4%CE%AE%CF%83%CE%B5%CE%B9%CF%82%29&utm_medium=feed&utm_content=FaceBook (accessed 23 October 2018). [in Greek]

Miller, Carolyn R. 1994. Genre as social action. In Aviva Freedman & Peter Medway (eds.), *Genre and the New Rhetoric* (Critical Perspectives on Literacy and Education), 20–36. London: Taylor and Francis.

Milner, Ryan M. 2013. Pop polyvocality: Internet memes, public participation, and the Occupy Wall Street Movement. *International Journal of Communication* 7. 2357–2390.

Milner Davis, Jessica & Sharyn Roach Anleu (eds.). 2018. *Judges, judging and humor.* New York: Palgrave Macmillan.

Miltner, Kate M. 2014. "There's no place for lulz on LOLCats": The role of genre, gender and group identity in the interpretation and enjoyment of an internet meme. *First Monday* 19(8). http://firstmonday.org/ojs/index.php/fm/article/view/5391/4103 (accessed 23 October 2018).

Moalla, Asma. 2013. Tunisia in the aftermath of the revolution: Insights into the use of humor on Facebook to create social bonds and develop relational identity. *SAGE Open* 3(3). 1–7.

Morreall, John. 1983. *Taking laughter seriously.* Albany: State University of New York Press.

Morreall, John. 2008. Philosophy and religion. In Victor Raskin (ed.), *The primer of humor research* (Humor Research 8), 211–242. Berlin: Mouton de Gruyter.

Morreall, John. 2009. *Comic relief: A comprehensive philosophy of humor* (New Directions in Aesthetics 9). Chichester: Wiley-Blackwell.
Morreall, John. 2010. Comic vices and comic virtues. *Humor: International Journal of Humor Research* 23(1). 1–26.
Moschonas, Spiros A. 2005. *Ιδεολογία και γλώσσα* [Ideology and language]. Athens: Patakis. [in Greek]
Mulkay, Michael. 1988. *On humor: Its nature and its place in modern society*. Cambridge: Polity Press.
Naked men on the beach. 2011. http://antres-gumnoi.blogspot.com/2011/03/blog-post_04.html (accessed 28 June 2011).
Neff, Peter & John Rucynski. 2017. Japanese perceptions of humor in the English language classroom. *Humor: International Journal of Humor Research* 30(3). 279–301.
Nesi, Hilary. 2012. Laughter in university lectures. *Journal of English for Academic Purposes* 11(2). 79–89.
Norrick, Neal R. 1993. *Conversational joking: Humor in everyday talk*. Bloomington: Indiana University Press.
Norrick, Neal R. 2001. On the conversational performance of narrative jokes: Toward an account of timing. *Humor: International Journal of Humor Research* 14(3). 255–274.
Norrick, Neal R. 2004. Non-verbal humor and joke performance. *Humor: International Journal of Humor Research* 17(4). 401–409.
Norrick, Neal R. & Delia Chiaro (eds.). 2009. *Humor in interaction* (Pragmatics and Beyond New Series 182). Amsterdam: John Benjamins.
Norrick, Neal R. & Janine Klein. 2008. Class clowns: Talking out of turn with an orientation toward humor. *Lodz Papers in Pragmatics* 4(1). 83–107.
North, Sarah. 2006. Making connections with new technologies. In Janet Maybin & Joan Swann (eds.), *The art of English: Everyday creativity*, 209–260. Basingstoke: Palgrave Macmillan and The Open University.
Norton, Bonny. 2008. Identity, language learning and critical pedagogies. In Jasone Cenoz and Nancy H. Hornberger (eds.), *Encyclopedia of language and education, Volume 6: Knowledge about language*, 45–58. New York: Springer.
Obrdlik, Antonin J. 1942. "Gallows humor" – A sociological phenomenon. *American Journal of Sociology* 47(5). 709–716.
Olson, David R. 1990. When a learner attempts to become literate in a second language, what is he or she attempting? *TESL TALK* 20(1). 18–22.
Oring, Elliott. 2008. Humor in anthropology and folklore. In Victor Raskin (ed.), *The primer of humor research* (Humor Research 8), 183–210. Berlin: Mouton De Gruyter.
Özdemir, Özlem & Emrah Özdemir. 2017. Whose problem is it anyway? The depiction of Syrian refugee influx in political cartoons. *Syria Studies* 9(1). 33–63.
Palmer, Jerry. 1994. *Taking humor seriously*. London: Routledge.
Park, Ji Hoon, Nadine G. Gabbadon & Ariel R. Chernin. 2006. Naturalizing racial differences through comedy: Asian, Black, and White views on racial stereotypes in *Rush Hour 2*. *Journal of Communication* 56 (1). 157–177.
Parker, Christina A. 2012. Conflicts and "Canadian" identities embedded in citizenship education: Diverse immigrant students' experiences. In Peter Cunningham & Nathan Fretwell (eds.), *Creating communities: Local, national and global*, 623–635. London: CiCe.

Parker, Christina A. 2016. *Peacebuilding, citizenship, and identity: Empowering conflict and dialogue in multicultural classrooms* (Transnational Education and Migration 2). Rotterdam: Sense.

Paximadaki, Sofianna. 2016. *Πολυγραμματισμοί: Αξιοποίηση γελοιογραφιών στη διδασκαλία της νεοελληνικής γλώσσας* [Multililteracies: The exploitation of cartoons in Modern Greek language teaching]. Educartoon. [in Greek]

Peck, Andrew M. 2014. A laugh riot: Photoshopping as vernacular discursive practice. *International Journal of Communication* 8. 1638–1662.

Piata, Anna. 2018. On-line humorous representations of the 2015 Greek national elections: Acting and interacting about politics on social media. In Villy Tsakona & Jan Chovanec (eds.), *The dynamics of interactional humor: Creating and negotiating humor in everyday encounters* (Topics in Humor Research 7), 258–282. Amsterdam: John Benjamins.

Piata, Anna. to appear. Stylistic humor across modalities: The case of Classical Art memes. *Internet Pragmatics*.

Pickering, Michael & Sharon Lockyer. 2005. Introduction: The ethics and aesthetics of humor and comedy. In Sharon Lockyer & Michael Pickering (eds.), *Beyond a joke: The limits of humor*, 1–24. Basingstoke: Palgrave Macmillan.

Pike, Kenneth L. 1967 [1954]. *Language in relation to a unified theory of the structure of human behavior*, 2nd revised edn. The Hague: Mouton.

Politis, Periklis & Maria Kakavoulia. 2010. Pastiche and parody in Greek radio advertisements. *Journal of Modern Greek Studies* 28(1). 121–145.

Pomerantz, Anne & Nancy D. Bell. 2007. Learning to play, playing to learn: FL learners as multicompetent language users. *Applied Linguistics* 28(4). 556–578.

Pomerantz, Anne & Nancy D. Bell. 2011. Humor as safe house in the foreign language classroom. *The Modern Language Journal* 95(s1). 148–161.

Pozsonyi, Kriszta & Seth Soulstein. 2019. Classroom clowning: Teaching (with) humor in the media classroom. *Journal of Cinema and Media Studies* 58(3). 148–154.

Predelli, Stefano. 2005. *Contexts: Meaning, truth, and the use of language*. Oxford: Clarendon Press.

Preston, Dennis R. 2004. Folk metalanguage. In Adam Jaworski, Nikolas Coupland & Dariusz Galasiński (eds.), *Metalanguage: Social and ideological perspectives* (Language, Power and Social Process 11), 75–101. Berlin: Mouton de Gruyter.

Priego-Valverde, Beatrice. 2006. How funny it is when everybody gets going! A case of co-construction of humor in conversation. *CÍRCULO de Lingüística Aplicada a la Comunicación (CLAC)* 27. 72–100.

Ramoz-Leslie, Nigel J. 2011. Doin' it for the LULZ: A contemporary analysis of internet humor. Walla Walla, Washington: Whitman College graduate thesis. https://dspace.lasrworks.org/bitstream/handle/10349/1039/Ramoz-Leslie%2c%20NJ.pdf?sequence=1 (accessed 4 January 2015).

Raskin, Victor. 1985. *Semantic mechanisms of humor* (Studies in Linguistics and Philosophy 24). Dordrecht: D. Reidel.

Raskin, Victor. 2008a. On the political impotence of humor. In Paul Lewis (ed.), *The Muhammad cartoons and humor research: A collection of essays. Humor: International Journal of Humor Research* 21(1). 26–30.

Raskin, Victor. 2008b. Theory of humor and practice of humor research: Editor's notes and thoughts. In Victor Raskin (ed.), *The primer of humor research* (Humor Research 8), 1–15. Berlin: Mouton de Gruyter.

Raskin, Victor. 2012a. A theory's purview: What is reasonable to expect from a theory of humor. Paper presented at the 24th International Society of Humor Studies Conference, Jagellonian University Krakow, 25–29 June.

Raskin, Victor. 2012b. The hidden media humor and hidden theory. In Jan Chovanec & Isabel Ermida (eds.), *Language and humor in the media*, 45–64. Newcastle upon Tyne: Cambridge Scholars Publishing.

Raskin, Victor. 2017a. Humor theory: What is and what is not. In Władysław Chłopicki and Dorota Brzozowska (eds.), *Humorous discourse* (Humor Research 11), 11–22. Berlin: Mouton De Gruyter.

Raskin, Victor. 2017b. Script-based semantic and ontological theories of humor. In Salvatore Attardo (ed.), *The Routledge handbook of language and humor* (Routledge Handbooks in Linguistics), 109–125. New York: Routledge.

Raskin, Victor, Christian F. Hempelmann & Julia M. Taylor. 2009. How to understand and assess a theory: The evolution of the SSTH into the GTVH and now into the OSTH. *Journal of Literary Theory* 3(2). 285–312.

Reddington, Elizabeth & Hansun Zhang Waring. 2015. Understanding the sequential resources for doing humor in the language classroom. *Humor: International Journal of Humor Research* 28(1). 1–23.

Rogers, Rebecca & Melissa Mosley Wetzel. 2014. *Designing critical literacy education through critical discourse analysis: Pedagogical and research tools for teacher researchers*. New York: Routledge.

Ross, Alison. 1998. *The language of humor* (The Intertext Series). London: Routledge.

Ruch, Willibald. 1998. Foreword and overview. Sense of humor: A new look at an old concept. In Willibald Ruch (ed.), *The sense of humor: Explorations of a personality characteristic* (Humor Research 3), 3–14. Berlin: Mouton De Gruyter.

Rucynski, John Jr. 2011. Using The Simpsons in EFL classes. *English Teaching Forum* 49(1). 8–17.

Ruiz-Gurillo, Leonor. 2012. *La lingüística del humor en español* [The linguistics of humor in Spanish]. Madrid: Arco Libros. [in Spanish]

Ruiz-Gurillo, Leonor. 2013. Narrative strategies in Buenafuente's humorous monologues. In Leonor Ruiz-Gurillo & M. Belén Alvarado Ortega (eds.), *Irony and humor: From pragmatics to discourse* (Pragmatics and Beyond New Series 231), 107–140. Amsterdam: John Benjamins.

Ruiz-Gurillo, Leonor. 2016a. Exploring metapragmatics of humor. In Leonor Ruiz-Gurillo (ed.), *Metapragmatics of humor: Current research trends* (IVITRA: Research in Linguistics and Literature 14), 1–8. Amsterdam: John Benjamins.

Ruiz-Gurillo, Leonor (ed.). 2016b. *Metapragmatics of humor: Current research trends* (IVITRA: Research in Linguistics and Literature 14). Amsterdam: John Benjamins.

Ruiz-Gurillo, Leonor. 2016c. Metapragmatics of humor: Variability, negotiability and adaptability in humorous monologues. In Leonor Ruiz-Gurillo (ed.), *Metapragmatics of humor: Current research trends* (IVITRA: Research in Linguistics and Literature 14), 79–101. Amsterdam: John Benjamins.

Rutter, Jason. 2001. Rhetoric in stand-up comedy: Exploring performer-audience interaction. *Stylistyka* X. 307–325.

Saelid Gilhus, Ingvild. 2011. Why did Jesus laugh? Laughing in Biblical-Demiurgical texts. In Hans Geybels & Walter Van Herck (eds.), *Humor and religion: Challenges and ambiguities* (Continuum Religious Studies), 123–140. London: Continuum.

Santa Ana, Otto. 2009. Did you call in Mexican? The racial politics of Jay Leno immigrant jokes. *Language in Society* 38(1). 23–45.

Saussure, Ferdinand de. 1959 [1916]. *Course in General Linguistics* [Cours de linguistique générale]. New York: Philosophical Library.

Schank, Roger C. & Robert P. Abelson. 1977. *Scripts, plans, goals, and understanding: An inquiry into human knowledge structures* (The Artificial Intelligence Series). Hillsdale: Lawrence Erlbaum Associates.

Schmitz, John Robert. 2002. Humor as a pedagogical tool in foreign language and translation courses. *Humor: International Journal of Humor Research* 15(1). 89–113.

Seewoester Cain, Sarah. 2018. Teasing as audience engagement: Setting up the unexpected during television comedy monologues. In Villy Tsakona & Jan Chovanec (eds.), *The dynamics of interactional humor: Creating and negotiating humor in everyday encounters* (Topics in Humor Research 7), 127–152. Amsterdam: John Benjamins.

Semfe.gr. 2011. http://www.semfe.gr/forum/viewtopic.php?f=7&t=4077 (accessed 28 June 2011).

Sheftel, Anna. 2011. "Monument to the international community, from the grateful citizens of Serajevo": Dark humor as counter-memory in post-conflict Bosnia-Herzegovina. *Memory Studies* 5(2). 145–164.

Shehata, Samer S. 1992. The politics of laughter: Nasser, Sadat, and Mubarek in Egyptian political jokes. *Folklore* 103(1). 75–91.

Shifman, Limor. 2007. Humor in the age of digital reproduction: Continuity and change in internet-based comic texts. *International Journal of Communication* 1. 187–209.

Shifman, Limor. 2013. Memes in a digital world: Reconciling with a conceptual troublemaker. *Journal of Computer-Mediated Communication* 18(3). 362–377.

Shifman, Limor. 2014a. *Memes in digital culture* (The MIT Essential Knowledge Series). Cambridge: MIT Press.

Shifman, Limor. 2014b. The cultural logic of photo-based meme genres. *Journal of Visual Culture* 13(3). 340–358.

Shilikhina, Ksenia. 2017. Metapragmatic markers of the *bona fide* and *non-bona fide* modes of communication. In Władysław Chłopicki & Dorota Brzozowska (eds.), *Humorous discourse* (Humor Research 11), 107–130. Berlin: Mouton De Gruyter.

Shilikhina, Ksenia. 2018. Discourse markers as guides to understanding spontaneous humor and irony. In Villy Tsakona & Jan Chovanec (eds.), *The dynamics of interactional humor: Creating and negotiating humor in everyday encounters* (Topics in Humor Research 7), 57–75. Amsterdam: John Benjamins.

Shively, Rachel L. 2013. Learning to be funny in Spanish during study abroad: L2 humor development. *The Modern Language Journal* 97(4). 930–946.

Shor, Ira. 1999. What is critical literacy? *The Journal of Pedagogy, Pluralism and Practice* 1(4). https://digitalcommons.lesley.edu/cgi/viewcontent.cgi?article=1052&context=jppp (accessed 13 November 2018).

Sierra, Sylvia. 2019. Linguistic and ethnic media stereotypes in everyday talk: Humor and identity construction among friends. *Journal of Pragmatics* 152. 186–199.

Silvers, Penny, Mary Shorey & Linda Crafton. 2007. Critical literacy in a primary multiliteracies classroom: The hurricane group. *Journal of Early Childhood Literacy* 10(4). 379–409.

Silverstein, Michael. 1993. Metapragmatic discourse and metapragmatic function. In John A. Lucy (ed.), *Reflexive language: Reported speech and metapragmatics*, 33–58. Cambridge: Cambridge University Press.

Simpson, Paul. 2001. "Reason" and "tickle" as pragmatic constructs in the discourse of advertising. *Journal of Pragmatics* 33(4). 589–607.

Simpson, Paul. 2003. *On the discourse of satire: Towards a stylistic model of satirical humor* (Linguistic Approaches to Literature 2). Amsterdam: John Benjamins.

Sinkeviciute, Valeria. 2017. Funniness and "the preferred reaction" to jocularity in Australian and British English: An analysis of interviewees' metapragmatic comments. *Language and Communication* 55. 41–54.

Sinkeviciute, Valeria. 2019. Juggling identities in interviews: The metapragmatics of "doing humor". *Journal of Pragmatics* 152. 216–227.

Smith, Moira. 2009. Humor, unlaughter, and boundary maintenance. *Journal of American Folklore* 122(484). 148–171.

Solin, Anna. 2011. Genre. In Jan Zienkowski, Jan-Ola Östman & Jef Verscheuren (eds.), *Discursive pragmatics* (Handbook of Pragmatics Highlights 8), 119–134. Amsterdam: John Benjamins.

Sørensen, Majken Jul. 2016. *Humor in political activism: Creative nonviolent resistance*. Basingstoke: Palgrave Macmillan.

Spilioti, Tereza. 2016. Radio talks, pranks, and multilingualism: Styling Greek identities at a time of crisis. In Janus Mortensen, Nikolas Coupland & Jacob Thøgersen (eds.), *Style, mediation, and change: Sociolinguistic perspectives on talking media* (Oxford Studies in Sociolinguistics), 51–76. Oxford: Oxford University Press.

Stallone, Letícia & Michael Haugh. 2017. Joint fantasizing as relational practice in Brazilian Portuguese interactions. *Language and Communication* 55. 10–23.

Stamou, Anastasia G. 2011. Speech style and the construction of social division: Evidence from Greek television. *Language and Communication* 31(4). 329–344.

Stamou, Anastasia G. 2012. Representations of linguistic variation in children's books: Register stylization as a resource for (critical) language awareness. *Language Awareness* 21(4). 313–329.

Stamou, Anastasia G., Argiris Archakis & Periklis Politis. 2016. Γλωσσική ποικιλότητα και κριτικοί γραμματισμοί στον λόγο της μαζικής κουλτούρας: Χαρτογραφώντας το πεδίο [Sociolinguistic diversity and critical literacies in popular culture discourse: Mapping the field]. In Anastasia G. Stamou, Periklis Politis & Argiris Archakis (eds.), *Γλωσσική ποικιλότητα και κριτικοί γραμματισμοί στον λόγο της μαζικής κουλτούρας: Εκπαιδευτικές προτάσεις για το γλωσσικό μάθημα* [Sociolinguistic diversity and critical literacies in popular culture discourse: Suggestions for language teaching], 13–55. Kavala: Saita. [in Greek]

Stanoev, Stanoy. 2009. Totalitarian political jokes in Bulgaria. In Arvo Krikmann & Liisi Laineste (eds.), *Permitted laughter: Socialist, post-socialist and never-socialist humor*, 185–207. Tartu: ELM Scholarly Press.

Stein, Mary Beth. 1989. The politics of humor: The Berlin Wall in jokes and graffiti. *Western Folklore* 48(2). 85–108.

Stein, Pippa. 2001. Classrooms as sites of textual, cultural, and linguistic reappropriation. In Barbara Comber & Anne Simpson (eds.), *Negotiating critical literacies in classrooms*, 151–169. Mahwah: Laurence Erlbaum Associates.

Stewart, Craig O. 2013. Strategies of verbal irony in visual satire: Reading *The New Yorker's* "Politics of Fear" cover. *Humor: International Journal of Humor Research* 26(2). 197–217.

Street, Brian V. 1984. *Literacy in theory and practice* (Cambridge Studies in Oral and Literate Culture). Cambridge: Cambridge University Press.

Street, Brian. V. 1995. *Social literacies: Critical approaches to literacy in development, ethnography and education* (Real Language Series). London: Longman.

Sue, Christina A. & Tanya Golash-Boza. 2013. "It was only a joke": How racial humor fuels color-blind ideologies in Mexico and Peru. *Ethnic and Racial Studies* 36(10). 1582–1598.

Taels, Johan. 2011. Humor as practical wisdom. In Hans Geybels & Walter Van Herck (eds.), *Humor and religion: Challenges and ambiguities* (Continuum Religious Studies), 22–34. London: Continuum.

Takouda, Christina. 2002. *Πραγματολογικές προσεγγίσεις του χιούμορ και οι δυνατότητες αξιοποίησής του στη διδασκαλία της ελληνικής ως δεύτερης/ξένης γλώσσας* [Pragmatic approaches to humor and the potential of its exploitation in teaching Greek as L2]. Thessaloniki: Aristotle University of Thessaloniki MA thesis. [in Greek]

Takovski, Aleksandar. 2016. The humor of Skopje 2014: Between effects and evaluations. *Humor: International Journal of Humor Research* 29(3). 381–412.

Taylor Rayz, Julia. 2017. Ontological Semantic Theory of Humor in a context of humorous discourse. In Władysław Chłopicki & Dorota Brzozowska (eds.), *Humorous discourse* (Humor Research 11), 205–218. Berlin: Mouton De Gruyter.

Tentolouris, Filippos & Sofronis Chatzisavvidis. 2014. Λόγοι του κριτικού γραμματισμού και η 'τοποθέτησή' τους στη σχολική πράξη: Προς μια γλωσσοδιδακτική αναστοχαστικότητα [Critical literacy discourses and their "positioning" in school practice: Towards a reflective language teaching]. *Studies in Greek Linguistics* 34. 411–421. http://ins.web.auth.gr/images/MEG_PLIRI/MEG_34_411_421.pdf (accessed 15 November 2018).

The New London Group. 1996. A pedagogy of multiliteracies: Designing social futures. *Harvard Educational Review* 66(1). 60–92.

Thompson, Geoff & Laura Alba-Juez (eds.). 2014. *Evaluation in context* (Pragmatics and Beyond New Series 242). Amsterdam: John Benjamins.

Thurlow, Crispin, Laura Lengel & Alice Tomic. 2004. *Computer mediated communication: Social interaction and the internet*. London: Sage.

Timofeeva-Timofeev, Larissa. 2016. Children using phraseology for humorous purposes: The case of 9-to-10-year-olds. In Leonor Ruiz-Gurillo (ed.), *Metapragmatics of humor: Current research trends* (IVITRA: Research in Linguistics and Literature 14), 273–298. Amsterdam: John Benjamins.

Trousdale, Rachel. 2018. Teaching comic narratives. In Richard Jacobs (ed.), *Teaching Narrative* (Teaching the New English Series), 71–85. Basingstoke: Palgrave Macmillan.

Tsakona, Villy. 2002. Οι γλωσσικοί και πραγματολογικοί παράγοντες επιτυχίας των ανεκδότων [Linguistic and pragmatic aspects of successful joke-telling]. *Studies in Greek Linguistics* 22. 659–670. [in Greek]

Tsakona, Villy. 2003a. Jab lines in narrative jokes. *Humor: International Journal of Humor Research* 16(3). 315–329.

Tsakona, Villy. 2003b. Η δομή των αφηγηματικών ανεκδότων στη συνομιλία [The organization of narrative jokes in conversation]. In the *Proceedings of the 1st Athens Postgraduate Conference, Department of Philology, National and Kapodistrian University of Athens, 12–13 May 2001*, 53–63. Athens: National and Kapodistrian University of Athens. [in Greek]

Tsakona, Villy. 2004. *Το χιούμορ στον γραπτό αφηγηματικό λόγο: Γλωσσολογική προσέγγιση* [Humor in written narratives: A linguistic approach]. Athens: National and Kapodistrian University of Athens dissertation. http://thesis.ekt.gr/thesisBookReader/id/17786?id=17786&lang=el#page/1/mode/2up (accessed 17 April 2014). [in Greek]

Tsakona, Villy. 2005. Τα μαργαριτάρια είναι παντοτινά: Η χιουμοριστική πλευρά του γλωσσικού λάθους [Pearls are forever: The humorous dimension of linguistic errors]. In the *Proceedings of the 2nd Athens Postgraduate Conference, Department of Philology,*

National and Kapodistrian University of Athens, 14–16 March 2003, 187–198. Athens: National and Kapodistrian University of Athens. [in Greek]

Tsakona, Villy. 2007. Towards a revised typology of humorous texts and humorous lines. In Diana Popa & Salvatore Attardo (eds.), *New approaches to the linguistics of humor*, 35–43. Galaţi: Academica.

Tsakona, Villy. 2009. Language and image interaction in cartoons: Towards a multimodal theory of humor. *Journal of Pragmatics* 41(6). 1171–1188.

Tsakona, Villy. 2013a. Okras and the metapragmatic stereotypes of humor: Towards an expansion of the GTVH. In Marta Dynel (ed.), *Developments in linguistic humor theory* (Topics in Humor Research 1), 25–48. Amsterdam: John Benjamins.

Tsakona, Villy. 2013b. *Η κοινωνιογλωσσολογία του χιούμορ: Θεωρία, λειτουργίες και διδασκαλία* [The sociolinguistics of humor: Theory, functions and teaching]. Athens: Grigoris Publications. [in Greek]

Tsakona, Villy. 2014. «Τ' αβγά παίρνω μόνη μου;»: Κριτικός γραμματισμός, επαγγελματικές συνδιαλλαγές και ευγένεια ["Can I help myself to some eggs?": Critical literacy, service encounters, and politeness]. *Glossologia* 22. 19–39. [in Greek]

Tsakona, Villy. 2015. "The doctor said I suffer from vitamin € deficiency": Investigating the multiple social functions of Greek crisis jokes. *Pragmatics* 25(2). 287–313.

Tsakona, Villy. 2016a. Book review of: Angelika Zirker & Esme Winter-Froemel (eds.) 2015. *Wordplay and metalinguistic/metadiscursive reflection: Authors, contexts, techniques, and meta-reflection*. Berlin: De Gruyter. *The Humorous Times: Newsletter of the International Society for Humor Studies* 29(1/2). 8–10.

Tsakona, Villy. 2016b. Teaching politeness strategies in the kindergarten: A critical literacy teaching proposal. *Journal of Politeness Research: Language, Behavior, Culture* 12(1). 27–54.

Tsakona, Villy. 2017a. Book review of: Leonor Ruiz-Gurillo (ed.) 2016. *Metapragmatics of humor: Current research trends*. Amsterdam: John Benjamins. *Linguist List* 28.3259. http://linguistlist.org/pubs/reviews/get-review.cfm?subid=36279697 (accessed 17 October 2018).

Tsakona, Villy. 2017b. Constructing local identities via/for humor: A Cretan-Greek case study. *Styles of Communication* 9(2). 118–147.

Tsakona, Villy. 2017c. «Δημοκρατία είναι 4 λύκοι και ένα πρόβατο να ψηφίζουν για φαγητό»: Αναλύοντας τα ανέκδοτα για τους/τις πολιτικούς στην οικονομική κρίση ["Democracy is 4 wolves and 1 sheep voting for food": Analyzing jokes about politicians in the financial crisis]. In Thanasis Georgakopoulos, Theodossia-Soula Pavlidou, Miltos Pechlivanos, Artemis Alexiadou, Jannis Androutsopoulos, Alexis Kalokairinos, Stavros Skopeteas & Katerina Stathi (eds.), *Proceedings of the 12th International Conference on Greek Linguistics, Volume 2*, 1035–1049. Berlin: Romiosini. http://www.cemog.fu-berlin.de/en/icgl12/offprints/tsakona/icgl12_Tsakona.pdf (accessed 17 October 2018). [in Greek]

Tsakona, Villy. 2017d. Genres of humor. In Salvatore Attardo (ed.), *The Routledge handbook of language and humor* (Routledge Handbooks in Linguistics), 489–503. New York: Routledge.

Tsakona, Villy. 2017e. Humor research and humor reception: Far away, so close. In Władysław Chłopicki & Dorota Brzozowska (eds.), *Humorous discourse* (Humor Research 11), 179–201. Berlin: Mouton De Gruyter.

Tsakona, Villy. 2017f. "This is not a political party, this is Facebook!": Political jokes and political (mis)trust in crisis-ridden Greece. *European Journal of Humor Research* 5(4). 136–157.

Tsakona, Villy. 2018a. Intertextuality and cultural literacy in contemporary political jokes. In Arie Sover (ed.), *The languages of humor: Verbal, visual, and physical humor* (Bloomsbury Advances in Semiotics), 86–104. London: Bloomsbury Academic.

Tsakona, Villy. 2018b. Intertextuality and/in political jokes. *Lingua* 203. 1–15.

Tsakona, Villy. 2018c. Online joint fictionalization. In Villy Tsakona & Jan Chovanec (eds.), *The dynamics of interactional humor: Creating and negotiating humor in everyday encounters* (Topics in Humor Research 7), 229–255. Amsterdam: John Benjamins.

Tsakona, Villy & Jan Chovanec (eds.). 2018. *The dynamics of interactional humor: Creating and negotiating humor in everyday encounters* (Topics in Humor Research 7). Amsterdam: John Benjamins.

Tsakona, Villy, Rania Karachaliou & Argiris Archakis. to appear. Liquid racism in the Greek anti-racist campaign #StopMindBorders. *Journal of Language Aggression and Conflict*.

Tsakona, Villy & Diana Elena Popa. 2011a. Humor in politics and the politics of humor: An introduction. In Villy Tsakona & Diana Elena Popa (eds.), *Studies in political humor: In between political critique and public entertainment* (Discourse Approaches to Politics, Society and Culture 46), 1–30. Amsterdam: John Benjamins.

Tsakona, Villy & Diana Elena Popa (eds.). 2011b. *Studies in political humor: In between political critique and public entertainment* (Discourse Approaches to Politics, Society and Culture 46). Amsterdam: John Benjamins.

Tsakona, Villy & Diana Elena Popa. 2013. Editorial: Confronting power with laughter. *European Journal of Humor Research* 1(2). 1–9.

Tsami, Vasia. 2018. *Κείμενα μαζικής κουλτούρας και γλωσσική ποικιλότητα: Κριτική ανάλυση και ανάπτυξη εκπαιδευτικού υλικού* [Mass culture texts and language variation: Critical analysis and development of teaching material]. Patras: University of Patras dissertation. https://www.didaktorika.gr/eadd/handle/10442/42689 (accessed 17 November 2018). [in Greek]

Tsami, Vasia, Argiris Archakis, Sofia Lampropoulou & Villy Tsakona. 2014. Η αναπαράσταση της γλωσσικής ποικιλότητας σε τηλεοπτικά κείμενα μαζικής κουλτούρας [The representation of linguistic variation in television mass cultural texts]. In George Kotzoglou, Kalomoira Nikolou, Eleni Karantzola, Katerina Frantzi, Ioannis Galantomos, Marianthi Georgalidou, Vasilia Kourti-Kazoullis, Chrysoula Papadopoulou & Evangelia Vlachou (eds.), *11th International Conference on Greek Linguistics (Rhodes, 26–29 September 2013): Selected papers*, 1716–1729. Rhodes: Laboratory of Linguistics of the Southeastern Mediterranean, Department of Mediterranean Studies, University of the Aegean. [in Greek]

Tsami, Vasia, Eleni Kapogianni, Villy Tsakona & Argiris Archakis. 2019. Το χιούμορ και η διδακτική του αξιοποίηση στο πλαίσιο του κριτικού γραμματισμού: Ανίχνευση των στάσεων των εκπαιδευτικών [Humor and its teaching exploitation within the framework of critical literacy: Tracing teachers' attitudes]. Paper presented at the 14th International Conference on Greek Linguistics, Patras, Greece, 5–8 September.

Tsiplakou, Stavroula & Elena Ioannidou. 2012. Stylizing stylization: The case of *Aigia Fuxia*. *Multilingua* 31(2). 277–299.

Van Boeschoten, Riki. 2006. Code-switching, linguistic jokes and ethnic identity: Reading hidden transcripts in a cross-cultural context. *Journal of Modern Greek Studies* 24(2). 347–377.

Van Dam, Jet & Anne Bannick. 2017. The first English (EFL) lesson: Initial settings or the emergence of a playful classroom culture. In Nancy D. Bell (ed.), *Multiple perspectives on language play* (Language Play and Creativity 1), 245–279. Boston: Mouton de Gruyter.
van Dijk, Teun A. 1992. Discourse and the denial of racism. *Discourse and Society* 3(1). 87–118.
van Dijk, Teun A. 2005. *Racism and discourse in Spain and Latin America* (Discourse Approaches to Politics, Society and Culture 14). Amsterdam: John Benjamins.
van Dijk, Teun A. 2008a. *Discourse and context: A sociocognitive approach*. Cambridge: Cambridge University Press.
van Dijk, Teun A. 2008b. *Discourse and power*. New York: Palgrave Macmillan.
van Leeuwen, Theo. 2005. *Introducing social semiotics*. London: Routledge.
Van Praag, Lore, Peter A. J. Stevens & Mieke Van Houtte. 2017. How humor makes or breaks student–teacher relationships: A classroom ethnography in Belgium. *Teaching and Teacher Education* 66. 393–401.
Van Sluys, Katie, Mitzi Lewison & Amy Seely Flint. 2006. Researching critical literacy: A critical study of analysis of classroom discourse. *Journal of Literacy Research* 38(2). 197–233.
Vandergriff, Ilona & Carolin Fuchs. 2009. Does CMC promote language play? Exploring humor in two modalities. *CALICO Journal* 27(1). 29–47.
Vandergriff, Ilona & Carolin Fuchs. 2012. Humor support in synchronous computer–mediated classroom discussions. *Humor: International Journal of Humor Research* 25(4). 437–458.
VanLoan Aguilar, Julia. 1997. Humor in crisis: Guadalupe Loaeza's caricature of the Mexican bourgeoisie. *Journal of American Culture* 20(2). 153–158.
Vasquez, Vivian Maria. 2004. *Negotiating critical literacies with young children* (Language, Culture and Teaching). Mahwah: Laurence Erlbaum Associates.
Vasquez, Vivian Maria. 2017. Critical literacy. In *Oxford Research Encyclopedia of Education*. http://education.oxfordre.com/view/10.1093/acrefore/9780190264093.001.0001/acrefore-9780190264093-e-20 (accessed 13 November 2018).
Vasquez, Vivian Maria, Stacie L. Tate & Jerome C. Harste. 2013. *Negotiating critical literacies with teachers: Theoretical foundations and pedagogical resources for pre–service and in–service contexts*. New York: Routledge.
Verschueren, Jef. 1999. *Understanding pragmatics*. London: Edward Arnold.
Verschueren, Jef. 2000. Notes on the role of metapragmatic awareness in language use. *Pragmatics* 10(4). 439–456.
Viktoroff, David. 1953. *Introduction à la psycho–sociologie du rire*. Paris: Presses Universitaires de France.
Vladimirou, Dimitra & Juliane House. 2018. Ludic impoliteness and globalization on Twitter: "I speak England very best" #agglika_Tsipra, #Tsipras #Clinton. *Journal of Pragmatics* 134. 149–162.
Wagner, Manuela & Eduardo Urios–Aparisi. 2008. Pragmatics of humor in the foreign language classroom: Learning (with) humor. In Martin Pütz & JoAnne Neff–van Aertselaer (eds.), *Developing contrastive pragmatics: Interlanguage and cross–cultural perspectives* (Studies on Language Acquisition 31), 209–228. Berlin: Mouton de Gruyter.
Wagner, Manuela & Eduardo Urios–Aparisi. 2011. The use of humor in the foreign language classroom: Funny and effective? *Humor: International Journal of Humor Research* 24(4). 399–434.
Wallace, Catherine. 2003. *Critical reading in language education*. Basingstoke: Palgrave Macmillan.

Wallace, Catherine. 2013. *Literacy and the bilingual learner: Texts and practices in London schools*. Basingstoke: Palgrave Macmillan.

Wallinger, Linda Moody. 1997. Don't smile before Christmas: The role of humor in education. *National Association of Secondary School Principals (NASSP) Bulletin* 81(589). 27–34.

Weaver, Simon. 2011. Jokes, rhetoric and embodied racism: A rhetorical discourse analysis of the logics of racist jokes on the internet. *Ethnicities* 11(4). 413–435.

Weaver, Simon. 2013. A rhetorical discourse analysis of online anti-Muslim and anti-Semitic jokes. *Ethnic and Racial Studies* 36(3). 483–499.

Weaver, Simon. 2016. *The rhetoric of racist humor: US, UK and global race joking*. London: Routledge.

Werner, Walt. 2004. On political cartoons and social studies textbooks: Visual analogies, intertextuality, and cultural memory. *Canadian Social Studies* 38(2). https://files.eric.ed.gov/fulltext/EJ1073912.pdf (accessed 14 November 2018).

Widdowson, Henry G. 2004. *Text, context, pretext: Critical issues in discourse analysis* (Language in Society 35). Malden: Blackwell.

Wiggins, Bradley E. & Bret G. Bowers. 2015. Memes as a genre: A structurational analysis of the memescape. *New Media & Society* 17(1). 1886–1906.

Willis, Ken. 2005. Merry Hell: Humor competence and social incompetence. In Sharon Lockyer & Michael Pickering (eds.), *Beyond a joke: The limits of humor*, 126–145. Basingstoke: Palgrave Macmillan.

Winchatz, Michaela R. & Alexander Kozin. 2008. Comical hypothetical: Arguing for a conversational phenomenon. *Discourse Studies* 10(3). 383–405.

Wodak, Ruth & Michael Meyer (eds.). 2001. *Methods of Critical Discourse Analysis* (Introducing Qualitative Methods). London: Sage.

Woolard, Kathryn A. 1987. Code-switching and comedy in Catalonia. *Pragmatics* 1(1). 106–122.

"World's greatest crocodile hunter" fails to catch "Sifis" – Crete's fugitive reptile. 2014. *The Guardian*, 2 September. http://www.theguardian.com/world/2014/sep/02/crocodile-hunter-olivier-behra-fails-catch-sifis-crete-rethymnon (accessed 23 October 2018).

Χιούμορ και κριτικός γραμματισμός [Humor and critical literacy]. 2018. https://www.humor-literacy.eu/index-en.html (accessed 15 November 2018). [in Greek]

Yates, Joanne & Wanda J. Orlikowski. 1992. Genres of organizational communication: A structurational approach to studying communication and media. *Academy of Management Review* 17(2). 299–326.

Zachariadis, Nikos. 2011. Οι μπάμιες στον πλανήτη των αγανακτισμένων [Okras in the planet of the indignant]. *My Name is Nikos Zachariadis and This Is the Way I See Things*. http://www.nikos-zachariadis.org/?p=62 (accessed 28 June 2011). [in Greek]

Zacher Pandya, Jessica & JuliAnna Ávila (eds.). 2014. *Moving critical literacies forward: A new look at praxis across contexts*. New York: Routledge.

Zhang, Lawrence Jun. 2009. Teaching critical reading to in-service EFL teachers in Singapore. *TESOL TEIS Newsletter* 24(1). 1–10.

Zinkgraf, Magdalena. 2003. Assessing the development of critical language awareness in a foreign language environment. https://eric.ed.gov/?id=ED479811 (accessed 13 November 2018).

Subject Index

aggression 1, 2, 18, 31, 32, 48, 106, 156, 169, 174, 181, 186
aggressive 12, 18, 29, 41, 48, 124, 127, 135, 146, 147, 156, 158, 160, 172, 182
ambiguity 109, 136, 146, 161, 177, 187
ambiguous 29, 129, 157, 178
Analytical Focus/Foci 123–126, 128–129, 130–138, 171, 180, 191–192

canned joke 1, 3, 4, 7, 59, 69, 70, 71, 78, 79, 80, 81, 82, 85, 104, 105, 107, 108, 109, 115, 116, 117, 123, 137, 167, 182, 187, 189
carnival 46, 47
cartoon 30, 33, 70, 87, 89, 90, 93, 116, 117, 124, 128, 163–165, 167, 168, 171
classroom management 139, 141, 142, 143, 144, 155
code-switching 10
comics 164, 167
communicative competence 145–148, 155, 161
conflict 23, 28, 32, 52, 67, 141, 144, 151, 153, 155, 160, 161, 170, 181, 187, 188
contextualization cues 10, 11, 14, 15, 21, 24, 110, 112, 118, 119, 120, 122, 124, 125, 127, 129, 135, 136, 145, 189, 191
creativity 2, 68, 85, 88, 127, 141
critical language awareness 148–149, 159
critical literacy 5, 148–171
critical reading 146, 154, 193
critical skills 138, 161, 162, 165, 188
curriculum 139, 142, 152, 153, 154, 161

decontextual(ization/ize) 3, 7, 62, 108, 127, 157, 189, 190
Discourse Theory of Humor (DTH) 103, 123–126, 128, 129, 130–138, 171–188, 191, 192
discrimination 55, 150, 154, 156, 157, 168, 187
discriminatory 59, 60, 136, 153, 154, 156, 159, 182

emic 30, 31, 32, 45, 47, 63, 108
etic 30, 31, 32, 41, 45, 47, 63, 108

Facebook 35, 36, 88, 89, 90, 91, 99, 116
face-threatening act 12, 24, 124, 126
facial expression 12, 28, 132, 135, 180
failed humor 126, 127
fantasy 40, 82, 99, 130, 133, 135, 178
fictionalization 4, 81–89, 101, 173
framing device(s) 12, 15, 121

gender 5, 12, 13, 50, 62, 88, 89, 104, 124, 136, 156, 175–180, 192
General Theory of Verbal Humor (GTVH) 1–2, 4, 65, 69, 103, 104–109, 110, 111, 112, 113, 114, 115, 117–122, 126, 137, 138, 190
generic conventions 67, 68, 69, 79–102, 125, 156, 180, 190, 192, 193
genre 3, 4, 5, 7, 8, 9, 10, 11, 13, 14, 15, 16, 17, 26, 65–102, 106, 109, 113, 115–119, 121–125, 129, 132, 134–135, 136, 138, 148, 149, 152, 156, 157, 162, 167, 169, 170, 171, 173–174, 179, 186–187, 189, 190, 191, 192
gesture 12, 109, 110, 125, 132, 135, 180

humor failure 4, 6, 103, 118, 126–130, 138, 144, 191
humor quality 4, 103, 126–130
hyperdetermination 108

identity 12, 13, 24, 29, 31, 62, 88, 89, 96, 99, 124, 140, 141, 147, 151, 158, 166, 167, 168, 175, 177, 178, 180
ideological 22, 27, 45, 46, 109, 111, 149, 151, 156, 158, 164, 165, 167, 168, 181
ideology 23, 29, 61, 88, 112, 113, 149, 151, 153, 154, 155, 160, 166, 167, 181, 182, 186, 188
incongruity 1, 8, 36, 43, 77, 79, 89, 90, 96, 99, 100, 105, 106, 114, 134, 135, 158, 164, 165, 169, 173, 182

incongruous 2, 35, 36, 37, 38, 40, 46, 50, 55, 74, 76, 79, 82, 84, 86, 90, 101, 114, 123, 130, 132, 133, 135, 136, 157, 165, 166, 169, 175, 177, 178, 179, 180, 184, 186, 187, 191
ingroup 12, 33, 63, 124, 126
interaction 2, 9, 10, 14, 15, 16, 20, 24, 26, 31, 61, 62, 65, 66, 69, 71, 74, 75, 81, 85, 86, 87, 90, 99, 100, 101, 109, 115, 116, 117, 119–120, 125, 136, 137, 140, 141, 144, 155, 158, 167, 193
interactional 9, 65, 99, 116, 136
intertextual joke 81, 82, 84, 85, 173
intertextuality 68, 82, 164
intimacy 3, 12, 19, 124, 140, 175
intonation 10, 12, 21, 109, 110, 125, 132, 135, 136, 179, 180

jab line 70, 71, 72, 74, 101, 107, 124, 126, 136, 138, 180

Knowledge Resource 65, 105, 106, 107, 110, 111, 112, 113, 114, 117, 118, 122, 123, 124, 125, 126, 132, 133, 134, 135, 138

language awareness 21
language teaching 4, 139, 140, 143-148, 152, 153, 159, 161, 166, 168, 188
laughter 9, 10, 12, 29, 30, 32, 42, 43, 44, 45, 54, 74, 86, 87, 101, 109, 110, 125, 133, 158, 159, 177, 179, 180, 182

meme 17, 34, 70, 87, 88, 90, 91, 93, 96, 97, 99, 116, 167, 171, 173, 182, 183, 187
metalanguage 20–22
metalinguistic awareness 9, 144–148, 155, 162
metalinguistic device 12
metapragmatic awareness 20, 21, 22, 23, 24, 25, 26, 28, 113, 144–146, 148, 155, 162
metapragmatic comment 3, 19, 20, 24, 27, 28, 29, 30, 31, 32, 33–35, 41, 42, 43, 44, 45, 46, 47, 48, 52–57, 62–63, 189
metapragmatic indicator 21–26, 28, 33, 62, 63
metapragmatic stereotype 16, 21, 22, 23, 24, 25, 27, 28, 29, 30, 32, 33, 34, 41, 44, 45–48, 52, 53, 56, 57, 58–63, 65, 68, 69, 70, 78, 109, 111, 113, 118, 123, 132, 135, 136, 179, 180, 189, 190, 191
metapragmatics 17, 19–64, 103, 189, 192
Meta-Knowledge Resource 110, 112, 118, 122, 124, 125, 133, 135
migrant 60, 181–188, 192
multiliteracies 146, 164, 167

narrative 71–74, 81, 82, 109, 167, 175–180
narrative joke 70, 79, 80, 85, 173, 187
narrative strategy 65, 106, 113, 114, 118, 122, 124, 125, 132, 134
normative communities of humor 12, 58, 59, 61, 62, 63, 78, 111

offensive 27, 29, 32, 48, 60, 127, 135, 160
one-liner 70, 71, 78, 79, 80, 81, 85, 173, 182, 187
outgroup 12, 33, 63, 124, 126

performance 2, 4, 22, 31, 46, 102, 103, 104, 107, 109, 110, 111, 112, 113, 114–126, 127, 128, 138, 166
political joke 33–41, 44, 45–48, 62, 80, 171–175
prosody 10, 21, 28, 109, 132, 135, 136, 179, 180
punch line 35, 40, 44, 69, 70, 71, 79, 80, 81, 104, 106, 107, 126, 138

racism 28, 150, 154, 168, 181, 182
racist 59, 140, 163, 181, 182, 185, 186, 187
reaction 2, 3, 4, 11, 12, 13–17, 19, 24, 28, 29, 30, 31, 34, 50, 52, 57, 74, 87, 94, 103, 108, 109, 110, 112, 114, 116–122, 124, 129, 130, 132, 135, 146, 158, 160, 169, 174, 180, 187, 189, 190, 191, 192
recontextualization 68, 69, 78, 79–102
recontextualize 10, 20, 24, 69, 71, 102, 116, 170, 192
register 19, 86, 113, 124, 152, 165, 189
relief 1, 60, 144, 169, 174
resistant perspective 151
resistant reading 129, 130, 137, 151, 157
riddle-joke 70, 79, 80, 81, 84, 85, 173, 187

script 9, 46, 59, 71, 87, 104–109, 122, 128, 129, 131, 184
script opposition 8, 71, 89, 90, 96, 97, 99, 105, 107, 108, 109, 110, 111, 122, 123, 124, 125, 127, 128, 133, 136, 138, 158, 185, 190, 191
Semantic Script Theory of Humor (SSTH) 1, 2, 4, 9, 103, 104–108, 125, 137, 138, 190
sexism 55, 133, 150, 154, 164
sexist 48, 51, 53, 54, 55–57, 59, 62, 69, 103, 130, 131, 132, 133, 134, 135, 136, 137, 175
smile 10, 12, 32, 112, 125
sociocultural assumptions 13, 14, 16, 17, 33, 58, 118, 119, 122, 123, 124, 125, 129, 130–132, 133–135, 136, 138, 143, 171–173, 177–180, 189, 191
sociocultural presuppositions 11, 15, 111, 118, 120, 167

sociopragmatic function 2, 24, 25, 29, 30, 31, 33, 34, 35, 41–47, 52, 53–56, 58, 59, 61–65, 87, 117, 137, 145, 156, 158, 162, 167, 168, 169, 173, 179, 180, 189
solidarity 3, 12, 19, 33, 45, 63, 79, 81, 124, 141, 144, 179
style 163, 166, 168, 174
stylistic 68, 100, 106, 124, 165, 166, 191
superiority 1, 60, 106, 156, 169, 174, 186

target 1, 2, 5, 11, 12, 31, 34, 39, 41, 60, 63, 65, 105, 106, 109, 111, 114, 122, 123, 124, 125, 128, 129, 130, 133, 136, 141, 156, 157, 164, 167, 169, 170, 172, 173, 174, 177, 178, 181, 186, 187, 191
teaching about humor 4, 5, 139, 140, 142, 143, 145–148, 155, 156, 159, 160, 168, 171–188, 191, 192
teaching with humor 139, 145, 147, 168

Author Index

Ávila, JuliAnna 150
İçmez, Simla 154
Özdemir, Özlem 181
Özdemir, Emrah 181

Abelson, Robert P. 104
Adetunji, Akin 165
Agha, Asif 3, 16, 20, 22
Ahn, So-Yeon 144, 145
Akinola, Ayodele James 35
Alba-Juez, Laura 114
Alexander, Richard J. 69
Alexander, Stephanie 144
Anderson, Benedict 58
Antonopoulou, Eleni 68, 75, 100, 109, 128
Archakis, Argiris 48, 60, 68, 72, 74, 82, 86, 100, 101, 106, 109, 110, 116, 132, 134, 141, 144, 145, 146, 148, 149, 150, 151, 152, 153, 154, 156, 159, 160, 164, 165, 167, 168, 171, 175, 176, 181, 182, 187, 193
Aronsson, Karin 141, 162
Attardo, Salvatore 1, 2, 13, 17, 27, 65, 68, 69, 70, 71, 79, 100, 103, 104, 105, 106, 107, 108, 109, 110, 111, 112, 113, 114, 115, 118, 119, 120, 127, 128, 144, 156, 165, 186, 190

Badarneh, Muhammad A. 45, 46
Bainschab, Alexandra Corinna Damaris 165
Bakhtin, Mikhail 46, 47, 67, 68, 117
Balirano, Giuseppe 106, 109
Bannick, Anne 144
Bateson, Gregory 21
Bauman, Richard 67
Bawarshi, Anis S. 67
Baym, Nancy K. 86, 115, 116
Baynham, Mike 148, 150, 151
Bean, Thomas W. 148, 151
Beck, Ann S. 153, 159, 161
Behrman, Edward H. 148, 150, 151, 153
Bell, Nancy D. 1, 3, 4, 13, 77, 126, 127, 128, 129, 148, 151, 155, 156, 157, 158, 159, 160, 162, 169, 140, 141, 142, 144, 145, 146, 147
Berglin, Ieva Tūna 165

Bergson, Henri 1, 134
Bhatia, Vijay K. 67, 68
Billig, Michael 1, 29, 46, 59, 60, 62, 129, 141, 156
Bishop, Elizabeth 149, 150, 159, 193
Blommaert, Jan 150
Boespflug, François 128
Bowers, Bret G. 88
Boxman-Shabtai, Lillian 46, 79, 85
Brandes, Stanley H. 45, 46
Briggs, Charles L. 67
Brown, Gillian 7
Brown, Kristine 159, 161
Bublitz, Wolfram 3, 20, 21, 24, 26
Bushnell, Cade 144

Cadiero-Kaplan, Karen 150, 154, 193
Caffi, Claudia 20, 21, 26
Cameron, Deborah 23, 24, 27
Canagarajah, A. Suresh 146
Canakis, Kostas 165
Canestrari, Carla 10, 11, 13, 15, 110, 120
Capelotti, João Paolo 76
Carr, Jimmy 101
Cekaite, Asta 141, 162
Cervetti, Gina 148, 149, 157
Chabanne, Jean-Charles 79
Chaniotakis, Nikos I. 141
Charalambous, Constadina 182
Chatzisavvidis, Sofronis 148
Chen, Khin Wee 60, 79
Chernin, Ariel R 29, 156, 182
Chiaro, Delia 2, 65, 66, 69, 71
Chłopicki, Władysław 107, 128
Chomsky, Noam 2, 8, 104, 108, 145, 190
Chovanec, Jan 3, 12, 13, 15, 32, 75, 82, 85, 86, 115, 116, 117, 121, 156
Chun, Elaine W. 21, 29, 156, 182
Clark, Romy 149
Clarke, Lane W. 151, 152
Coe, Richard M. 151
Comber, Barbara 148, 150, 154
Constantinou, Maria 28, 59, 115, 116, 129, 181

Coogan, Peter 67
Cook, Guy 140, 145, 159
Cope, Bill 153, 164
Corduas, Marcella 106, 109, 128
Correia, Rosane 154
Cots, Josep M. 154
Coupland, Nikolas 3, 20, 21, 23, 24, 26, 27
Coutinho, Maria Antónia 68, 100
Crafton, Linda 153, 164
Crossley, Scott 77
Culpeper, Jonathan 3, 20, 21, 22, 24, 26, 27, 32
Curdt-Christiansen, Xiao Lan 22, 24, 148, 154, 159, 160

Damico, James S. 148, 149, 157
Davies, Catherine Evans 7, 109, 145
Davies, Christie 10, 45, 46, 59, 60
de Jongste, Henri 76
Deliroka, Sideri 148, 150, 151, 152, 154
Di Maio, Sara 105
Dilmaç, Julie Alev 181
Dooley, Karen T. 148
Dore, Margherita 106, 109, 116, 132, 134
Dowling, Jacqueline S. 162
Duranti, Alessandro 7
Dynel, Marta 28, 31, 32, 59, 69, 78, 85, 90, 110, 115, 129

Eggleston, Alyson 109, 128
Ekdale, Brian 88
El Refaie, Elisabeth 10, 59
Ermida, Isabel 107
Evans, Janet 148, 154

Fairclough, Norman 5, 68, 129, 133, 148, 149, 151, 193
Farias, Miguel 149, 154
Felipe Fajardo, Margarita 148, 153, 154, 159, 160, 161
Fetzer, Anita 7
Filani, Ibukun 11, 13, 15, 47, 121
Finkbeiner, Rita 7
Flint, Amy Seely 148
Forman, Ross 144
Freedman, Aviva 151
Freire, Paulo 149

Freud, Sigmund 1, 9
Fterniati, Anna 164, 166, 168
Fuchs, Carolin 82, 86

Gabbadon, Nadine G. 29, 156, 182
Gal, Susan 181
Galasiński, Dariusz 3, 21
Gardner, Scott 165
Gasteratou, Spyridoula 144, 164, 168
Georgakopoulou, Alexandra 7, 82, 114, 165
Gérin, Annie 106, 109
Geybels, Hans 76
Goatly, Andrew 65, 69, 101
Golash-Boza, Tanya 156, 182
Gonulal, Talip 141, 142
Goodwin, Charles 7
Goutsos, Dionysis 7
Greeves, Lucy 101
Grice, H. Paul 104, 113
Gruner, Charles R. 156, 186
Gumperz, John J. 10

Hale, Adrian 59, 62, 126, 127, 128, 129, 141, 142
Hann, David 144
Harste, Jerome C. 150, 151, 153, 155, 156
Harwood, Debbie 154
Hatzithomas, Leonidas D. 132, 134
Haugh, Michael 3, 20, 21, 22, 23, 24, 26, 32, 82
Hay, Jennifer 82, 86, 127
Hedgcock, John S. 142
Hempelmann, Christian F. 32, 77, 105, 146, 147, 148, 158, 162
Hill, Jane H. 156
Hiramoto, Mie 165
Hlynka, Anthony 127
Hobbs, Pamela 17, 76, 77
Hoicka, Elena 162
Holcomb, Christopher 141
Hong, Nathaniel 45, 46
House, Juliane 39
Howitt, Dennis 156
Hübler, Axel 3, 20, 21, 24, 26
Hunston, Susan 114
Huth, Thorsten 144
Hymes, Dell H. 145

Ioannidou, Elena 68, 100, 159, 165
Irvine, Judith T. 181
Ivanič, Roz 149

Jakobson, Roman 20, 21
Janks, Hilary 148, 149, 151, 163, 164, 168
Jaspers, Jürgen 142
Jaworski, Adam 3, 20, 21, 23, 24, 26, 27
Johns, Ann M. 67
Jones, Rodney 68
Jones, Stephanie 151, 152
Jonsson, Rickard 142

Kádár, Dániel Z. 20, 22, 23, 24, 26, 32
Kakavoulia, Maria 132, 134
Kalantzis, Mary 153, 164
Kanaana, Sharif 45
Karachaliou, Rania 116, 187
Karagiannaki, Evanthia 154
Kerkkänen, Paavo 29
Kersten, Holger 30, 46
Kim, Jiyun 144, 146
Klumbytė, Neringa 45, 46
Knupfer, Nancy Nelson 127
Kocadal, Özker 181
Kolek, Leszek S. 128
Kontio, Janne 141
Kontovourki, Stavroula 159
Kotthoff, Helga 4, 72, 81, 82, 85, 86, 100
Koupaee Dar, Zeinab 154
Koutsogiannis, Dimitris 148, 159
Kozin, Alexander 82, 86, 87, 90
Kramer, Elise 28, 29, 59, 115, 129
Kramsch, Claire 157
Kristiansen, Tore 26, 27
Kuipers, Giselinde 10, 12, 17, 29, 58, 78, 111, 127, 128, 129
Kyriakou, Maria 162

Labov, William 26, 114
Laineste, Liisi 28, 29, 41, 45, 59, 88, 115, 116, 129, 181, 184
Lam, Wan Shun Eva 148
Lampropoulou, Sofia 132, 134, 187
Larkin–Galiñanes, Cristina 1, 105, 140
Lau, Man Chu 148, 159

Lefkowitz, Natalie 142
Lengel, Laura 85
Lentin, Alana 181
Lewis, Paul 60, 115, 116, 128
Lewison, Mitzi 148
Linell, Per 3, 146
Lockyer, Sharon 16, 29, 32, 59, 60, 62, 66, 156, 158, 193
Loizou, Eleni 162
Lucy, John A. 20, 21
Luke, Allan 148, 150
Lytra, Vally 141, 162

Majors, Yolanda J. 151
Malinowski, Bronislaw 7
Malmquist, Karl 29, 156, 182
Manteli, Vicky 106, 109
Marciniak, Przemysław 140
Marone, Vittorio 115
Maroniti, Katerina 154, 165, 168
Mauranen, Anna 20, 24
McBride, Keally D. 58
McKinney, Julia 29
Medway, Peter 67, 151
Meibauer, Jörg 7
Meyer, Michael 150
Miller, Carolyn R. 67
Milner Davis, Jessica 76
Milner, Ryan M. 88
Miltner, Kate M. 88
Miranda, Florencia 68, 100
Moalla, Asma 46, 79, 80
Moni, Karen 148, 151
Morreall, John 1, 59, 60, 134, 140, 141, 156, 186
Moschonas, Spiros A. 22, 23
Mosley Wetzel, Melissa 149, 151, 192
Mulkay, Michael 61, 62

Neff, Peter 141, 159
Nesi, Hilary 142
Nikiforidou, Kiki 68, 100
Norrick, Neal R. 2, 3, 9, 10, 11, 13, 14, 69, 71, 76, 109, 119, 128, 141, 142
North, Sarah 85
Norton, Bonny 159

Obrdlik, Antonin J. 45, 46
Oishi, Etsuko 7
Olson, David R. 158
Oring, Elliott 3, 10, 11, 13, 15, 78, 120
Orlikowski, Wanda J. 85
Owusu-Bempah, Kwame 156

Palmer, Jerry 1
Pardales, Michael J. 148, 149, 157
Park, Ji Hoon 29, 156, 182
Parker, Christina A. 159, 160, 161
Paximadaki, Sofianna 164, 165
Peck, Andrew M. 88
Piata, Anna 42, 68, 88, 100, 106, 116, 165
Pickering, Lucy 110
Pickering, Michael 17, 29, 32, 59, 60, 66, 156, 158, 193
Pike, Kenneth L. 30, 108
Politis, Periklis 132, 134, 148, 159
Pomerantz, Anne 140, 141, 142, 144, 145, 146, 147, 148, 151, 155, 156, 157, 158, 159, 160, 169
Popa, Diana Elena 46, 60
Poppi, Fabio I. M. 28, 59, 115, 129
Pozsonyi, Kriszta 141, 158, 160
Predelli, Stefano 7
Preston, Dennis R. 20, 21, 23, 24, 26, 27
Priego-Valverde, Beatrice 82

Rahimi, Ali 154
Ramoz-Leslie, Nigel J. 88
Raskin, Victor 1, 3, 8, 9, 10, 14, 19, 34, 59, 60, 69, 79, 103, 104, 105, 106, 107, 108, 109, 111, 119, 122, 127, 128, 135, 136, 137, 156, 186, 190
Reddington, Elizabeth 145
Reiff, Mary Jo 67
Roach Anleu, Sharyn 76
Rogers, Rebecca 149, 151, 192
Ross, Alison 69
Ruch, Willibald 27
Rucynski, John 141, 144, 159
Ruiz-Gurillo, Leonor 21, 28, 109, 113, 118
Rutter, Jason 116

Saelid Gilhus, Ingvild 140
Santa Ana, Otto 156, 182

Saussure, Ferdinand de 104
Schank, Roger C. 104
Schmitz, John Robert 144, 156
Schumacher, Petra B. 7
Seewoester Cain, Sarah 116
Shams, Mohammad Reza 154
Sheftel, Anna 45
Shehata, Samer S. 45, 46
Shifman, Limor 46, 85, 87, 88, 116
Shilikhina, Ksenia 11, 12, 110, 117
Shively, Rachel L. 144, 145
Shor, Ira 148, 153
Shorey, Mary 153, 164
Sierra, Sylvia 31
Sifianou, Maria 109
Silvers, Penny 153, 164
Silverstein, Michael 21
Simpson, Anne 148, 154
Simpson, Paul 68, 100, 132, 134
Sinkeviciute, Valeria 26, 27, 30, 31
Smith, Moira 60, 62, 129
Solin, Anna 67, 68
Sørensen, Majken Jul 31, 46
Soulstein, Seth 141, 158, 160
Spilioti, Tereza 39
Stallone, Letícia 82
Stamou, Anastasia G. 148, 154, 159, 165, 168
Stanoev, Stanoy 45, 46
Stein, Mary Beth 46
Stein, Pippa 162, 166, 168
Stevens, Peter A. J. 141, 142
Stewart, Craig O. 28, 59, 115, 116, 129
Street, Brian V. 148
Sue, Christina A. 156, 182

Taels, Johan 140
Takouda, Christina 144, 156
Takovski, Aleksandar 46, 60
Tate, Stacie L. 150, 151, 153, 155, 156
Taylor Rayz, Julia 105
Tentolouris, Filippos 148
The New London Group 153, 164
Thompson, Geoff 114
Thurlow, Crispin 85
Timofeeva-Timofeev, Larissa 20, 162
Tomic, Alice 85
Trousdale, Rachel 140, 155, 173

Tsakona, Villy 3, 10, 11, 12, 13, 17, 22, 26, 27, 30, 32, 33, 45, 46, 48, 60, 66, 68, 70, 71, 72, 74, 75, 82, 86, 88, 100, 101, 106, 107, 109, 110, 111, 115, 116, 117, 118, 120, 121, 128, 132, 134, 140, 141, 144, 145, 146, 148, 149, 150, 151, 152, 153, 154, 156, 157, 159, 160, 164, 167, 168, 171, 175, 176, 181, 182, 187, 193
Tsami, Vasia 68, 100, 106, 109, 164, 165, 166, 168
Tsiplakou, Stavroula 68, 100, 165
Tully, Melissa 88

Urios–Aparisi, Eduardo 110, 144

Van Boeschoten, Riki 45, 46
Van Dam, Jet 144
van Dijk, Teun A. 7, 150, 181
Van Herck, Walter 76
Van Houtte, Mieke 141, 142
van Leeuwen, Theo 67
Van Praag, Lore 141, 142
Van Sluys, Katie 148
Vandergriff, Ilona 82, 86
VanLoan Aguilar, Julia 45
Vasquez, Vivian Maria 148, 150, 151, 153, 154, 155, 156
Verschueren, Jef 20, 21, 22, 23, 26, 27, 28, 30, 113

Viktoroff, David 8
Vladimirou, Dimitra 39
Voolaid, Piret 88, 181, 184

Wagner, Manuela 110, 144
Wallace, Catherine 5, 148, 149, 151, 153, 154, 158, 160, 193
Wallinger, Linda Moody 141
Walters, Keith 29, 156, 182
Waring, Hansun Zhang 145
Weaver, Simon 60, 62, 156, 182, 184, 193
Werner, Walt 164, 168
Widdowson, Henry G. 7
Wiggins, Bradley E. 88
Willis, Ken 59
Winchatz, Michaela R. 82, 86, 87, 90
Wodak, Ruth 149
Wood, Lana Mariko 144
Woolard, Kathryn A. 165

Yates, Joanne 85
Yule, George 7

Zacher Pandya, Jessica 150
Zhang, Lawrence Jun 154
Zinkgraf, Magdalena 154

www.ingramcontent.com/pod-product-compliance
Lightning Source LLC
Chambersburg PA
CBHW071817230426
43670CB00013B/2478